STORY
as TORAH

STORY *as* TORAH

Reading Old Testament Narrative Ethically

GORDON J. WENHAM

Baker Academic
A Division of Baker Book House Co
Grand Rapids, Michigan 49516

Published by Baker Academic
a division of Baker Book House Company
P.O. Box 6287, Grand Rapids, MI 49516-6287
www.bakeracademic.com

North American paperback edition published in 2004 by Baker Academic
Previously published in 2000 by T & T Clark

Printed in the United States of America

Library of Congress Cataloging-in-Publication Data is on file at the Library of Congress, Washington, D.C.

ISBN 0-8010-2783-7

The LORD is merciful and gracious,
slow to anger and abounding in steadfast love.
He does not deal with us according to our sins,
nor requite us according to our iniquities.

Psalm 103:8, 10

CONTENTS

ACKNOWLEDGEMENTS

I should like to thank my friends and colleagues, Andrew Lincoln, Katharine Martin, Robin Parry, David Reimer and Peter Widdowson, who have been kind enough to read all or part of the manuscript and offer their advice. I should also like to express my gratitude to the Bible House Research Fund for a grant that enabled me to take a sabbatical to write this book.

ABBREVIATIONS

AB	Anchor Bible
AnBib	Analecta Biblica
ANET	*Ancient Near Eastern Texts*
Bib	*Biblica*
Bib Int	*Biblical Interpretation*
BN	*Biblische Notizen*
BZAW	Beihefte zur Zeitschrift für die alttestamentliche Wissenschaft
CBQ	*Catholic Biblical Quarterly*
ConBOT	Coniectanea Biblica Old Testament Series
ET	English translation
EvQ	*Evangelical Quarterly*
Exp Tim	*Expository Times*
ICC	International Critical Commentary
Int	*Interpretation*
JBL	*Journal of Biblical Literature*
JETS	*Journal of the Evangelical Theological Society*
JJS	*Journal of Jewish Studies*
JPS	Jewish Publication Society
JSNT	*Journal for the Study of the New Testament*
JSOT	*Journal for the Study of the Old Testament*
JSOTSup	JSOT Supplement Series
OTL	Old Testament Library
RIDA	*Revue Internationale des Droits de l'Antiquité*
TDOT	*Theological Dictionary of the Old Testament*
TynBul	*Tyndale Bulletin*
UF	*Ugarit-Forschungen*
VT	*Vetus Testamentum*
VTSup	Vetus Testamentum Supplements
WBC	Word Biblical Commentary
WTJ	*Westminster Theological Journal*
ZAW	*Zeitschrift für die alttestamentliche Wissenschaft*

1

INTRODUCTION

For centuries Jews have read the Bible didactically drawing from its stories moral and legal principles to guide daily life. Encouraged by Jesus and Paul (Matt 19:4; 1 Cor 10:11) and common ancient practice,[1] Christian teachers and preachers have similarly read the Old Testament with a view to using its stories to instil ethical principles in their hearers.

However, some of the lessons drawn from these texts are arbitrary and whimsical at the one extreme and banal at the other. Augustine's delightful and witty interpretation of the flood story may be right to compare the ark to the Church, for both act as means for saving the human race, but to suggest that the occupants of the three decks of the ark represent 'chaste marriage dwelling in the ground floor, chaste widowhood in the upper, and chaste virginity in the top storey'[2] is a trifle fanciful. But he would allow even 'better' interpretations, so long as the connection with the Church is recognised.

Augustine thus implicitly allows that his allegorical interpretation is subjective, a stance that has recently become most evident in postmodern approaches to Scripture which stress that the reader creates the meaning of the text. At times this leads to bizarre and counter-intuitive readings. The contemporary stress on the reader's involvement in the interpretative process is of course valid, but to argue that it is entirely subjective is misguided. A text is essentially a message from an author to its first readers, which the author hoped would be understood and acted on. Because both readers and author shared a common language and culture, there was a reasonable chance that the writer's intentions would be realised and the message understood correctly. Our distance in time and space from the author and first readers makes it much more difficult to pick up the original sense of the message. However, just as readers of modern texts, whether they be e-mails or scholarly tomes, do their best to grasp the author's intended sense, so responsible interpreters of ancient texts have tried to do the same.

But there are formidable difficulties. In narrative it is often unclear whether the writer is making an ethical comment at all: he may be describing an action because it happened, or because it was a link in a

[1] 'In all those cultures, Greek, medieval or Renaissance . . . the chief means of moral education is the telling of stories.' Alasdair MacIntyre, *After Virtue* (London: Duckworth, 1981), 114.

[2] Augustine, *City of God*, 15.26.

chain of events, which led to something significant. Furthermore, in those cases where narratives appear more than descriptive and seem to be offering ethical advice, it is often very difficult to be sure where the writer and his 'implied reader'[3] stand ethically. We have difficulty determining their moral standpoint, so we often cannot be sure whether deeds recounted are meant to serve as examples to imitate or mistakes to avoid.

Partly for these reasons systematic discussions of Old Testament ethics have avoided the narratives, focusing instead on the direct ethical teaching that is found in the legal codes in the Pentateuch, the exhortations of the Wisdom literature and the preaching of the prophets.[4] These texts of course provide invaluable insights into the ethical outlook of the biblical writers, but there have been surprisingly few attempts made to integrate these insights with the storytellers' purposes and perspectives except on an *ad hoc* basis to interpret individual stories. Serious biblical scholarship has traditionally been concerned almost entirely with historical questions, how and when the text originated, what it tells us about Israel's political and religious history, and so on. The purpose of the writer in telling particular stories and the message that a particular book was intended to convey has been given a low profile in biblical study, and where it has been discussed the focus has been on a work's theology rather than its ethical stance.

Thus interpretations of Genesis tend to see it as a book about creation, fall and the call of the patriarchs. Yet in the Bible Genesis is seen as the first book of the *law* (*Torah*), although it is nearly all narrative. Jesus and Paul, Jewish rabbis and Christian preachers, all appeal to Genesis to demonstrate truths about human behaviour and draw out principles of ethics. More adventurous souls try to use books like Judges to illuminate both theology and ethics despite its horrendous storyline and generally depressing conclusions. Genesis certainly looks as though it may be trying to teach ethics as well as theology, but there are quite contradictory conclusions drawn by eminent scholars as to what that ethic is. And as for more popular expositors the comment of Judges on the chaos of its own times might well be applied to interpretations of Genesis! 'In those days there was no king in Israel; every man did what was right in his own eyes' (Judg 21:25).

This book will try to trace a path through this tangled area. While fully recognising that the reader makes an indispensable contribution to interpretation and that the whole issue of authorial intentionality is fraught with difficulty, we shall employ the methods of historical,

[3] For a definition of 'implied reader' see Chapter 2.

[4] The otherwise most useful volume E. Otto, *Theologische Ethik des Alten Testaments* (Stuttgart: Kohlhammer, 1994) has nothing about the ethics implicitly taught in the narratives.

literary and rhetorical criticism to investigate what the original author of a biblical book was trying to communicate to his first readers. Historical criticism is required because every work originated at a specific time in a particular culture, so that if we do not understand the sense of the words in that period and what concepts and institutions they refer to we shall never grasp the message the work was written to convey. The techniques of literary criticism are necessary to appreciate the organisation of a piece of literature, the ideas it embodies, and the standpoint of the writer. Rhetorical criticism links the concerns of literary and historical criticism. It attempts to show how an author writing in a particular context organised his work to try to persuade his readers to respond in the way he wanted. Rhetorical criticism uses the observations of literary critics to illuminate the communicative and persuasive techniques built into every text.[5]

This will lead us to conclude that Old Testament narrative books do have a didactic purpose, that is, they are trying to instil both theological truths and ethical ideals into their readers. A closer examination of Genesis and Judges will attempt to elucidate what the purposes of these two books are. I shall argue that the Bible storytellers are not advocating a minimalist conformity to the demands of the law in their storytelling, rather that they have an ideal of godly behaviour that they hoped their heroes and heroines would typify.[6] But the attainment of these ideals seems to be erratic, and this has important implications for the theology of the storytellers: they appear to relate a story of success despite the frequent moral failings of the principal actors in the story.

Before exploring this in more depth, it is necessary to fill out the picture of the ethical ideals of the writers. This involves an examination of a variety of texts. Most important for an understanding of Genesis are the opening chapters, particularly chapters 1–2, which describe the world as it was first created, before mankind disobeyed: it thus serves as a vision of God's ideals for the human race, a vision that is presumably shared by the author of Genesis. But this is not enough to cover all aspects of human existence and the appropriate ethical approach to them. We shall try to identify patterns of behaviour in the narratives which the authors seem to be implicitly commending and so draw out what they consider to be virtues. Further light on these issues may be derived from the exhortations and other expressions of moral ideals,

[5] In this respect M. Sternberg, *The Poetics of Biblical Narrative* (Bloomington: Indiana University Press, 1985) offers the best general synthesis of the methods of historical, literary, and rhetorical criticism, and Y. Amit, *The Book of Judges: The Art of Editing* (Hebrew) (Jerusalem: Bialik, 1992; ET, J. Chipman, Biblical Interpretation Series 38, Leiden: Brill, 1999) its most convincing application to a Bible narrative book.

[6] This idea is hinted at in the paradigms of behaviour in W. Janzen, *Old Testament Ethics: A Paradigmatic Approach* (Louisville: Westminster/John Knox, 1994).

which are scattered through the pentateuchal law codes, the Psalms and the Wisdom literature. These originated at different times and in different circles, so it is not at all certain that they have the same ethical outlook as each other or as the narrative texts, but given the sparsity of information on some aspects of thought we shall assume homogeneity of outlook if heterogeneity is not demonstrable. Notwithstanding the critical problems of potentially different ethical standards in different periods, it emerges that throughout the Old Testament much more is expected of the righteous than merely keeping the letter of the law. Its writers hoped that in some way man, made in the image of God, would in some measure imitate God, his creator, in maintaining creation and in loving his fellow man. 'Be holy, for I am holy', the motto of Leviticus, sums up this aspect of Old Testament ethics.

This reconstruction of the ethical world-view of some Old Testament writers provides the background for a rereading of some problematic stories of Genesis and Judges, such as the Rape of Dinah (Gen 34), and the Gideon cycle (Judg 6–9). It will become apparent that the biblical writers do not merely assess these characters against the requirements of the law codes but against the ideals we have sketched in the preceding chapter (Chapter 5).

Obviously the behaviour of the chief actors in many instances falls miserably short of the ideal, and they often suffer in some way for their mistakes. Yet it is clear too that they are not deserted by God despite their sinfulness. So there is a paradox in Old Testament narrative ethics: on the one hand God is terribly demanding, he looks for nothing less than godlike perfect behaviour, yet on the other, despite human failings, he does not forget his covenant loyalty to his people, and ultimately brings them through the suffering that their sin has brought about. Old Testament ethics are therefore as much about grace as about law: they declare that God, the all-holy, is also God, the all-merciful.

Thus in many ways the fundamental principles of Old Testament ethics are much closer to the New Testament than is often perceived. Both look for divine attributes to be replicated in humanity, but both realise that this rarely occurs and that the overwhelming need for the human race is divine mercy. In this way the incarnation fulfils the goals of the Old Testament system of ethics. But in other more subtle ways it modifies both the vision of God and attitudes to food, marriage and violence. In the final chapter we sketch some of the continuities and differences between the two testaments.

2

CRITICAL METHODOLOGY

In this work we shall investigate the ethical norms and values embodied in the stories of the Old Testament. This though is a field of intense debate, where historical and literary theories are locked in conflict. It would make our task easier if there were more agreement by biblical scholars on historical issues and by literary critics on methods of interpretation. But until the curse of Babel is reversed, and all again share the same scholarly discourse, we shall have to put up with a diversity of critical methods and pick our way carefully through the hubbub. Others of course may prefer a different path. So it is not the purpose of this chapter to claim that the methods and solutions proposed here are the only ones possible, but simply to clarify what approach is being followed.

Since the Enlightenment, biblical study has been dominated by the historical-critical method. As the term suggests, this method is chiefly concerned with historical issues, which are vital to an informed understanding of the Bible. We need to know as much as possible about the historical environment in which the biblical narratives are set in order to understand them properly. Their marriage customs and family structures were so different from ours, that if we do not recognise these differences we shall be in great danger of misreading even the most straightforward family stories. Similarly their attitudes to women, authority, work and God differ markedly from the outlook of modern Western readers. Without the historical awareness brought by a critical approach these texts are liable to serious misinterpretation, especially in the realm of ethics. Detailed historical studies of ancient Israel's social structure are a prerequisite to understanding the ethics of the Old Testament.[1] We have to have some understanding of life in Bible times to appreciate what the texts are saying about the situations of which they speak.

An historical approach is also required to understand the language of the Bible exactly. Like all languages Hebrew has evolved down the

[1] Roland de Vaux, *Ancient Israel* (ET, J. McHugh, London: Darton, Longman & Todd, 1961); H. W. Wolff, *The Anthropology of the Old Testament* (ET, M. Kohl. London: SCM Press, 1974) and S. Bendor, *The Social Structure of Ancient Israel: The Institution of the Family from the Settlement to the End of the Monarchy* (Jerusalem: Simor, 1996) discuss in depth the social structures of Old Testament society.

years in its morphology, syntax, and lexicon: words changed their meaning over time, so that the meaning a word has in an early text may not be the same in a later text. It makes a difference, for example, whether the word *betulah* should be translated 'virgin' or 'teenage girl'.[2] Thus in the last hundred years the discovery of many texts in languages akin to biblical Hebrew, e.g. Ugaritic and Akkadian, has shed light on many terms in the Bible as well as illuminating the society and assumptions of the ancient Near East in the era in which the Bible was written.[3] Here the contribution of historical criticism has been invaluable.

Historical criticism is also essential for the dating of the biblical material. The main Old Testament story from Abraham to Malachi covers nearly two millennia, and unless we suppose that there was no historical development, it seems likely that language, attitudes and customs altered during this period. It is therefore vital to date the different biblical texts so that they are interpreted in a way that is appropriate both to the periods in which the texts originated and to the periods which they describe. Often too the date of composition may give a clue to the purpose of a text.

Historical criticism is often used to evaluate the historical reliability of a document or to distinguish the sources which have been used in the composition of a biblical book. But though many monographs have been devoted to these issues, they are marginal to a study of Old Testament narrative ethics. For we are not trying to write a history of behaviour in ancient Israel, answering such questions as: Was there a crime wave in the days of the judges? When was polygamy tolerated? or How did they wage war?[4] These are perfectly legitimate topics to explore, but they are incidental to the heart of the issue addressed here. What interests us is the stance of the biblical writers to the deeds they describe. Writers, whether of fact or fiction, write with a view to influencing their readers to think or act in a certain way. Authors convey their own outlook through their poetry or prose and seek to share it with their readers; they hope that as a result of their writing their readers will come to accept their own point of view to a greater or lesser extent. Indeed arguably one of the marks of great writers is that they write with persuasiveness convincing the reader of the rightness of their viewpoint. Since a study of narrative ethics is essentially an attempt to elucidate the writer's outlook, it usually matters very little whether the

[2] For discussion see M. Tsevat, 'Bethulah', *TDOT* 2: 338–43; G. J. Wenham, 'Betulah, "A Girl of Marriageable Age"', *VT* 22 (1972), 326–48.

[3] For discussion of principles see James Barr, *Comparative Philology and the Text of the Old Testament* (Oxford: Clarendon Press, 1968).

[4] For this sort of discussion see de Vaux, *Ancient Israel*; Gordon P. Hugenberger, *Marriage as Covenant* (VTSup 52, Leiden: Brill, 1994); Susan Niditch, *War in the Hebrew Bible* (New York: Oxford University Press, 1993).

story that is told is fiction or history.[5] From an ethical perspective at least it makes little difference whether the book of Jonah is historical or fictional: in either case the author delights in mocking Jonah's folly at believing he could run away from God and in challenging his narrow-mindedness in supposing God cares only about the salvation of Israel.[6] Thus the preoccupation with historicity and fictionality that has characterised much historical criticism is quite peripheral to our study.

Source criticism is also marginal to a study of narrative ethics. It goes without saying that all but the shortest narrative works, from Genesis to Chronicles, drew on a variety of longer or shorter sources. Sometimes these sources can be specified with some degree of probability, at others it appears to be mere speculation. But very rarely does it matter. Whether the author of Genesis was working with three major sources, J, E and P, or with umpteen independent short stories, or with just one oral tradition which he committed to writing, the message of the book is the same, and we can still study the book in the same way to elucidate the author's ethical stance. If we were confident that we could distinguish one of the sources of Genesis in its entirety by dissecting the present text, we could theoretically study the ethics of that source. But this is easier said than done. We do not know what the author of Genesis has omitted from the source, but we do know that what he has preserved is refracted through his own ethical lens. This makes the attempt to discuss the stance of a source very problematic. It is also regarded by most readers of the Old Testament as unimportant. For both Jews and Christians it is the present books of the Hebrew Bible that are canonical, not their putative sources. They read the life of David as it is told in the books of Samuel and Kings, not in the so-called Succession Narrative (2 Sam 9 – 1 Kgs 2). The pious reader wants to know what the canonical author thought about the deeds of David and his entourage, not what the author of the Succession Narrative thought. This popular focus on the final form of the story is one that is shared by most modern scholarly narrative studies of these books.[7]

In the last twenty years biblical study has been transformed by the application of literary criticism to many texts. Numerous books and articles have appeared discussing specific texts[8] while many others have

[5] Cf. MacIntyre, *After Virtue*, 114.

[6] For a careful assessment of the genre of Jonah and its messages see J. Limburg, *Jonah: A Commentary* (London: SCM Press, 1993).

[7] E.g. David M. Gunn, *The Story of King David: Genre and Interpretation* (JSOTSup 6, Sheffield: JSOT Press, 1978); *The Fate of King Saul: An Interpretation of a Biblical Story* (JSOTSup 14, Sheffield: JSOT Press, 1980); Lyle M. Eslinger, *Kingship of God in Crisis: A Close Reading of 1 Samuel 1–12* (Sheffield: Almond Press, 1985).

[8] Cf. works mentioned in footnote 7; on Judges, Lillian R. Klein, *The Triumph of Irony in the Book of Judges* (JSOTSup 68, Sheffield: JSOT Press, 1988); Barry G. Webb, *The Book of the Judges: An Integrated Reading* (JSOTSup 46, Sheffield: JSOT

explored the techniques of biblical writers more generally, illustrating their observations by frequent reference to specific texts.[9] This type of study often draws attention to the ethical positions of the biblical writers, and where scholars have embraced standpoints quite different from the Bible (e.g. feminism or Marxism) it leads to very interesting critiques of assumptions embedded in the biblical texts. But it is rarely tackled systematically.[10]

I shall therefore in the rest of this chapter attempt to do three things. First, explain the insights and terminology that literary critics have brought to the understanding of texts. Second, explore the way in which writers seek to persuade their readers to adopt their ethical norms. Third, draw attention to some of these techniques at work in the Bible.

Texts are part of a communication process. In speech we can distinguish three main stages. In face-to-face conversation:

Speaker > Message > Listener

In this situation the possibility of a listener misunderstanding the message is reduced to a minimum, because he can always question the speaker if the message is obscure. But this may well not be the case if the message is written down: the reader has to read more carefully, for if the text came from a dead author, he cannot be questioned to check what he really meant. Interpreting texts is therefore intrinsically more difficult than understanding live speech. It may be represented as follows:

Author > Text > Reader

But literary critics hold that this is too simple a picture of the communication process especially when written texts are involved. They reformulate the situation thus:

Author > (Implied Author) > Text > (Implied Reader) > Reader

How does the implied author differ from the real author, and the implied reader from the real reader? When someone speaks or writes,

---

Press, 1987); on Genesis, H. C. White, *Narration and Discourse in the Book of Genesis* (Cambridge: Cambridge University Press, 1991).

[9] Some of the most valuable studies are E. M. Good, *Irony in the Old Testament*[2] (Sheffield: Almond Press, 1981); Jacob Licht, *Storytelling in the Bible* (Jerusalem: Magnes Press, 1978); Robert Alter, *The Art of Biblical Narrative* (New York: Basic Books, 1981); Adele Berlin, *Poetics and Interpretation of Biblical Narrative* (Sheffield: Almond Press, 1983); Meir Sternberg, *The Poetics of Biblical Narrative* (Bloomington: Indiana University Press, 1985); and Shimon Bar-Efrat, *Narrative Art in the Bible* (ET, D. Shefer-Vanson, JSOTSup 70, Sheffield: Almond Press, 1989).

[10] Sternberg in chapters 12–13 of his *Poetics* comes closest to what I am looking for.

he projects an image of himself and his attitudes that may differ considerably from what he is like in real life. Usually one suspects that the implied author is better than the real author. Politicians' speeches are full of high-flown rhetoric presenting themselves as trustworthy and devoted to social justice: sadly in real life some politicians do not live up to the image they project. If we rely solely on their speeches or writings to build up a picture of them and their views, we construct the 'implied author' as opposed to the real author. In dealing with biblical texts we are always dealing with the implied author not the real author, because all our knowledge of the author and his mind is derived from the texts themselves. We have no way of independently assessing whether the real Amos matched the Amos implied by the text of his prophecy. However the inaccessibility of the real authors to readers of the Bible is no obstacle to discussing its ethics, for it is precisely the norms and values embodied in the texts that we are trying to elucidate. These are the views of the implied author, which may or may not correspond to those of the real authors. Establishing the stance of the implied author is often difficult, but it is no problem for our study that we cannot reconstruct the real authors of our texts. Since in dealing with biblical texts we are always discussing only the implied author not the real author, we shall often for the sake of brevity refer to the 'author' where 'implied author' would be more exact.

The implied reader is a mirror image of the implied author. It is the reader presupposed by the author. There may be all sorts of readers who actually read the text, but when a writer writes or a preacher preaches a sermon he has a certain sort of reader or listener in mind. The writer makes a guess at his reader's knowledge, experience, and outlook and pitches his presentation to appeal to this implied reader. If a real reader is to grasp accurately what the writer is saying, he must approximate to this implied reader, otherwise he is likely to pick up the wrong end of the stick. 'It is only as I read that I become the self whose beliefs must coincide with the author's. Regardless of my real beliefs and practices, I must subordinate my mind and heart to the book if I am to enjoy it to the full.'[11]

But the central critical problem is to discover the implied author and his outlook. How do we determine his standpoint? We can illustrate the problem from the book of Job. In it we meet several characters, Job, God, the Satan, Job's wife, the comforters, and Elihu, as well as the narrator who sets the scene in chapters 1 and 2 telling us what happened in heaven and on earth. The narrator is also responsible for introducing each speech, 'Then Job (Bildad) answered', etc. and for the concluding summary in chapter 42.

[11] Wayne C. Booth, *The Rhetoric of Fiction* (Chicago and London: University of Chicago Press, 1961), 138.

The implied author of Job is responsible for the whole text. Though he may be supposed to be recording the words of Job or his friends, it is ultimately the author's version of their speeches that we have. The author decided what to include and what to omit, so in a real sense all the words are his. But that does not mean he agrees with what every character says or even with what the narrator says: in modern fiction 'unreliable narrators' who do not represent the author's outlook are well known. The task of the reader of Job is to weigh the comments of the different characters and decide how far they reflect the author's views. Presumably the Satan, Job's wife, and Job's friends are unreliable, since they are condemned by God himself. God's words must surely be regarded as reliable, and as the narrator claims knowledge of what happens in heaven as well as on earth, it would appear that he too is reliable in this book. It is more difficult to assess the status of the speeches of Job and Elihu and whether they reflect the implied author's view, but this is what constitutes the reader's task.[12]

The status of the narrator in biblical texts has been much discussed. Though in modern novels the narrator may be unreliable, especially when he or she speaks in the first person, in classic realist fiction the third-person narrator was both reliable, in that he or she accurately reflected the implied author's views, and also omniscient, in that the narrator appears to know everything about the characters portrayed, their psychology and inner emotions, that would never be apparent to the ordinary human observer such as the other actors in the story.

In most Old Testament narrative the narrator is apparently omniscient. He informs the reader about what people think, what they do in secret, and most importantly what God thinks. For Alter this is a clear indication that the Old Testament is fiction, but for Sternberg it is a claim to divine inspiration.[13] Though Sternberg's interpretation of the 'omniscience' phenomenon in the Bible would seem to fit the nature of this ancient text better, it is not vital to our discussion. For as mentioned above, it makes little difference to the ethical stance of the implied author whether he is recording history or creating fiction. Much more germane to our discussion is Sternberg's insistence that the voice of the biblical narrator is to be identified with the implied author. The biblical 'narrator is absolutely and straightforwardly reliable. Historians may quarrel with his facts and others call them fiction; but in context

[12] For two modern attempts to do justice to the different standpoints in the book of Job see David J. A. Clines, *Job 1–20* (WBC, Dallas: Word, 1989) and Norman C. Habel, *The Book of Job* (OTL, London: SCM Press, 1985).

[13] 'Prose fiction is the best general rubric for describing biblical narrative.' Alter, *Art of Biblical Narrative*, 24. Sternberg, *Poetics*, 25–35.

his remain accounts of the truth communicated on the highest authority.'[14] However, Sternberg allows that the narrator's comments, though reliable, do not present the full views of the author: to obtain a fuller picture further reflection on the total story is required. As a general principle Sternberg is correct in holding that in most cases the narrator does reflect the position of the implied author: there are arguably a few passages where the statements of the narrator conflict with other data in the text[15] which could suggest the author does not endorse every word of the narrator, but they do not affect our study of ethics. The narrator's comments on moral issues will be central to our discussion.

Having clarified the understanding of such a term as the implied author, we are ready to have a preliminary look at how his norms are embodied in texts and in particular how we discover them. But we must digress briefly to argue the case that literary works do have ethical values of which they are explicitly or implicitly trying to convince their readers. The case has been put most eloquently by Wayne Booth in *The Company We Keep: An Ethics of Fiction*.[16] Though Booth's work focuses on the great classics of modern English literature, his argument applies to other forms of writing, poetry, history, journalism, and indeed to other narrative media such as film.

The title of the book is taken from *David Copperfield*, where the lonely David describes his books as his friends. More precisely the reader is always conducting a sort of conversation with the implied author of the work. It is the implied author who is in charge of the conversation. He or she dictates the course of the conversation, but it is the reader's decision whether to continue it. If we do not like the subject of the conversation or the author's attitude to the subject, we may well give up reading. But to continue requires us to submit at least partially to the interests and values of the author. 'Whenever I work my way into a narrative . . . the "I" that is "me" becomes increasingly like my picture of the implied author: I succumb – I begin to see as he or she sees, to feel as she feels, to love what he loves, or to mock what she mocks.'[17]

Booth illustrates his point by looking at the values of popular fiction as well as more serious works. To appreciate *Jaws* for example, we must both fear spectacular bloodshed and desire it. We must want the shark to eat someone, yet also be glad when the good guys escape. We must accept that for the characters in the story happiness consists in

[14] Sternberg, *Poetics*, 51. For a critique of this view see David M. Gunn, 'Reading Right', in *The Bible in Three Dimensions* (ed. David J. A. Clines, Stephen E. Fowl and Stanley E. Porter; JSOTSup 87, Sheffield: JSOT Press, 1990), 53–64.

[15] E.g. in Joshua.

[16] Wayne C. Booth, *The Company We Keep: An Ethics of Fiction* (Berkeley and Los Angeles: University of California Press, 1988).

[17] Booth, *Company*, 256.

escaping from danger, whereas for me, the reader or viewer, pleasure consists in seeing others endangered and then miraculously escaping.[18]

Similarly if we are to enjoy a Jane Austen novel or one of Hardy's we must, as we read, identify with their values. We must want Elizabeth Bennet to marry Darcy in *Pride and Prejudice* or when reading *Tess of the Durbervilles*, if we desire her happiness we must share the author's vision of that happiness, which is to meet a man like the implied Thomas Hardy who would appreciate her and protect her.[19]

Because continuing to read or listen to a story involves the consent of the reader, there is an active involvement of the reader with the implied author. As Poulet observes: 'As soon as I replace my direct perception of reality by the words of a book, I deliver myself, bound hand and foot, to the omnipotence of fiction . . . I am thinking the thoughts of another.'[20] This means that all storytelling is implicitly didactic, and because it involves the reader's imaginative involvement, powerfully so.[21] Furthermore the images we derive from narrative become part of us, so that it becomes difficult to distinguish what we were before we read from what we have become through reading stories.

> Anyone who conducts honest introspection knows that 'real life' is lived *in* images derived in part from stories. Though usually our imitations are not highly dramatic, especially once past adolescence, everyone who reads knows that whether or not we *should* imitate narrative heroes and heroines, we in fact do.[22]

Booth makes these points about fiction, and does not discuss in what way they apply to historical narrative. It is evident that historical writing makes a much stronger claim on its readers than fiction: this is what *really* happened and is important, is at least implied by every historian. Their heroes were real people, who actually did what is recorded, not the make-believe creations of novelists. Thus intrinsically history is a much more authoritative narrative than fiction. This is especially so when the history of a nation is being recounted. English schoolchildren are taught the significance of the Norman Conquest, Reformation, Spanish Armada and so on with the implication that this is what made us who we are and this is what we are like. 'The medium for this shaping of character in community is encounter with the stories those communities tell.'[23] There is thus a normative claim in historical narrative

[18] Booth, *Company*, 202–3.

[19] Booth, *Company*, 206.

[20] G. Poulet, in *The Structuralist Controversy* (ed. R. Macksey and E. Donato, Baltimore, 1972), 58, 59 quoted in Booth, *Company*, 139.

[21] Booth, *Company*, 201.

[22] Booth, *Company*, 228–9.

[23] B. C. Birch in *The Bible in Ethics: The Second Sheffield Colloquium* (ed. John W. Rogerson, M. Davies and M. D. Carroll R. (JSOTSup 207, Sheffield: JSOT Press, 1995), 123.

that fiction for all its interest rarely makes. As far as the Old Testament is concerned, despite modern scholars' doubts about their historical reliability, there is no doubt that most of the Old Testament narratives claim to be historical and were read that way by their first readers. Because these accounts profess to be dealing with the historical origins and later experiences of the nation, they were doubtless perceived by their readers as having intrinsic authority. Therefore to identify their ethical norms and values should clarify their didactic purpose.

In his broad survey of modern literature Booth argues for the ubiquity of ethical norms in literature, though these of course vary widely from work to work, but he gives relatively few examples of what these norms and values are: that of course would involve a detailed commentary on each work. He observes that jokes about stupidity depend on and reinforce stereotypes about the sort of people likely to be stupid. Detective stories assume that crimes deserve to be punished, should be solved and that the world will be a happier place when they are.[24] Booth argues that great works like Shakespeare's have universal appeal partly because their norms are very widely shared,[25] a synthesis of biblical and classical norms. Whereas the high modernism of James Joyce and others 'was a direct and often deliberate attempt to depose "the good" as the sovereign served by both classical philosophy and the Judeo-Christian tradition, and to crown in its place the individual and his creative works'.[26]

While recognising the value of many of Booth's insights Martha Nussbaum has criticised him for his pluralism. He not only recognises that there are diverse ethical stances taken by different writers, but refuses to choose between them, whereas an Aristotelian like Nussbaum wants to affirm the objectivity of certain virtues.[27] For her part Nussbaum has explored the connections between Greek tragedy and philosophy and the novel. Tragedians and philosophers 'agreed that the aim of their work was to provide illumination concerning how one should live'.[28] But she argues that the poets' preference for tragedy as opposed to philosophy was not merely aesthetic: it was based on their belief in the importance of emotion and chance events.[29] It also allowed for a sense of openness in moral decision: not everything could be decided by rules. Fiction allows the reader to develop perception

[24] Booth, *Company*, 152.

[25] Booth, *Rhetoric of Fiction*, 141–2.

[26] Booth, *Company*, 251.

[27] Marxist critics accuse Booth of favouring middle-class Victorian values, cf. Raman Selden, Peter Widdowson and Peter Brooker, *A Reader's Guide to Contemporary Literary Theory*[4] (Hemel Hempstead: Prentice-Hall, 1997), 113.

[28] Martha C. Nussbaum, *Love's Knowledge: Essays on Philosophy and Literature* (Oxford/New York: Oxford University Press, 1990), 23.

[29] Nussbaum, *Love's Knowledge*, 26.

into the salient features of situations and develop an ethic that is not based exclusively on general rules, but one that is responsive to concrete situations.[30]

These observations are pertinent to a reading of Old Testament narratives, which seldom contain explicit moral judgements, but much more often leave the events to speak for themselves, thereby encouraging the reader to reflect on and relate past events to him- or herself in the present. Where however there is a danger that the reader might misjudge the situation, an authoritative comment may be heard. Some oriental despots might be permitted to have affairs and eliminate awkward subjects, but to avoid such a misunderstanding of David's treatment of Uriah, the narrator comments: 'the thing that David had done displeased the LORD' (2 Sam 11:27). The remark 'the LORD saw that the wickedness of man was great in the earth' (Gen 6:5) presages the flood and explains God's motives for sending it. Simultaneously it denies the common Near Eastern view that the flood was simply an attempt by the gods to curb human population growth.

Sometimes the author's viewpoint is expressed by one of the actors in the story. The author surely concurs with the Levite, who described the rape of his concubine as 'they have committed abomination and wantonness in Israel' (Judg 20:6) or with Tamar's impassioned rebuke of her brother Amnon 'you would be one of the wanton fools in Israel' (2 Sam 13:13).[31] On other occasions the choice of word is enough to alert us to the author's views. The scenic mode of storytelling[32] so beloved of the biblical narrators may appear to be showing us just what happened in quite objective fashion, but an evaluative adjective or verb gives the narrator's own judgement on the behaviour.[33] 'A *wise* woman called from the city' (2 Sam 20:16), 'Sarai *ill-treated* her' (Gen 16:6) or 'the people of Israel *played the harlot* after the Baals' (Judg 8:33).

Comments by the narrator remind the reader that it is a story he or she is reading: they put a distance between the narrator and reader and reduce the emotional involvement of the latter.

> A reader who is totally absorbed in the plot will be able neither to see the events dispassionately, nor to judge them and assess their significance. A certain emotional distance is a precondition for clear thinking, and without it it is impossible to grasp the ideas in the narrative. The explanations help in understanding the narrative, emphasising certain points and influencing

[30] Nussbaum, *Love's Knowledge*, 37.

[31] 'There can be scarcely any doubt that by placing this statement in Tamar's mouth the narrator's opinion of Amnon is being expressed and conveyed to the reader.' Bar-Efrat, *Narrative Art*, 55.

[32] For a definition see Licht, *Storytelling*, 29.

[33] Bar-Efrat, *Narrative Art*, 33.

the formation of the reader's opinion in accordance with the author's ideas and values.[34]

On the other hand it is most important to keep the reader emotionally involved and identifying with the actors in the story, otherwise he or she will not care about the outcome of the story or adopt its values. This is one reason why scenic representation of events is preferred in the Bible. 'This has the effect of dramatising the action before our eyes, but in a narrative, or film-like, manner.'[35]

Just as in a film, scenic narrative allows for different points of view to be shown. In the Isaac deathbed blessing episode in Genesis 27, the first scene has just Esau and Isaac on stage (vv. 1–4), the next has Rebekah and Jacob plotting to deceive Isaac (vv. 5–17), then comes the central scene when Jacob goes in to Isaac, persuades him that he is Esau, and then receives the first-born's blessing (vv. 18–29), and finally we are back with Isaac and Esau to hear the bitter cry 'Bless me, even me also, O my father!' (v. 34). By switching viewpoints the narrator makes us understand and sympathise with each party's outlook. We are made to realise that no one in this incident is without blame. Our last glimpse of Isaac is of an old blind man, 'ill at ease with every single member of his family, all (like himself) sinning and sinned against as a result of his folly'.[36]

This episode is most revealing in the way it brings out the viewpoints of the different actors. It is also one of many in the Old Testament which show the depth of its moral insight and its avoidance of simple black-and-white judgements. It deals with a world where there are few perfect saints and few unredeemable sinners: most of its heroes and heroines have both virtues and vices, they mix obedience and unbelief. Their behaviour and attitudes must parallel those of the ancient Israelite readers in so many ways that they could identify with them quite easily. But can one be more specific? What ethical ideals are these authors implying in their narratives to which they hope their readers will aspire? By focusing on two quite different narrative works, Genesis and Judges, we hope to establish principles that may help the understanding of other Old Testament books as well.

[34] Bar-Efrat, *Narrative Art*, 31. Similarly B. Brecht's 'alienation effect' seeks to shatter the audience's illusion that the play is reality. Selden, Widdowson and Brooker, *Reader's Guide*, 97–8.

[35] Berlin, *Poetics and Interpretation*, 46.

[36] Sternberg, *Poetics*, 350.

3

THE RHETORICAL FUNCTION OF GENESIS

The previous chapter has introduced the concept of the implied author and the system of ethical norms that this notion entails. We noted a few remarks in a variety of stories which put these norms into words. But these are insufficient by themselves to establish the ethics of the biblical storytellers: we need to see individual stories within the context of complete books. To take an individual episode in the life of Abraham on its own could be as misleading as just focusing on the speeches of one character in the book of Job. Before attempting to explore the ethics of the implied author, it is necessary to reach an understanding of the message of the whole book. Whether the writer is trying to glorify the past or damn it makes a profound difference to our understanding of his ethical stance towards the deeds he relates. Instinctively we suppose the author of Genesis is endorsing its heroes, while we feel the author of Judges is much less impressed with the deeds he recounts. But these preliminary judgements need to be checked by a careful analysis of each book and its overall message.

In recent years the revival of rhetorical criticism and its application to the Bible has served to elucidate the message of several biblical texts.[1] The principles of rhetoric have been discussed from the time of Aristotle, so that it is clearly appropriate to suppose that they might have influenced consciously or unconsciously the composition of New Testament books. Unless one postulates a very late origin for the Old Testament no such assumption is plausible here. However, though the formal principles of Greek rhetoric cannot have influenced the composition of the Old Testament, Hebrew writers like others were in the business of persuasive communication: they were seeking to impart an important message and presumably organised their books to make their points as effectively as they could. Rhetorical criticism may thus serve to elucidate the message of an Old Testament book even though the Hebrew writers were not following all the rules of Greek rhetoric.

Rhetorical criticism combines the insights of the critical methods discussed in Chapter 2. On the one hand, literary criticism illuminates the compositional techniques of the biblical writers, e.g. their use of parallelism, repetition, chiasmus, metaphor and paronomasia, and seeks

[1] For a review of the approach see Dale Patrick and Allen Scult, *Rhetoric and Biblical Interpretation* (JSOTSup 82, Sheffield: Almond Press, 1990).

to elucidate the structure of texts with a view to understanding the writer's message. On the other hand, historical criticism aims to explain the date and circumstances of the composition of different books. Rhetorical criticism, however, uses the insights of literary criticism to shed light, not simply on the writer's literary genius and artistic skills, but on the argument that the writer is developing in a work. What kind of a work are we dealing with?[2] How does one section of a work lead logically into the next? How does each part contribute to the argument of the whole work? These are the primary questions asked by the rhetorical critic.

But they lead into a second set of questions that in biblical studies have been primarily the concern of historical criticism. Who are the implied readers? For what audience is the book intended? What was their point of view? What were their attitudes and assumptions? How does the book address the audience's concerns? When is it likely to have been written, i.e. when is the implied readership likely to have existed? Rhetorical criticism attempts to integrate these two types of question, the message of the book on the one hand and the intended readership on the other. By synthesising the two it has offered some convincing interpretations of biblical texts.

There have been two full-scale rhetorical critical studies of Judges,[3] but surprisingly no comparable studies of Genesis.[4] This is probably because the dominant approaches to Genesis have seen its parts in isolation rather than looking at the book as a whole.[5] Whereas Christian theologians have concentrated on chapters 1–11, the primeval history, and Jews on chapters 12–50, the story of the patriarchs, biblical critics have focused on the underlying sources with studies such as 'The Kerygma of the Yahwist',[6] or 'The Kerygma of the "Priestly Writers"',[7]

[2] Classical rhetoric classified works into three main categories. *Deliberative* oratory was concerned with future actions and was aimed at encouraging or discouraging certain courses of action. *Forensic* oratory was concerned with the past and aimed to justify or condemn past behaviour. *Epideictic* oratory was the most ornate form 'not so much concerned with persuading an audience as with pleasing and inspiring it'. E. P. J. Corbett, *Classical Rhetoric for the Modern Student*[3] (Oxford: Oxford University Press, 1990), 29. Biblical books often do not fit neatly into one category or another. Whereas Deuteronomy is essentially a deliberative discourse, the prophets contain both deliberative and forensic discourse, whereas the narrative books are a mixture of epideictic and forensic discourse.

[3] Y. Amit, *The Book of Judges: The Art of Editing* (Leiden: Brill, 1999); R. H. O'Connell, *The Rhetoric of the Book of Judges* (VTSup 63, Leiden: Brill, 1996).

[4] T. E. Fretheim, *The Pentateuch* (Nashville: Abingdon Press, 1996) uses some rhetorical critical insights, but a more rigorous application is needed.

[5] D. Carr, '*Biblos geneseos* Revisited: A Synchronic Analysis of Patterns in Genesis as Part of the Torah', *ZAW* 110 (1998), 159–72, 327–47.

[6] H. W. Wolff, *Int* 20 (1966), 131–58.

[7] W. Brueggemann, *ZAW* 84 (1972), 397–414.

but studies of the theology of Genesis or the rhetorical strategy of Genesis have not appeared. Closest to what is needed is D. J. A. Clines, *The Theme of the Pentateuch*,[8] but as the title suggests its brief is much wider than the book of Genesis. In what follows therefore we must make our own way adapting the methodology of Amit[9] on the book of Judges to a study of Genesis.

The major problem facing a rhetorical study of Genesis is the relationship between the primeval history from creation to the tower of Babel (chs 1–11) and the main part of the book, the story of the patriarchs from the call of Abraham to the death of Joseph in Egypt (chs 12–50). How do these major sections relate to each other, and what light do they shed on each other? Is it simply chronological sequence that unites them, or are there connecting motifs and themes that tie both parts together? To this end we shall look at features and keywords that occur in both the primeval and patriarchal stories. Then we shall look at the divine promises made to the patriarchs, which are clearly of prime importance to the author, and ask how these promises relate to the stories of the patriarchs and also back to the primeval history. This will allow us to read Genesis 1–11 as an introductory exposition to the main cycles dealing with Abraham, Jacob and Joseph in the rest of the book. Finally we shall look at possible settings for the book of Genesis in the history of Israel. In what periods could one imagine its ideas being entertained and in what circumstances would its ideas be most relevant? This will sharpen our appreciation of the ethical stance of the implied author and help to determine whether Genesis is simply a panegyric for the patriarchs or is somewhat more nuanced in its appreciation of their achievements.

The structure of Genesis

The clearest structural marker in Genesis is the formula that occurs ten times, traditionally translated 'These are the generations of'. This so-called *toledot*-formula might be better rendered 'This is the family history of'. Five times in Genesis it introduces a genealogy (5:1; 10:1; 11:10; 25:12; 36:1),[10] and five times it introduces a major cycle of stories (2:4 the story of Adam; 6:9 the flood; 11:27, 25:19, 37:2 the stories of Abraham, Jacob and Joseph). The short genealogies alternate with the long narratives centred on key actors in the overall story. This pattern invites us to compare the careers of the leading figures in the story with

[8] JSOTSup 10, Sheffield: JSOT Press, 1978.

[9] See footnote 3 above.

[10] Repeated in 36:9 for some reason, perhaps because 36:9–43 was added later, cf. Claus Westermann, *Genesis 12–36: A Commentary* (ET, J. J. Scullion, London: SPCK, 1986), 561.

each other. Most obviously Adam's and Noah's careers echo each other, but Abraham and Jacob also have similar experiences, and there are hints from time to time of parallels between the antediluvians and the later patriarchs. Furthermore these genealogies serve not simply to show how all the nations of the world known to ancient Israel were descended from Adam, but how they were related to Israel. This interest in lines of descent is not confined to the genealogies. The longer cycles often go into greater detail about Israel's relationship with its closest neighbours, e.g. Moab and Ammon (19:30–38), the Ishmaelites and the Philistines (chs 20–21), the Hittites (ch. 23), the Edomites (i.e. Esau) (chs 25–28, 31–33), the Hivites (ch. 34), the Canaanites (ch. 38), and the Egyptians (chs 39–50). For the most part Israel's relationship with these other peoples is portrayed quite positively. There is an atmosphere of ecumenical bonhomie between the patriarchs and the other inhabitants of Canaan,[11] while Egypt and Israel are portrayed as mutually indebted to each other for survival.

With the birth of Jacob's sons in chapter 30 the focus moves from relationships between Israel and the other peoples to those between the sons, the ancestors of the twelve tribes. Maternal jealousy marks their birth, and sibling rivalry mars subsequent family life. Only after the death of Jacob is there a whole-hearted reconciliation between them, which is ascribed to the will of God (50:19–20).

Keywords in Genesis

The book's interest in genealogy is shown too by the keyword *zeraʿ*, traditionally translated 'seed' or 'offspring', which occurs more frequently in Genesis than any other book.[12] It is used first of human seed in 3:15, of Seth, Adam and Eve's third son, in 4:25, several times in the flood story, and many times in the patriarchal promises, e.g. 12:7 'to your seed I will give this land'. 'Seed' in Hebrew and English is a collective, so while it usually refers to descendants in the plural, 'your seed will be like the dust of the earth' (28:14), it may refer to a single individual, such as Ishmael (21:13). It may well be that when the sense is individual and distant, there is a reference to the ruler descended from Judah who is foretold in 49:8–12. Certainly 17:6 and 35:11 envisage kings descended from the patriarchs.

Another term used more often in Genesis than in any other biblical book is 'bless, blessing' (Hebrew *berek*, *berakah*).[13] It is especially

[11] Cf. R. W. L. Moberly, *The Old Testament of the Old Testament* (Minneapolis: Fortress Press, 1992), 99–103.

[12] It is used 59 times in Genesis as opposed to 229 uses in the whole Old Testament. T. Desmond Alexander, 'Genealogies, Seed and the Compositional Unity of Genesis', *TynBul* 44 (1993), 255–70. Statistic, 259.

[13] Used 88 times in Genesis out of 398 uses in the whole Old Testament.

frequent in the context of the patriarchal narratives, but it makes several significant appearances in the introductory chapters, where God blesses the birds and fishes (1:22), mankind (1:28), the Sabbath (2:3), and Noah (9:1). Once again Genesis' interest in procreation is evident, for God's blessing is linked with his command to 'be fruitful and multiply' in 1:22, 28 and 9:1. The importance of blessing is of course central to the patriarchal stories. The idyllic picture of Isaac's enjoyment of God's blessing in chapter 26 is followed by the bitter struggle to inherit it in chapter 27. But this does not exhaust Genesis' enthusiasm for blessing. Paronomasia is a favourite device of Hebrew writers, and there are many puns in Genesis on significant words, and it seems hardly a coincidence that Abraham's name contains the letters b and r, two of the three Hebrew letters in the root for blessing.[14] It has also been noted that the first two words of the book 'in the beginning' (*br'št*) 'he created' (*br'*) also begin with these two letters.[15] Genesis begins as it were with an allusion to blessing and comes to a climax with Jacob on his deathbed blessing the twelve tribes in their future holdings (ch. 49).

The third word in Genesis used so often that it has become a keyword or *leitmotif* is 'land, earth' (*'ereṣ*) and the associated term 'ground' (*'adamah*).[16] *'ereṣ* refers to the earth as opposed to the heavens in 1:1, the dry land as opposed to the sea in 1:10, political territory such as Egypt, 45:19, but specially Canaan the promised land, e.g. 12:1, 5. In some contexts *'adamah* and *'ereṣ* are interchangeable, but more usually *'adamah* refers to the soil from which Adam was taken, which is cursed because of his sin, and to which he will return (2:19; 3:17, 19). It is the soil that grows crops for Cain and for Noah (4:2; 9:20) but fails to crop for the Egyptians during the famine (47:19).

Most of these keywords occur together in 12:1–3, the call of Abraham, generally regarded as programmatic for the whole of Genesis:

> Go from your *country* . . . to the *land* that I will show you. And I will make of you a great nation, and I will *bless* you, and make your name great, so that you will be a *blessing*. I will *bless* those who *bless* you, and him who curses you I will curse; and in you all the families of the *earth* will find *blessing*.

'Bless' or 'blessing' occurs five times here, 'land' or 'earth' three times, and though the word 'seed' is not found here, that is clearly presupposed by the promise of nationhood.

[14] A. Strus, *Nomen-Omen* (AnBib 80, Rome: Biblical Institute Press, 1978).

[15] D. F. Pennant, *Bib* 68 (1987), 390–2.

[16] *'adamah* occurs 43 times in Genesis out of a total of 225 occurrences, and *'ereṣ* 311 times out of 2,504. Genesis contains about 1/18 of the OT text, so even *'ereṣ* occurs twice as often as might be expected, and *'adamah* about four times as often.

From this point in Genesis nearly all the speeches attributed to God are concerned with these promises, developing them, elaborating them, and making them more explicit and definite. Much of the human dialogue too is explicitly or implicitly concerned with them. There are four elements within these promises that keep recurring: (1) descendants/nationhood; (2) land; (3) covenantal relationship; and (4) blessing to the nations. The development of each promise may be traced through Genesis. For example the land promise starts out very vague: 'a land I will show you' (12:1). It becomes more precise in 12:7 'this land', and yet more in 13:15 'all the land which you see'. Its boundaries are defined in 15:18, 'from the river of Egypt to the . . . river Euphrates', and finally it is named in 17:8, 'all the land of Canaan' and said to be 'for an everlasting possession'. Similar developments can be traced in the elaboration of the other aspects of the promise. These promise elements of land, descendants and covenantal relationship are the most visible components of blessing, which is the overarching concept in the book of Genesis.

The theme of Genesis

The story line of Genesis 12–50 could be summed up as the gradual and partial fulfilment of these promises. All the couples in the chosen line, Abraham and Sarah, Isaac and Rebekah, Jacob and Rachel, have difficulty in conceiving, but by the end of the book Jacob and his descendants have reached the magic number seventy, and if not quite a great nation, they are at least a significant clan (46:27). Similarly Genesis notes carefully the acquisition of various territorial rights in the land of Canaan, particularly wells, a burial ground, and an altar plot (21:25–34; 23:1–20; 26:12–33; 33:19–20). The narrator is very concerned to point out that these rights were either bought outright or recognised in public legal ceremonies, as was the border with the Aramaean Laban (31:52). But at the end of Genesis they are living in Egypt not in Canaan, and were it not for the express wish of Jacob and Joseph to be buried in Canaan, one might conclude that Goshen would be the long-term homeland of Israel.

These features have led David Clines to define the theme of the Pentateuch as follows: 'the partial fulfilment – which implies the partial non-fulfilment – of the promise to or blessing of the patriarchs. The promise or blessing is both the divine initiative in a world where human initiatives always lead to disaster, and a re-affirmation of the primal divine intentions for man.'[17]

[17] David J. A. Clines, *The Theme of the Pentateuch* (JSOTSup 10, Sheffield: JSOT Press, 1978), 29.

This is an excellent summary of the theme of Genesis at least. Strangely in his detailed discussion of the promises Clines omits the promise of blessing to the nations, which is very prominent in the most programmatic statements of the promise in 12:1–3; 22:16–18; 26:2–5; 28:13–14. Though there is little explicit reference to its fulfilment in Genesis, there are some notable examples of divine blessing on the nations through the actions of Abraham or his descendants in the book (chs 14, 20, 26, 47), so that it should not be ignored. It also serves as an important connection with the opening chapters, which sets Israel within the context of world history and relates its destiny to the other nations.

Theological interpreters of Genesis 1–11 have traditionally seen it to be making statements about the nature of God and the world. Creation and fall is the most popular model: the good world created by God in chapters 1–2 is ruined by human sin in chapter 3 and the after-effects of the fall are portrayed in the succeeding chapters. Von Rad nuanced this view somewhat by suggesting that chapters 3 onwards portray an avalanche of sin: the sins become more serious and so do the consequences. Cain's murder is more serious than Adam's disobedience and his penalty, perpetual nomadism, is more severe than Adam's exclusion from the garden. Von Rad also noted a theme in counterpoint to this spread-of-sin theme – a spread-of-grace theme. In his punishment of sin God shows mercy, for example providing clothes for Adam and Eve, and guaranteeing Cain that no one will kill him. The flood story concludes with a divine assurance that the world will never again be destroyed by water (9:15). 'What is described, therefore, is a story of God with man, the story of continuously new punishment and at the same time gracious preservation.'[18]

More recently it has been observed that Genesis 1–7 parallels Genesis 8–11, in a creation–decreation pattern. The land emerges from the primeval ocean in 1:9, is submerged again in the flood, and re-emerges after the flood in 8:5–14. Noah is a second Adam in being the father of all mankind, initially perfect (6:9), but then like Adam he succumbs to sin in an episode echoing the fall (9:20–27).[19]

These insights into the recurrent patterns in Genesis 1–11 are useful, but they do little to illuminate the connection of the opening chapters with the rest of the book. But here Clines' observation is pregnant with possibilities, especially for ethical studies. He states that the promises to the patriarchs are 'a re-affirmation of the primal divine intentions for man'. Unfortunately he does not unpack this at all fully. Genesis 1:26–28 states that man is made in God's image to fill the earth and

[18] G. von Rad, *Genesis*[2] (OTL, London: SCM Press, 1972), 153.

[19] A. J. Tomasino, 'History Repeats Itself: the "Fall" and Noah's Drunkenness', *VT* 42 (1992), 128–30.

subdue it and is blessed. These ideas are of course central to the promises to the patriarchs, who are promised land, numerous descendants, and divine blessing. In the light of Genesis 1–11 one might wonder whether mankind would ever fulfil the original divine mandate. The opening chapters 'may be read as a story of how things go wrong when men take the initiatives; mankind tends to destroy what God has made good. Perhaps only the addition of a divine promise (Gen. 12) to a divine command (ch. 1) can counteract that tendency'.[20]

In trying to develop a coherent view of the relationship between the opening chapters and the main body of Genesis, we must certainly give full weight to Clines' observations. However, we prefer to read Genesis 1–11 as an exposition for the rest of the book. Indeed it could said to consist of a bipartite exposition; 1:1 – 2:3 is a hymnic overture to the book, and in 2:4 with the first use of the *toledot*-formula, 'These are the generations of', the primeval history begins in earnest.

The first exposition (1:1 – 2:3)

In reading a book special attention needs to be devoted to the opening, for as Rimmon-Kenan says: 'information and attitudes presented at an early stage of the text tend to encourage the reader to interpret everything in their light'.[21]

Genesis 1 does this very effectively. 'In the beginning God created the heavens and the earth' introduces one God, not a pantheon, who takes the initiative and orders[22] all that happens in the whole universe. The implied monotheism of Genesis 1 is one example of the persistent critique of Near Eastern theology that runs throughout Genesis 1–11 culminating in its trenchant attack on the religious pretensions of Babylon and its tower.

This picture of one God in total control is reaffirmed repeatedly in Genesis, most obviously in the flood story and at turning points in history, when God 'remembers' people and intervenes on their behalf (cf. 8:1; 19:29; 30:22). Just before the end of Genesis, another key point for interpretation, Joseph reminds his brothers of God's sovereign control of human affairs: 'you meant evil against me; but God meant it for good' (50:20).

God's sovereignty is further underlined by the acts of creation that follow. Each time God speaks, his command is obeyed; there is light, the dry land appears, fish swarm in the seas and so on. God is a speaking

[20] Clines, *Theme of the Pentateuch*, 79.

[21] Shlomith Rimmon-Kenan, *Narrative Fiction: Contemporary Poetics* (London: Routledge, 1983), 120.

[22] The debate about *ex nihilo* creation is irrelevant to our discussion here. For a justification of the views assumed here see Gordon J. Wenham, *Genesis 1–15* (WBC, Waco: Word Books, 1987).

God, and what he says happens. This speaking anticipates his promises to the patriarchs, the theme of Genesis, and serves to give the reader confidence that they too will be fulfilled as assuredly as God's creative words have been (cf. Jer 31:35–36; Ps 89:35–37).

The acts of creation on the first five days have a polemical thrust in denying the divinity of the sun, moon, and sea monsters as much of the ancient Orient believed,[23] but their chief purpose is preparing a world suitable for human habitation, for the whole story reaches a climax with the creation of mankind on the sixth day. However already the creation of the environment hints at concerns that run through Genesis: the plants and fruit trees bear 'seed' (a Genesis keyword), while the birds and fish are 'blessed' (another keyword) and commanded to 'be fruitful and multiply' (1:11, 22).

Against the background of ancient Near Eastern mythology Genesis' account of the creation of mankind is strikingly original and distinctive. According to the Atrahasis epic,[24] the fullest and closest Babylonian parallel to Genesis 1–9, the gods created mankind as an afterthought to provide them with food. The subsequent population explosion led the gods to send famine, plague, and finally a flood to destroy the human race. Only the dissent of one of the gods enabled Atrahasis (=Noah) to escape in an ark. But Genesis portrays the one God as in favour of the human race.

Though this critique of ancient Near Eastern thinking emerges most clearly in the flood story, it is already evident in 1:26–31. Here the creation of mankind is seen as the culmination of the six days' work, and God pronounces all that he has made very good. Mankind is created in two sexes, male and female: he is blessed and commanded to be fruitful and multiply. God gives the plants to man for food; it is not man's duty to supply the gods with food. Finally and most significantly, man is made in God's image. The nature of this image is elusive,[25] but the function of the image is clear: it enables mankind to rule over the earth and the other creatures. In ancient oriental myth kings were made in the gods' image, but Genesis democratises the idea; every human being is a king and responsible for managing[26] the world on God's behalf.

[23] Cf. Gerhard F. Hasel, 'The Polemic Nature of the Genesis Cosmology', *EvQ* 46 (1974), 81–102.

[24] For an up-to-date translation of these texts see Stephanie Dalley, *The Myths of Mesopotamia* (Oxford: Oxford University Press, 1990).

[25] For discussions see Claus Westermann, *Genesis 1–11: A Commentary* (ET, J. J. Scullion, London: SPCK, 1984), 147–61, and other commentaries.

[26] Benevolence towards the governed, not exploitation, was the mark of the good ruler according to oriental and biblical thought: see Psalm 72, which is rich in allusions to Genesis 1–3. For a review of the main interpretations of the image of God see Gunnlaugur A. Jónsson, *The Image of God: Gen 1:26–28 in a Century of OT Research* (ConBOT 26, Lund: Almqvist & Wiksell International, 1988).

This positive vision of humanity's place in the divine economy echoes on through Genesis. Whereas in 1:28 God commands mankind to be fruitful and multiply, the genealogies in chapters 5 and 11 repeatedly observe that so-and-so 'had other sons and daughters', and the patriarchs are repeatedly assured that they will have numerous descendants. Conversely homicide is viewed as the gravest of crimes, itself warranting the death penalty at human hands, and Onan's attempt to frustrate the procreation of descendants leads to the LORD slaying him (4:1–16; 9:1–7; 38:9–10).

The image of God is not just invoked to underline the sanctity of human life, but it also signifies man's royal role as God's vice-gerent on earth. Here is a foreshadowing of the promise that among Abraham's descendants there will be kings (17:6) and more particularly that 'the sceptre will not depart from Judah' (49:10). Kings were supposed to act benevolently towards their subjects and seek their welfare, and Genesis 1:28 gives man dominion over the other creatures. In 2:19 Adam names the animals, demonstrating his authority over them, but the fall introduces tension between man and the animals (3:14–15; 9:5). However, Noah the perfect man is charged to bring pairs of animals into the ark 'to keep them alive' (6:19–20). The patriarchs are portrayed as shepherds whose flocks prosper under their care, most spectacularly in the case of Isaac and Jacob (26:12–14; 30:25 – 31:42). And Joseph's famine-relief measures save the lives not just of the Egyptians but their flocks and cattle too (47:15–18). Joseph is surely portrayed as very much the model ruler in Genesis, the ideal king.

God's provision of food for man is a distinctive feature of Genesis, when it is compared with its oriental predecessors which speak of humans feeding the gods. This provision is of course most evident in the Joseph story, where 'God revealed to Pharaoh what he is about to do' (41:25) and gave Joseph the ability to advise the Pharaoh how to cope with the famine. God's blessing of Isaac ensured bumper crops (26:12), but also right back in Eden Adam was provided with every kind of tree that was 'good for food' (2:9). Admittedly the fall complicated the food situation, and this is reflected in the various famines which are mentioned in the book (3:17; 12:10; 26:1, etc.), but however dire these famines were, the patriarchs survived.

The first account of creation concludes with God resting from all his work on the seventh day and blessing and sanctifying it (2:1–3). This shows that while the creation of man may be the climax of creation, its goal is rest. Though the seventh day is not called the Sabbath, the word used for 'rest' sounds almost the same (*šabat*), so that any Hebrew reader would say that God was observing the sabbath. Remarkably too the seventh day is blessed, a keyword in Genesis, but elsewhere God blesses only animate creatures, whether animal or human. And apart from the sabbath only one festival day is ever declared a holy day (Neh

8:9). This accumulation of unusual terms shows the prominence given to the sabbath here. Coming so soon after the comment that man is made in the image of God, God's rest on the seventh day is clearly being set out as model for mankind to follow (cf. Exod 20:11). This paragraph then has the clearest ethical implications of the whole section.

But strangely there are no other clear references to the sabbath in Genesis. The idyllic portrayal of the Garden of Eden in chapter 2 conveys an air of sabbatical bliss, though the mention that Adam would have to till the ground implies that not every day would be a sabbath for him! Interestingly in the flood story both God and Noah work on a weekly cycle, which suggests they both observe the sabbath (7:4, 10; 8:10, 12).[27] Here the righteous Noah is following God's working practices. But though we may infer Noah kept the sabbath, there are no hints that the patriarchs did. This is striking in the light of the prominence given to the sabbath in 1:1 – 2:3.

The second exposition (2:4 – 11:26)

The second exposition of Genesis runs from 2:4 to 11:26.[28] It consists of five sections, each headed by the formula 'These are the generations of . . .', alternating longish narratives (2:4; 6:9; 10:1) and short genealogies (5:1; 11:10), a pattern that closely parallels the structure of the core patriarchal narratives in 11:27 – 50:26. The contents of this second exposition also more closely resemble the core of the book, largely because human actors are prominent in both parts.

Certain motifs link the exposition and core. For example, beginning with Cain and Abel God often seems to prefer the younger brother, Isaac not Ishmael, Jacob not Esau, Ephraim not Manasseh. The same preference is hinted at in the case of Zerah and Perez (38:27–30), the ancestor of David (Ruth 4:18–22). Another link between exposition and core may be seen in the illicit union of the 'sons of God' with the daughters of men, which foreshadows the aversion to intermarriage with Canaanites and Hittites, a recurrent theme in the patriarchal stories (6:1–4; 24:3; 26:34; 28:1; 34:14; 38:2). Interestingly Joseph's marriage to an Egyptian is not censured (41:45). There are many echoes of the theme and vocabulary of the flood story in the Sodom and Gomorrah story.[29] Both tell of a universal destruction from which one family

[27] This is even clearer if Genesis presupposes the Jubilees calendar, for then the flood starts on a Sunday (the act of decreation starts on Sunday just as creation started on Sunday), and Noah sends out the birds on Sundays. Further discussion, Wenham, *Genesis 1–15*, 180–1.

[28] For a justification of breaking between 2:3 and 2:4 see T. Stordalen, 'Genesis 2, 4: Restudying a locus classicus', *ZAW* 104 (1992), 163–77.

[29] Cf. Gordon J. Wenham, 'Method in Pentateuchal Source Criticism', *VT* 41 (1991), 84–109.

escapes thanks to the father's righteousness, but after their rescue he drinks too much and is abused by his children (9:21–22; 19:32–35). Exploitation of a father's weakness is also seen in Jacob deceiving his blind father Isaac, and in Reuben sleeping with his father's concubine (27:18–27; 35:22). Noah's blessing and cursing of his sons foreshadows both Isaac's and Jacob's similar actions (9:25–27; 27:27–40; 49:3–27). Parallels between Noah and Abraham are numerous. Noah is said to be perfect, and Abraham is told to be perfect (6:9; 17:1). Both are in covenant relationship with God, and both offer sacrifices which change the course of human history; Noah's sacrifice saves the world from the threat of destruction by another flood, while Abraham's changes the promises into a guarantee based on God's oath (8:21; 22:16–18). In all these ways the second exposition adumbrates ideas put more fully in the core of the book.

The second exposition also serves to tie the first exposition to the core. Genesis 1 ended with the creation of mankind in two sexes to rule the other living creatures and supplied by God with food. In reverse order these three topics, food, dominion and sexuality, are the central topics of chapters 2–3. Chapter 2 reinforces the message of chapter 1 about food, that contrary to Babylonian views food is not given by man to the gods to keep them alive, but it is God's gift to man. He 'made to grow every tree that is pleasant to the sight and good for food' (2:9) and permitted Adam to eat of every tree except the tree of the knowledge of good and evil. It is of course Adam's eating of the one forbidden tree that leads to his expulsion from Eden, so that

> cursed is the ground because of you
> in toil you shall eat of it all the days of your life;
> thorns and thistles it shall bring forth to you
> and you shall eat the plants of the field.
> In the sweat of your face
> you shall eat bread. (3:17–19)

This curse on the ground clearly describes the experience of the typical Palestinian peasant in biblical times who eked out a precarious existence in the face of drought and famine. From the beginning to the end of the stories of the patriarchs famine threatens their existence in the promised land. No sooner does Abraham arrive in Canaan than he must leave it to go to Egypt in search of food (12:10), and it is famine that forces all Jacob's descendants to settle in Egypt at the end of Genesis. Yet there are glimmers of 'primal divine intentions for man' in these very stories. As we have already observed 'blessing' is a central motif in them, and this involves not just human and animal fecundity and God's protective presence, but also rain in its season and good crops (Lev 26:3–5). Noah was obviously a successful vine grower (Gen 9:20)! Isaac himself is blessed with hundred-fold yields and when blessing his son Jacob assures him that God will give him 'of the dew of heaven, the fatness of the earth and plenty of grain and wine' (26:12; 27:28). According to Joseph God sent him to Egypt to keep alive many people (45:5; 50:20), and Jacob pictures the future tribe of Judah so flush with grapes that he will wash 'his garments in wine and his vesture in the blood of grapes' (49:11). If the disobedience of Adam reduced mankind to precarious subsistence, the promise to the patriarchs offers the hope of a return to the plenty of Eden.

Dominion over the rest of creation was also part of the initial blessing bestowed on the human race according to 1:26, 28, and in 2:19 Adam is portrayed as fulfilling this mandate as each newly created animal is brought to him to be named. This establishes a hierarchy of authority with God as supreme, man answerable to God, and the animals subordinate to man and God. But by following the snake's suggestion and thereby disobeying God, Eve inverted this order of authority.[30] Once again the harmonious coexistence of mankind and the rest of creation in chapter 2 is replaced by a state of unending warfare poetically summed up in the curse on the snake:

> I will put enmity between you and the woman,
> and between your seed and her seed;
> he shall bruise your head,
> and you shall bruise his heel. (3:15)

This reflects the experience of ancient Israel where snakes, other wild animals and a variety of bugs posed a threat to human well-being. The ongoing struggle is alluded to after the flood, where the blessing on Noah includes the promise that the animal kingdom will be frightened of man, and animals that kill humans should be put to death. The fear of being killed by animals is reflected in Jacob's cry when his sons show him Joseph's blood-stained robe, 'a wild beast has devoured him' (37:33).

But just as the realism about the danger of crop failure is gilded with the hope of future abundance, so the curse on the snake in Genesis 3:15 hints at the certainty of ultimate human triumph. As it is a curse on the snake, Genesis 3:15 implies that the snake will ultimately come off worse in the struggle with man. This conclusion is reinforced by the wording 'he shall bruise your head', which implies a more serious injury than 'you shall bruise his heel'.[31] This hope is reinforced by the post-

[30] J. T. Walsh, 'Genesis 2:4b – 3:24: A Synchronic Reading', *JBL* 96 (1977), 161–77.

[31] Exegetes debate whether this is the first messianic prophecy in the Old Testament, but this is not really germane to our discussion; see further T. D. Alexander, 'Messianic Ideology in the Book of Genesis', in *The Lord's Anointed: Interpretation of Old Testament Messianic Texts* (ed. Philip E. Satterthwaite, Richard S. Hess and Gordon J. Wenham, Carlisle: Paternoster Press, 1995), 19–39.

flood comment to Noah that from now on the wild animals will be frightened of man.

Nevertheless this jars with the picture in Genesis 2 which implies a much more harmonious relationship. It is notable too that Noah, the only blameless or perfect person in Genesis, is the one who does most to preserve animal life by bringing them into the ark, while the description of his care for the dove he sent out to survey the subsiding waters is 'unsurpassed for tenderness and beauty'.[32] The patriarchs are shown to be concerned for the welfare of their animals giving their camels water, food and shelter at the end of their journey (24:19–20, 31–32) and worried lest their flocks and herds are driven too far and fast (33:13–14). Genesis also notes that Jacob's selective breeding techniques led to his sheep and goats being much more vigorous than Laban's (30:42). In this way the patriarchs are pictured as benevolent rulers of the animal kingdom, thus reaffirming God's primal intentions for the world.

Genesis thus presents a mixture of realism and idealism in discussing the creation mandates about food and dominion. On the one hand human beings always face the threat of famine and animal attacks, but the patriarchs, while not exempt from such risks, do survive and do show concern for the lives of their beasts (Prov 12:10). A similar ambivalence is apparent in Genesis' handling of sexuality.

We have already noted that Genesis 1 views human reproduction positively.[33] But in Genesis 2 it is the relationship of husband and wife that is central, not the procreation of children. In a narrative rich in symbolism a strikingly original view of the relationship of the sexes is set out. The writer also makes it quite plain at the end of the chapter that the story has universal relevance, for he appeals to it to explain a general principle: 'Therefore a man leaves his father and his mother and cleaves to his wife, and they become one flesh' (2:24). That this applies to every couple not just the *Ur*-couple is shown by the mention of father and mother, which neither Adam nor Eve had.

Some of the points Genesis makes about this primal relationship are not surprising in a patriarchal culture such as that of ancient Israel. The woman was created to meet the man's need of companionship, and to be a helper matching him (*ʿezer kenegdo*). A helper is one who meets someone's need; the relative strength of helped and helper is not at

[32] John Skinner, *A Critical and Exegetical Commentary on Genesis*² (ICC, Edinburgh: T&T Clark, 1930), 156.

[33] Not only is 'Be fruitful and multiply' the first command given to the human race, but it is repeated no less than four times to Noah after the flood, whereas at the corresponding point in the Atrahasis Epic the Babylonian gods introduce infertility and miscarriage to inhibit population growth. Of course, later in Genesis the blessing of numerous descendants is central to the patriarchal promise.

stake, simply that the helped is too weak on his own to achieve something. In other words a married couple can achieve what a single man cannot do on his own; in the context of 1:28 this obviously applies to having children,[34] but the very generality of 2:18 implies much more than this. 'Matching him' implies a relationship of complementarity rather than identity, which would have been expressed by 'like him'. Man and woman interlock, so that the strengths of the one complement the weaknesses of the other. If Adam's naming of the animals represents an expression of his authority over them, it seems likely that his naming of Eve in 2:23 implies a degree of authority over her too.

But this patriarchy is moderated by other features in the story which put male–female relationships on a more equal footing. First it is striking that the LORD God created only one Eve for Adam. Polygamy was an accepted feature of life in ancient Israel especially among the leaders of society, yet Adam is provided with just one wife. This is not meanness on God's part, for the rest of the story shows him keen to supply Adam's every need, and Adam's shout of greeting when he meets Eve shows he is perfectly satisfied with just one wife. The rest of Genesis seems to confirm monogamy as the most desirable situation, as all the polygamous marriages it describes are marred by strife. Finally, had Adam been supplied with several wives, he could have been fruitful and multiplied even quicker! The creation of one Eve thus shows that monogamy is more important than rapid multiplication.

Second, Eve's creation from Adam's rib[35] expresses the closeness of relationship that exists between man and wife. She is 'bone of my bones and flesh of my flesh' (2:23). This is the terminology used elsewhere to define close blood relatives (29:14). In other words marriage initiates a relationship that should be as durable as that between relatives ('a man . . . cleaves to his wife') and be characterised by the mutual affection and protection that is expected in a strong family society.

Third, and most surprising, is the generalising comment applying this story to all marriages: 'Therefore a man leaves his father and his mother and cleaves to his wife' (2:24). A Western reader may wrongly suppose that this is referring to the son leaving his parents and setting up home elsewhere with his wife. But Israelite marriage was patrilocal, that is the sons continued to live in or near the parental home when

[34] Cf. David J. A. Clines, *What Does Eve Do to Help?* (JSOTSup 94, Sheffield: JSOT Press, 1990), 34–5.

[35] Commentators speculate why the rib should have been chosen rather than some other part of Adam's body. There is no obvious answer, but Jewish and Christian readers have often thought along Matthew Henry's lines: 'Not made out of his head to top him, not out of his feet to be trampled on by him, but out of his side to be equal with him, under his arm to be protected, and near his heart to be beloved.'

they married. It was the bride who physically left her family and became part of her father-in-law's extended family. The 'leaving' of parents must therefore be taken figuratively: it implies a changed order of loyalties. In traditional societies the supreme social duty was to your parents. In the Ten Commandments 'Honour your father and mother' heads the list of manward obligations. What Genesis 2:24 means by leaving one's parents is putting their interests second to the needs of one's wife. Loyalty to one's spouse is even more important than loyalty to one's parents.

Finally this first marriage was characterised by uninhibited openness and harmony. 'The man and his wife were both naked, and were not embarrassed' (2:25).

Sadly the idealism of chapter 2 is soon replaced by the realism of chapter 3. Just as chapter 3 describes the problems facing mankind in dealing with agriculture and wild-life, so it describes present reality in relations between the sexes. Eve is hardly Adam's helper in encouraging him to eat the forbidden fruit. Immediately harmony and openness are replaced by disguise and shame, as they make loincloths from fig-leaves and hide from God among the trees of the garden. Their disloyalty to God in eating of the forbidden fruit spills over into disloyalty to each other, as Adam blames Eve for giving him the fruit.

But more than short-term disharmony blights male–female relationships, for 3:16 spells out long-term problems for women, such as pain in pregnancy and childbirth, and ongoing conflict with men. 'Your desire shall be for your husband' is obscure. It may be suggesting that women will go to unreasonable lengths to please their man, or that they will seek a degree of independence. Both situations are described in the patriarchal stories (e.g. chs 30, 16), but the latter meaning fits better in 4:7, the only other mention of 'desire' in Genesis.[36] 'He shall rule over you' may suggest a harsh use of male authority as opposed to the more benign patriarchy envisaged in chapter 2.

Reading further in Genesis, the harsh realism of chapter 3 seems more in evidence than the ideals of chapter 2. Lamech, the first bigamist, is a vicious thug, boasting that he will take seventy-sevenfold vengeance on those who attack him (4:23–24). Sarah's resort to surrogate motherhood, though a well-known practice in the ancient Near East, is described in terms that echo Genesis 3 and causes great tension between Sarah, Hagar and Abraham.[37] Jacob's involuntary bigamy leads to a most unhappy marriage for all concerned. As

[36] Susan T. Foh, 'What is the Woman's Desire?' *WTJ* 37 (1974/75), 376–83. For a sensitive reading of Gen 3:16 see Carol L. Meyers, *Discovering Eve* (New York: Oxford University Press, 1988), 109–17.

[37] W. Berg, 'Der Sündenfall Abrahams und Saras nach Gen 16:1–6', *BN* 19 (1982), 7–14.

Leah and Rachel name their sons, they pour out their feelings of rejection on the one hand and their desire for more children on the other (29:32 – 30:24).

But polygamy is not the only problem between the sexes. Husbands too frequently seem to put their own interests before their wife's: twice Sarah lands up in a foreign harem because of Abraham's lack of candour about their marriage (12:10–20; 20) and Rebekah nearly suffers the same way (26:6–11). For her part it is Sarah who persuades Abraham to go in for surrogacy and it is Rebekah who persuades Jacob to deceive his father Isaac (27:5–17) – hardly the action of a loyal wife. Most of the patriarchs' wives have difficulty in becoming pregnant, and when they succeed they suffer as 3:16 predicts. Rebekah experiences the pain of pregnancy as Esau and Jacob smash into each other inside her womb, while Rachel dies in childbirth (25:22; 35:16–19). Thus the gloomy picture of married life in Genesis 3 is illustrated in the following narratives. However there are glimpses of joy, showing that the idealism of Genesis 2 is not completely overshadowed. Eve ascribes the birth of both Cain and Seth to God's help. The birth of children to the patriarchs is not merely the fulfilment of God's promises but an answer to their prayers (15:2; 25:21; 30:22, 24). Birth is an occasion for joy as the names given to children at birth show (21:6; 29:32, 35; 41:51, 52). And as for happiness between partners, we are told that Jacob's seven years of engagement to Rachel 'seemed to him but a few days because of the love he had for her' (29:20). Thus the 'primal divine intentions for man' are not entirely forgotten in the tensions and conflict of patriarchal family life.

However the immediate sequel to the Garden of Eden story is gloomy. The Cain and Abel story contains many echoes of Genesis 2 and 3, all to the detriment of Cain. His offence is not only more serious than his father's, but he is the more brazen and impenitent sinner. But if he was bad, Lamech several generations later was much worse still, bragging to his two wives 'If Cain is avenged sevenfold, truly Lamech seventy-sevenfold'(4:24).

The avalanche of sin continues and climaxes with the sons of God marrying the daughters of men. Much debate has raged around the nature of this affair, but while this is uncertain,[38] its significance in the primeval history is clear, for it precipitates the flood. In Mesopotamian mythology the flood was sent to cure the population explosion, in Genesis it is sent because of mankind's sin. Genesis 6:5–6 is probably the strongest statement on this subject in the Bible: 'The LORD saw that the wickedness of man was great in the earth, and that every imagination of the thoughts of his heart was only evil continually. And the LORD was sorry that he had made man.'

[38] See commentaries for full discussion.

In particular the earth 'was filled with violence', a point first made by the narrator and then emphasised by God himself (6:11, 13). Even after the flood the danger persists that man and the animals will revert to violence (9:1–6).

Reading the biblical account of the flood against the background of Mesopotamian parallels one can trace many polemical changes that reflect the biblical storyteller's theology. There is only one God responsible for the flood, he is not scared by it, he controls it, and he oversees all that goes on. In particular it is the God who unleashed the flood who was responsible for telling Noah to escape by building the ark, whereas in the Gilgamesh epic it was a god who disagreed with the pantheon's decision to send the flood who tipped off his devotee. Noah's escape was not because of divine favouritism but because he was blameless in his generation and walked with God. He is one of the few 'saints' in the era between Adam and the flood, like Seth in whose days 'men began to call on the name of the LORD' and Enoch who 'walked with God' (4:26; 5:22).

We have already observed that the flood is presented as a great act of decreation, destroying human and animal life, covering the plants and mountains, so that the earth returns to the watery chaos that existed before the second day of creation. Noah, the survivor of this chaos, becomes as it were another Adam, the forefather of the human race after the flood. As befits a perfectly righteous person, he is portrayed as completely obeying every command of God in making the ark and embarking the animals. He also apparently observes the sabbath. When he disembarks from the ark, he builds an altar and offers sacrifices, which profoundly alter God's attitude to the human race. He now declares: 'I will never again curse the ground because of man, for the imagination of man's heart is evil from his youth' (8:21). Cursing the ground, as 9:8–17 makes plain, means sending another flood. But this is averted by Noah's sacrifice and instead an eternal covenant is established between God and all living creatures that there will never be another flood to destroy all life on earth.

The peroration about this eternal covenant is very reassuring to the reader, but it does pose a question: why, if the only family to survive the flood is headed by a perfectly righteous man, is there any threat of the flood recurring? Indeed this question is hinted at right at the beginning of the story, when it is said 'every imagination of man's heart is only evil continually' and then Noah is said to be 'blameless in his generation'. The author of Genesis draws attention to this issue by mentioning the evil of man's heart in 6:5 as the reason for the flood, but then after the flood he cites the evil of the human heart as a reason for not sending another flood. There is admittedly a slight variation in phraseology. Before the flood 'every imagination of the thoughts of his heart was only evil continually', whereas afterwards 'the imagination of man's heart is evil from his youth' (8:21). Essentially the same thing is being said on both occasions; every human thought from its inception tends towards evil. But it is put more gently the second time to explain God's mercy towards human sin, whereas on the first occasion it was explaining his determination to destroy mankind.[39] The text ascribes God's changed attitude to the burnt offerings sacrificed by Noah when he emerged from the ark. That sacrifice can so profoundly alter God's attitude to human sin shows how much weight Genesis attaches to the practice.[40] In this respect it is also evident that Genesis expects sin to characterise human behaviour after the flood, just as it did beforehand: in particular 9:5–6 shows that God is concerned to curb fresh outbreaks of violence.

It is not long before the ubiquity of sin is illustrated. The blameless Noah falls victim to the fruit of the vine. The ironic similarities to and differences from Adam's eating of another fruit show that we are dealing with another fall.[41] For example whereas Adam's fruit made him aware of his nakedness so that he tried to cover it up, Noah's fruit led him to uncover himself unwittingly. As in Adam's case the son's behaviour is even more reprehensible than the father's and leads to dissension among the three brothers. And just as Cain's descendants appear to be the ungodly line in Genesis 4, Ham's descendant Canaan is cursed by Noah.

This curse on Canaan is most important in the structure of Genesis as it encapsulates its vision of Israel's neighbours, but we should note first its importance for the book's understanding of character. Noah is the only person in Genesis described as blameless or perfect. Abraham is told to be perfect and walk before me (17:1), but he is never said to have achieved it. Indeed, that he has to be told to be perfect suggests he was not. Yet Noah, the perfect man, does lapse, not in a serious way, but enough to make a fool of himself and to lead his son Ham into a serious sin. In this way this episode illustrates the universality of sin which Genesis insists was the cause of the flood (6:5–7; 8:21). It also implies that if the one perfect man lapsed, no one else in Genesis may be beyond reproach in their conduct.

Important as this is to the broader reading of Genesis, it is not the main point being made by this episode. Ham's disrespect for his father,

[39] R. W. L. Moberly, *At the Mountain of God* (JSOTSup 22, Sheffield: JSOT Press, 1983), 90–1.

[40] Cf. Gordon J. Wenham, 'The Akedah: A Paradigm of Sacrifice', in *Pomegranates and Golden Bells: Studies in Honor of Jacob Milgrom* (ed. David P. Wright, David N. Freedman and Avi Hurvitz, Winona Lake: Eisenbrauns, 1995), 93–102.

[41] *Pace* Westermann, *Genesis 1–11*, 487–8 we do not think the Old Testament sees drunkenness as unexceptionable. Rather it is a lapse the righteous should avoid, not a major fault – see Wenham, *Genesis 1–15*, 198–9. On the echoes of the fall here, cf. Tomasino, 'History Repeats Itself', footnote 19.

which leads to Noah cursing Ham's son Canaan, prefigures Israel's relationship with her neighbours. From Noah descended the seventy nations of the world known to ancient Israel, which are listed in the table of nations in Genesis 10. Israel was one of the descendants of Shem, and among his other descendants there are a variety of Aramaean and Arabian tribes with whom Israel enjoyed close relations (10:21–31). The descendants of Japhet (10:2–5) are peoples on Israel's northern horizon, with whom she had little to do.

Most illuminating is the list of the descendants of Ham (10:6–20), for it includes many of Israel's traditional foes. It not only includes the Canaanites and their various sub-groups such as the Hittites, Jebusites, Amorites, Gergashites, Hivites and others familiar from other lists of the pre-Israelite inhabitants of the land, it also includes nations like the Egyptians, Babylonians and Assyrians, Israel's great rivals and indeed oppressors in the ancient world. It is this list of Ham's descendants that explains Noah's curse on Ham in 9:26: 'Blessed by the LORD my God be Shem; and let Canaan be his slave.' Just as later Isaac was to predict Esau's (i.e. Edom's) subservience to Jacob (i.e. Israel) and Jacob was to foresee the future of the individual tribes (27:29; 49:3–27), so here Noah predicts Canaan's subjection to Shem (i.e. Israel). It has often been thought odd that Noah does not curse Ham, who was the guilty son, but instead singles out Ham's son, Canaan, who did not do anything. However once the curse is read in the light of chapter 10, it is apparent that nations like Egypt and Assyria were never Israel's slaves as the Canaanites and their sub-groups were. In this respect it would certainly have been inappropriate for Noah to have said 'let Ham be Shem's slave', but 'let Canaan be his slave' does describe the fate of the Canaanites.

Chapter 10, the table of nations, shares the ambivalence of earlier genealogies in the book, in that it shows the fulfilment of the command to be fruitful on the one hand and hints at the dispersal of the nations on the other. This dispersion is of course the ultimate judgement in the primeval history prompted by the building of the tower of Babel. Building a tower that would reach up to heaven has analogies with the intermarriage of the sons of God and human women in 6:1–4; both acts illicitly blur the boundary between God and mankind, and so attract divine wrath that affects the whole human race. The tower of Babel story at one level ridicules the pretensions of Babylon to be the home of true religion, but at another it is affirming that the divisions between nations in language and culture are a divine judgement on human pride. Mankind may have escaped extinction in another flood, but sin has once again blighted human existence so that the race seems destined to suffer international rivalry and warfare for the foreseeable future. On this gloomy note the primeval history ends.

The core of Genesis

The patriarchal stories which begin in chapter 12 are nearly five times as long as the preceding primeval history. This shows clearly where the author's interests lie: he wants to trace the origins of Israel and the twelve tribes. Chapters 1–11 are essentially background, though as we have argued they foreshadow in various ways the theme and motifs of the patriarchal stories. We have accepted Clines' definition of the theme as 'the partial fulfilment . . . of the promise to or blessing of the patriarchs'. This promise contains four elements, land, descendants, covenantal relationship, and blessing to the nations (12:1–3). Practically everything within chapters 12–50 may be seen as related to these topics. The patriarchs gradually acquire land rights in Canaan. Slowly and with difficulty they have children. They are certainly preserved and those who persecute them suffer. Finally through them some of the families of the world are blessed.

The promises to Abraham renew the vision for humanity set out in Genesis 1 and 2.[42] He, like Noah before him, is a second Adam figure. Adam was given the garden of Eden: Abraham is promised the land of Canaan. God told Adam to be fruitful and multiply: Abraham is promised descendants as numerous as the stars of heaven. God walked with Adam in Eden: Abraham was told to walk before God. In this way the advent of Abraham is seen as the answer to the problems set out in Genesis 1–11: through him all the families of the earth will be blessed.

Read this way Genesis is a tract justifying Israel's claim to the land of Canaan. Its basic message is that God promised the land to Abraham. Abraham and his descendants acquired parts of it quite legitimately. The earlier inhabitants, the Canaanites, behaved so badly that they do not deserve to live there. Thus Canaan is rightfully Israel's land.

This crude summary of Genesis' message fails to do justice to several important features. The book is undoubtedly concerned with Israel's relationship to its neighbours, but also with relationships between the sons of Jacob, the forefathers of Israel's tribes. Furthermore while criticising Canaanite practices and discouraging intermarriage with them, Genesis offers a much more nuanced approach to their occupation of the land.

Essentially both the Jacob cycle (25:19 – 35:29) and the Joseph story (37:2 – 50:26) are stories of family reconciliations.[43] Jacob and Esau start fighting in the womb (25:22) and continue the feud in later life (25:29–34). This reaches such a pitch that Esau plans to kill Jacob, so

[42] Cf. 'A re-affirmation of the primal divine intentions for man' (Clines, *Theme of the Pentateuch*, 29).

[43] On the centrality of reconciliation in the Joseph story see Theo L. Hettema, *Reading for Good: Narrative Theology and Ethics in the Joseph Story from the Perspective of Ricoeur's Hermeneutics* (Kampen: Kok Pharos, 1996), 270–4.

that he has to leave home (27:41 – 28:5). Similarly Joseph's brothers hate him, plan to kill him, but eventually sell him to slave traders who take him to Egypt (37:2–28). After twenty years Jacob returns home, and in a most touching scene makes his peace with Esau (33:4–14). The Jacob cycle ends with Esau and Jacob burying their father Isaac (35:29). Similarly, again after about twenty years of unresolved conflict, the Joseph story comes to a magnificent climax with Judah's great speech and Joseph making his identity known to his brothers. The rest of the story tells how he provides for the needs of his father and brothers when they migrate to Egypt. When their father dies, like Jacob and Esau in their day, Joseph and his brothers join together in burying him. Then the story concludes with another strong declaration by Joseph that despite all his brothers have done to him he has completely forgiven them. 'Fear not, for am I in the place of God? As for you, you meant evil against me; but God meant it for good, to bring it about that many people should be kept alive, as they are today. So do not fear; I will provide for you and your little ones' (50:19–21).

Both the Jacob and Joseph stories could be seen as offering a commentary on 'the imagination of man's heart is evil from his youth', which we argued was a most significant comment in the flood story. Certainly the animosity between Jacob and Esau is traced back to their earliest days, while Genesis also implies that the antipathy between Joseph and his brothers reflects the lack of love between their parents, with Leah and Rachel intensely jealous of each other and Jacob acknowledging only Rachel as his wife. Nevertheless Genesis shows that even such deep-rooted long-term hatred can be overcome, where the offended parties (Esau and Joseph) show generosity and the offenders (Jacob and Joseph's brothers) are truly penitent. Genesis is surely suggesting to its readers that they too should forgive even their long-term enemies, if they show sincere contrition.

Other stories in Genesis appear to make a similar point. The strife between Lot's herdsmen and Abraham's was so intense that they had to separate. Abraham the older man wants peace with his brethren (13:8), so he generously allows his nephew Lot to pick whatever part of the land he wants to settle in. Abraham, whose generosity apparently cost him dear because Lot chose the well-watered Jordan valley, is soon rewarded by a much enhanced promise of land and descendants (13:14–17; cf. 12:1–3). Lot's choice is soon shown to be misguided. He is carried off when the kings of the East sack Sodom, and has to be rescued by Abraham (14:1–16). Later in response to Abraham's prayers for Sodom, Lot and his family are rescued by angels (18:16 – 19:29). Throughout Abraham is portrayed as treating generously his kinsman who, even if he has not wronged him, has at least treated him meanly.

Later on Abraham prays for Abimelech, king of Gerar (called a Philistine in 26:1), after he had returned Sarah to him (20:17). He also agrees to make a treaty with Abimelech, even though for a time Abimelech's men had seized a well he had dug (21:22–33). Isaac too had a similar set of problems with Abimelech, but when they had been resolved, he too agrees to a peace treaty (26:6–31). Jacob suffered great exploitation and double-dealing at the hands of his Aramaean father-in-law Laban, but when he proposes a treaty between himself and Jacob, the latter readily agrees (31:43–54).

In all these episodes the patriarchs are depicted as being anxious to make peace and forgive past wrongs, especially with their kinsmen, but also with inhabitants of the land such as Abimelech. Tolerance of the Canaanites does not extend to intermarrying with them, but generally the patriarchs seem to want to live peaceably with them. The problems posed by Genesis 34 will be discussed in a later chapter. Generally the Egyptians are viewed even more positively. Apart from Sarah's unfortunate stay in the Egyptian harem right at the beginning of the patriarchal period, the Egyptians are painted as benign and helpful, and no adverse comment is made on Joseph's marriage to an Egyptian.

This patriarchal goodwill both to relatives and people of other nations shines the more brightly against the background of the earlier chapters. Cain kills Abel, and sounds distinctly impenitent if not impertinent when God questions him about his deed. Only subsequently when his sentence is announced does he start to whinge. Lamech boasts about the fact that he will not forgive, but will exact seventy-sevenfold revenge (4:8–24). The world is said to be full of violence before the flood (6:13). After the flood the unity of mankind is shattered at Babel with international failure to co-operate being God's judgement on human pride (11:1–9). The experience of the patriarchs suggests that it is possible to put aside past disputes and for nations to work together. Indeed that is the climax of the promises to them: 'In you shall all the families of the earth find blessing.'[44] Joseph saved not only the Egyptians from famine, but surrounding peoples too. This Genesis suggests is both the fulfilment of God's promise and the fruit of international co-operation.

Thus Genesis is not simply a justification for Israel's occupation of Canaan, it embodies a practical appeal as well. It urges brothers to make peace with each other and to forgive past wrongs. It insists that Israelites should live peaceably with their relatives, with fellow countrymen of different ethnic origins, and implies that as a nation it should not be afraid to make agreements with surrounding nations when they seek peace.

In evaluating the purpose of a book its conclusion is most important. 'The recency effect encourages the reader to assimilate all previous

[44] On reading the Niphal of *brk* as medio-passive see Wenham, *Genesis 1–15*, 276–8.

information to the item presented last.'[45] Genesis ends with the burial of Jacob by all his sons and a reaffirmation of Joseph's forgiveness of his brothers. It is preceded by Jacob's deathbed blessing on his assembled sons and grandsons. First Jacob blesses Joseph's sons Ephraim and Manasseh: by so doing he makes them equal inheritors with his sons and fathers of full tribes (48:5). This explains why two of the Israelite tribes are descended from Jacob's grandsons, whereas the others are descended from his sons. Then Jacob crosses his hands, placing his right on the younger son Ephraim's head, so putting him ahead of Manasseh. For the final time in Genesis the pattern of God's choice of the younger brother is illustrated.[46] The strength of these future tribes is underlined by the blessing pronounced over them. 'By you Israel will pronounce blessings, saying, "God make you as Ephraim and Manasseh"' (48:20).

This incident though is just a trailer to the climax of the book, Jacob's poetic last will and testament in which he declares the destiny of his sons, the future tribes of Israel (Genesis 49). 'This chapter, in that it is poetry seems to be intended to be a high point of . . . the whole book of Genesis.'[47] In it 'we have a glimpse of the embryonic nation – with the Judah and Joseph tribes destined to have pre-eminence in the south and the north respectively'.[48] Particularly significant is that the future king is said to come from Judah, yet a very fulsome blessing of Joseph comes at the end (49:22–26), as if to offset the privilege of Judah's dynastic leadership.

> The sceptre will not pass from Judah
> nor the staff from between his feet (i.e. from his descendants)
> until tribute is brought to him
> and the peoples obey him. (49:10)

Though Genesis 37–50 is conventionally called the story of Joseph,[49] the other important son in the story is Judah whose bad reputation (cf. ch. 38) is somewhat restored in chapter 44 by his fine speech and his offer to become Joseph's slave instead of Benjamin. Then in Jacob's last words he is granted the privilege of leadership. We noted that right at the beginning of Genesis mankind is granted rule over the rest of creation (1:28), and that 3:15 promises that a seed of Eve would bruise the serpent's head, and that Abraham and Jacob are both assured there would be kings among their descendants (17:6; 35:11). The

[45] Rimmon-Kenan, *Narrative Fiction*, 120.

[46] Note the first example occurs in Genesis 4 (Cain and Abel). Repetition of this pattern near the beginning and end of the book underlines its significance.

[47] R. E. Longacre, *Joseph: A Story of Divine Providence* (Winona Lake: Eisenbrauns, 1989), 23.

[48] Longacre, *Joseph*, 54.

[49] Note the editor of Genesis calls these chapters 'the family history of *Jacob*' (37:2).

blessing on Judah crowns this series of promises with an assurance that he will father a line of kings.

There are thus multiple thrusts to the book of Genesis. It is a claim to the land. It is a plea for peace and reconciliation between the tribes. It justifies peaceable relations with the Canaanites in the land, Egyptians, Aramaeans, Edomites, and others beyond Israel's borders. It predicts a Judaean royal dynasty, and justifies God's passing over older brothers in favour of the younger by many examples.

A setting for Genesis

Having tried to draw out the significant points in the message of Genesis, can we suggest an audience to whom it could be addressed? Who are the implied readers? Do these points help us to understand who its first readers may have been? There are many times in Israel's history when this message would have been relevant. Intertribal rivalry and tensions are attested at many points in Israel's history from Mosaic times to the post-exilic. The claim to the land was often contested from the conquest to the exile. So it is possible to postulate a variety of settings for the book. The three most often canvassed are the Mosaic era (thirteenth century B.C.), the united monarchy of David and Solomon (tenth century), and the fifth-century post-exilic era.

The Mosaic era certainly accounts for many of the key features in Genesis. In that period Israel was moving towards the land, and Israel made peaceful overtures towards Edom, but it was not as benevolently disposed towards Egypt and the Canaanites as Genesis suggests. Nor does a Judaean dynasty have much relevance in that era.

Critical orthodoxy has usually plumped for a sixth or fifth-century final redaction of the book. Certainly relationships with the Samaritans were difficult in that period, so we could read Joseph's appeals for brotherly forgiveness as a Samaritan plea. But it does not fit very well with Ezra and Nehemiah's rejection of these approaches and their hostility towards most of the peoples of the land. The post-exilic era was also marked by bitter hatred of the Edomites, which is totally at odds with Genesis' sympathetic portrayal of Esau. The mockery of Babylon and its pretensions also would be odd in this era: hatred and bitterness would be understandable (cf. Ps 137), but the dismissiveness of Genesis about Babylon's claims so soon after the Jews had experienced its power and culture is unlikely. Though the post-exilic era would certainly have endorsed the claim to the land and the hope of a Davidic dynasty, the book of Chronicles presents those hopes very differently as befitted a generation who had had its faith in the land and dynasty-promises shattered. But Genesis presents these claims with no hint that they fly in the face of recent historical experience. Finally by the post-exilic era Egypt was just a part of the Persian empire, so there would seem very little point in Genesis celebrating Israel's close relationship with Egypt.

None of these observations are problems for a date in the united monarchy period. Mainline historical criticism has for a long time dated the main source of Genesis to this period.[50] Our rhetorical analysis of the book suggests that it would all be at home in this era. The reign of David began with conflict between the tribe of Judah and the other tribes, and doubtless the northern tribes felt very sore about submitting to his rule. Yet Genesis points out that their great forefather Joseph had forgiven his brothers including their leader Judah. David conquered the Edomites and Aramaeans, yet their ancestors too had made peace with Israel. The boundaries of the land mentioned in Genesis seem to be closest to those of the Solomonic empire. Jacob's predictions of a Judaean dynasty offer powerful support for Davidic or Solomonic rule. Both kings had older brothers, who might have expected to have been anointed instead of them. But Genesis says: remember that God preferred Abel to Cain, Jacob to Esau, Perez to Zerah, and (if you northerners disagree) Ephraim to Manasseh. Israel enjoyed good relations with Egypt in the days of David and Solomon, indeed Solomon married an Egyptian princess. Again if northerners were disposed to carp at this foreign alliance, they are reminded that their forefather Joseph married an Egyptian. In this era too Babylon was very weak – indeed the ziggurat built by Nebuchadrezzar I was probably in ruins then, which would have given the tower of Babel story particular piquancy.[51] The importance of sacrifice for the future of mankind and the nation of Israel which emerges from Genesis 8 and 22 fits well with both kings' concern with temple building.[52]

[50] For a reassertion of this view see K. Berge, *Die Zeit des Jahwisten* (BZAW 186, Berlin: W. de Gruyter, 1990). Traditionally J, the Yahwistic source, which accounts for about half of Genesis, has been dated to the tenth century. E, the Elohistic source, was dated about a century later. Many modern critics now doubt the existence of E, preferring to see it as part of J. P, the priestly source, was dated to the sixth/fifth century. However there are good grounds for regarding P as preceding J, as older critics used to suppose. See G. J. Wenham, 'The Priority of P', *VT* 49 (1999), 240–58 and more briefly Joseph Blenkinsopp, *The Pentateuch* (London: SCM Press, 1992), e.g. 78. For a fuller review of the current state of pentateuchal criticism including the idea that the Pentateuch could have been edited as late as 300 B.C. see G. J. Wenham, 'Pondering the Pentateuch' in *The Face of OT Studies: A Survey of Contemporary Approaches* (ed. David W. Baker and Bill T. Arnold, Grand Rapids/Leicester: Baker/Apollos, 1999), 116–44.

[51] W. von Soden, 'Etemenanki von Asarhaddon nach der Erzählung vom Turmbau zu Babel und dem Erra-Mythos', *UF* 3 (1971), 253–63.

[52] Other interesting parallels between Genesis and the united monarchy which could be supposed to have rhetorical intent include Genesis 14, prefiguring David's northern victories and the blessing of Melchizedek on Jerusalem and Abraham's descendants. Reuben's sleeping with his father's concubine led to him forfeiting his first-born's privileges; a similar act by Adonijah led to his execution (Gen 35:22; 49:3–4; 1 Kgs 2:13–25). Genesis' encouragement of fertility chimes in with David's census concerns

A setting within the united monarchy period would thus seem a very appropriate context for the book of Genesis. This is not to say that it is not based on traditions of much older date. If it was written to justify the Davidic monarchy and as a call to the northern tribes to rally behind it, its appeal would have depended on their recognition of the validity of these traditions. If the stories of Esau's and Joseph's big-heartedness had been invented, they would have carried much less conviction for those tribes and their leaders to whom Genesis is appealing.

But ultimately the message of Genesis does not depend on finding an appropriate setting for it. The message must emerge from a close reading of the book itself. If we can find a historical situation into which it seems to fit snugly, that may support our reading. But ultimately it is the text of Genesis itself that counts. By trying to establish the main thrust of the book, we hope we have established parameters within which individual stories should be interpreted.

(2 Sam 24). The promises of blessing 'I will make you a great nation, and I will bless you, and make your name great, so that will be a blessing. I will bless those who bless you, and him who curses I will curse' would have sounded less over-blown in a period of national strength than in an era of national humiliation, such as the post-exilic era. Then they would have rung hollow. There are a number of indicators that Genesis was at least revised in the tenth century, including the table of nations, the mentions of Dan, Ur *of the Chaldees*, the Edomite royal archives in ch. 36, and details in the Joseph story. However claims that there are even later elements are not so strong. Our argument is not that Genesis was lightly revised in the tenth century, but that it was significantly edited then so that its relevance to tenth-century issues was apparent.

4

THE RHETORICAL FUNCTION OF JUDGES

The atmosphere of the book of Judges is quite different from the book of Genesis. The latter begins with the triumphant account of God creating the world in six days and declaring it 'very good', and it ends with Joseph confidently looking forward to his burial in the promised land. Judges by contrast opens with the rather ineffective efforts of the Israelite tribes to conquer that land and closes after a most dreadful civil war with the gloomy reflection, 'In those days there was no king in Israel; every man did what was right in his own eyes' (21:25). It is therefore immediately obvious that the implied author of Judges is approaching his subject-matter from a very different direction from the implied author of Genesis.

Whereas Genesis has a basically fairly positive attitude towards the past, Judges has a much darker one. Indeed most of the stories in Judges seem to be told to shock the reader or at least make the reader ask him- or herself about what the characters in the tales ought to have done. In other words the narrative embodies a set of values and ethical norms that the reader must somehow tune into if he or she is not to read the stories against the grain, i.e. in ways that are contrary to the message that the author intended to convey. But when a story is telling of action that the author disapproves of, it may often be very difficult to know what he thought ought to have been done, what canons of behaviour he is implicitly measuring his characters' deeds by. In a close-knit culture like ancient Israel where there was a much higher degree of agreement between its members about religion and ethics than there is in modern secularised and pluralist societies, there was correspondingly less reason to spell out authorial norms and values, because the reader was very likely to share them.[1] In the book of Judges we have fewer clues than usual in the Old Testament to give away the author's assumptions, and this coupled with its portrayal of non-normative behaviour makes it one of the most difficult books in the canon to interpret from an ethical perspective.

Since the work of Noth[2] (1943) it has been commonplace to view Judges as part of the deuteronomistic history, that is those books from

[1] Cf. Kenneth A. Stone, *Sex, Honor and Power in the Deuteronomistic History* (JSOTSup 234, Sheffield: JSOT Press, 1996), 32–3.

[2] Martin Noth, *Überlieferungsgeschichtliche Studien* (1943), partial ET = *The Deuteronomistic History* (JSOTSup 15, Sheffield: JSOT Press, 1981).

Deuteronomy to 2 Kings which tell the history of Israel from the conquest of the land to the fall of Jerusalem in 587 B.C. Read in this way the book of Judges is seen to exemplify the ideas of the book of Deuteronomy, particularly its message that disobedience to the law leads to divine displeasure and suffering for the nation. Repeatedly the book of Judges prefaces its account of the career of a major deliverer with the observation that 'the people of Israel did what was evil in the sight of the LORD, forgetting the LORD their God, and serving the Baals and the Asheroth. Therefore the anger of the LORD was kindled against Israel, and he sold them into the hand of . . .' (some enemy) (3:7–8; cf. 3:12; 4:1; 6:1; 10:6; 13:1).

The story then continues with an account of Israel's oppression for so many years, national prayer and repentance, and God's response in the form of raising up a military leader or judge who delivered the people from foreign oppression for so many years. Thus the bulk of the book from chapters 3 to 16 consists of a series of cycles of conquests by foreigners, national despair, and divine interventions to save Israel. An analysis of the formulae that frame these stories shows that for the editor of Judges the theological ideas of Deuteronomy were most important and this should be borne in mind as one seeks to evaluate the ethical dimensions of the book.

However, a recognition of the deuteronomic elements within Judges does not necessitate the view that the book is simply one volume within the deuteronomistic history. Deuteronomic ideas pervade the Old Testament, especially in the historical and prophetic books, but it would be mistaken to conclude that all these books showing deuteronomic features originated in the same school at the same time. Rather they witness to the abiding importance of this outlook in biblical times. Within the so-called deuteronomistic history of Deuteronomy to 2 Kings there are sufficient differences between different books to make it likely that they were not all out of the same literary mould. Though there is a theological outlook common to them all, which may be broadly termed deuteronomic/istic, the books have their own distinctive features which suggest that they are of diverse origin.[3] As far as Judges is concerned we shall be following the trend in modern studies to read the book as a work in its own right, not just as one volume in a unified history of pre-exilic Israel.

[3] Two prominent dissenters from Noth's deuteronomistic history view are Gerhard von Rad, who in his *OT Theology I* (ET, D. M. G. Stalker, Edinburgh: Oliver & Boyd, 1962), 334–47, pointed to Judges' pattern of cyclical judgements, which differs from Kings' picture of cumulative punishment, and C. Westermann, *Die Geschichtsbücher des Alten Testaments* (Gütersloh: C. Kaiser/Gütersloher Verlag, 1994), who emphasised the diversity of presentation within these books.

The structure of Judges

The book of Judges falls into three distinct sections:

Prologue/Exposition	1:1 – 3:6
Core/ Book of Deliverers	3:7 – 16:31
Epilogue	17:1 – 21:25

Both prologue and epilogue fall into two parts. The prologue consists of 1:1 – 2:5, a summary review of successful and unsuccessful attempts by different tribes to capture their allotted tribal territories concluding with an angelic rebuke for breaking the covenant, and 2:6 – 3:6, an editorial review of the apostasy of the judges' period and God's decision to allow the nations to remain in the land, to harry Israel and test their loyalty to the covenant. The epilogue is quite different in style. Like the core of Judges it relates in some detail two episodes, the first about a Levite who came from Bethlehem (17:1 – 18:31) and the second about a Levite whose concubine was a Bethlehemite (19:1 – 21:25). Both Levites trigger off outrageous behaviour by other tribes, and unlike the pattern in the rest of the book no judge arises to save the people. Instead the epilogue echoes with the refrain: 'In those days there was no king in Israel; every man did what was right in his own eyes' (17:6; 18:1; 19:1; 21:25). Not only do the prologue and epilogue both fall into two parts, but there are a number of cross-linkages between them so that they serve to frame the book.[4] For example the book opens with the question: 'Who shall go up first for us against the Canaanites, to fight against them?' and God replies, 'Judah shall go up' (1:1–2). Almost the same question is asked in 20:18: 'Which of us shall go up first to battle against the Benjaminites?' and the LORD said, 'Judah shall go up first.' The slight change from 'Canaanites' to 'Benjaminites' shouts. The nation that began by fighting external foes ends with an internecine civil war.

The core of the book consists of cycles of foreign oppression, which are countered by the raising up of a judge who rescues Israel: Othniel of Judah (3:7–11), Ehud of Benjamin (3:12–30), Shamgar of Anath (Judah?) (3:31), Barak of Naphtali (4:1 – 5:31), Gideon of Manasseh (6:1 – 9:57), Tola from Issachar (10:1–2), Jair from Gilead (Manasseh) (10:3–5), Jephthah from Gilead (10:6 – 12:7), Ibzan of Judah (12:8–10), Elon of Zebulon (12:11–12), Abdon of Ephraim (12:13–15), and Samson of Dan (13:1 – 16:31). Of the minor judges the book tells us nothing save that they lived, had numerous children, and died. The major judges, Othniel, Ehud, Barak, Gideon, Jephthah and Samson are treated differently. Not only are their deeds recounted in detail, but

[4] See Robert H. O'Connell, *The Rhetoric of the Book of Judges* (VTSup 63, Leiden: Brill, 1996), 231–66.

they are linked together by formulaic comments on the people doing what was evil in the LORD's eyes, being sold into their enemies' hands, praying to the LORD, and the LORD raising up a judge to deliver them.

But these major judges are not all the same. Just as the nation appears to be in a worse state at the end of the book than at the beginning, its saviours seem to degenerate as the story unfolds. Othniel escapes criticism. Ehud's single-handed bravery leads to a magnificent defeat of the Moabites, but the gloss is perhaps taken off it by his association with idols[5] (3:19, 26). Likewise Barak's splendid victory over the Canaanites is clouded by his own faintheartedness as leader,[6] Jael's dispatch of Sisera, the enemy general, and the dissension among the tribes (Judg 5:15–17). If Barak was reluctant to respond to God's call mediated by a prophetess, Gideon needed an angelic visit, two signs, and a dream before he led Israel to a sensational victory against the Midianites. However its aftermath was bitter: vengeance on Succoth (Judg 8:16), the manufacture of an ephod, which 'all Israel played the harlot after' (8:27), and a son Abimelech, whose rule was a disaster (Judg 9). Jephthah received no divine call but simply responded to the desperate plea of the elders of Gilead. Though his victory over the Ammonites is ascribed to the Spirit of the LORD, his success was followed by the sacrifice of his daughter and the death of forty-two thousand Ephraimites in a post-campaign vendetta (Judg 10:17 – 12:7). Finally comes the comic-tragic Samson. Set apart as a Nazirite from birth, he should have been as strict as the high priest in maintaining his holy status. But far from trying to save his people from the oppressive Philistines, he has a fascination with Philistine girls and keeps marrying them.[7] His acts of deliverance are not motivated by a desire to deliver his people, but by revenge for the way the Philistines have treated him personally. His own suicide, simultaneously killing seven thousand Philistines, sums up the ambiguity of his role (Judg 13:1 – 16:31).

This survey of the trends in Judges shows that the implied author takes a fairly negative view of the developments in the nation in the period he describes. But on the other hand he takes obvious delight in telling of the exciting triumphs the judges achieved and the unconventional tactics they employed to secure victory. Evidently he thought some of the judges' achievements praiseworthy, so we need to look more closely to discover the positive message he is trying to put over by recounting these events.

[5] 'Sculptured stones' (RSV, etc.) seems rather a euphemism for *pasil*, a term which in other passages clearly means idolatrous graven images (e.g. Deut 7:5, 25; 12:3).

[6] Judg 4:7–9. Note Deuteronomy's ban on the fearful going to war (Deut 20:8).

[7] Intermarriage with foreigners is the ultimate sin in covenant unfaithfulness according to Deut 7:3–4; Judg 3:5–6. Even Genesis which adopts a fairly relaxed attitude to foreigners disapproves of intermarriage (24:3–4, see our discussion above in Chapter 3).

The Deuteronomic formulae

One clue to the editor's interests is the set of formulae that he uses to introduce or conclude each account of a judge's activity. There are five elements in the formulae. First, the people's sin: 'The people of Israel did what was evil in the sight of the LORD, forgetting the LORD their God, and serving the Baals and the Asheroth' (3:7). Second, punishment: 'Therefore the anger of the LORD was kindled against Israel, and he sold them into the hand of . . . and the people of Israel served . . . eight years' (3:8). Third, appeal for help: 'the people of Israel cried to the LORD' (3:9). Fourth, deliverance: 'the LORD raised up a deliverer for the people of Israel, who delivered them . . . The Spirit of the LORD came upon him, and he judged Israel; he went out to war, and the LORD gave . . . into his hand' (3:9–10). Fifth, peace: 'So the land had rest forty years. Then . . . died' (3:11).

This cyclical pattern has been analysed more often to determine the extent of editorial intervention than to shed light on the writer's own perspective. Because the cycles repeat and the period of rest is followed by renewed declension, it is easy to miss the obvious point that everyone including the editor would have hoped that the rest would have been permanent. Long-term peace, not repeated bouts of warfare, however heroic the deeds of the participants, is what the author really would have liked to see.

We have illustrated the features from the first judge in the cycle, Othniel (3:7–11). The accounts of the other major judges contain most of these elements but not always so fully. Ehud (3:12–30), Barak (4:1 – 5:31), Gideon (6:1 – 8:28), and Jephthah (10:6 – 12:7) contain them all, but Tola[8] (8:33 – 10:5) lacks the appeal to God, and Samson (13:1 – 16:31) lacks both the appeal to God and the period of peace, and in his case it was promised only that 'he shall *begin* to deliver Israel from the hand of the Philistines' (13:5).

In the case of the minor judges, such as Shamgar and Jair, these formulae are rarely present, though one may see some similarities in the ideas. Shamgar delivered Israel from the Philistines (3:31). But in the case of Jair, Ibzan, Elon and Abdon (10:3–5; 12:8–15) all that is said is that they judged Israel for *x* years, died and were buried. The incidental references to their wealth and numerous children may suggest that the nation enjoyed relative peace in their days, but this is not certain.

These formulae, which are used to interpret the main stories of the judges, also appear in the prologues to the book, especially the second (2:6 – 3:6), thereby underlining their importance to the author. The

[8] This section is mainly about Abimelech's misdeeds, but Y. Amit, *The Book of Judges: The Art of Editing* (Leiden: Brill, 1999), 40–3, argues it forms part of the Tola cycle.

first prologue sums up the attempts of different tribes to possess their allotments, and their increasing accommodation with the Canaanites, so that instead of driving them out the tribes settle among them. This leads to the angel of the LORD rebuking them.

> I said, 'I will never break my covenant with you, and you shall make no covenant with the inhabitants of this land; you shall break down their altars.' But you have not obeyed my command. What is this you have done? So now I say, I will not drive them out before you: but they shall become adversaries to you, and their gods shall be a snare to you. (2:2–3)

Here the angel of the LORD predicts what the rest of the book will describe. Israel has broken the covenant by not expelling the Canaanites, and will go further and worship their gods. In turn the Canaanites will become their adversaries. Here we have implicit reference to two elements of the formula, national sin and divine punishment. A third element, appeal to the LORD, is foreshadowed by Israel's response to the warning: 'the people lifted up their voices and wept . . . and they sacrificed there to the LORD' (2:4–5). But this gloomy scenario is prefaced by a ray of hope: 'I will never break my covenant with you.' Despite the repeated tales of Israel's faithlessness that are about to begin, God's loyalty to Israel is not in doubt. So although the book's horizon becomes ever darker as the story progresses and it ends with the blackest of episodes, God's promise gives hope of new and better days.

The second prologue (2:6 – 3:6) sets the judges period in its historical context and at the same time explains the theological thinking that underlies its presentation. Israel had served the LORD as long as Joshua lived, indeed as long as the generation who had worked with Joshua lived, but then 'there arose another generation who did not know the LORD or the work which he had done for Israel' (2:10). There then follows a long section expanding the five elements of the deuteronomic formulae (sin, punishment, appeal for help, deliverance, peace). Most of the phraseology here seems to be drawn from Deuteronomy,[9] but there is new terminology, 'plunderers', 'being sold into the hand of',[10] and new emphases that set apart the book as distinctive. In particular the prologue stresses the progressive and cumulative nature of national sin: 'whenever the judge died, they turned back and behaved worse than their fathers' (2:19). This confirms the reader's impression that the situation deteriorates throughout the book. The second fresh emphasis of the prologue is that God allowed the Canaanites to stay in the land as a punishment for Israel's past covenant disloyalty and as a test of their future loyalty. 'Because this people . . . have not obeyed

[9] For a detailed analysis see O'Connell, *Rhetoric*, 72–80.

[10] E.g. 2:14: 'So the anger of the LORD was kindled against Israel, and he gave them over to plunderers . . . and he sold them into the power of their enemies round about.'

my voice, I will not henceforth drive out before them any of the nations that Joshua left when he died, that by them I may test Israel, whether they will take care to walk in the way of the LORD as their fathers did, or not' (2:20–22).

Anticipating the end of the book the prologue observes that Israel failed the test completely: the Israelites intermarried with the people of the land and worshipped their gods (3:6), the very thing that Deuteronomy had been most concerned should not happen (Deut 7:1–5).

Thus the double prologue highlights the importance of the deuteronomic formulae that recur throughout Judges. Though the formulae tend to be brief, they presuppose the much fuller statements in the prologue of Judges, which in turn reflect the ideology of Deuteronomy itself. Essentially the history of this period is set within a moral framework. Israel's oppression by Canaanites, Philistines and invaders from Transjordan is the result of covenant unfaithfulness, doing what was evil in the sight of the LORD and worshipping other gods. Yet in response to prayer, and occasionally without prayer, Yahweh intervenes to save his people by raising up a judge to lead them to victory in battle.

Amit argues that divine intervention and the nature of human leadership are the key themes of the book. According to Judges God is involved in both the punishment and the deliverance of Israel. He 'sells' them into the hands of Cushan-Rishathaim, Jabin, the Philistines and the Ammonites (3:8; 4:2; 10:7); he 'gave' them into the hand of Midian and the Philistines (6:1, 13; 13:1), and he 'strengthened' Eglon, king of Moab against Israel (3:12). There are several hints in the story of Abimelech that his turbulent rule in Shechem was divine punishment for the apostasy after Gideon's days (8:33–35; 9:23–24, 56–57).

If God's intervention to punish Israel is clear, his involvement in saving Israel is even more explicit. God raises up Othniel and Ehud as deliverers (3:9, 15). He gives Israel's enemies into their hands (3:10, 28; 4:7, 14; 7:2, 7, 9, 14, 15; 8:3, 7; 11:9, 30, 32; 12:3). The Spirit of the LORD falls on a judge before he goes into battle (3:10; 6:34; 11:29; 13:25; 14:6, 19; 15:14).

In the cases of Barak and Gideon the LORD's control is obvious. Barak is summoned by the prophetess Deborah, who gives him God's instructions (4:6–7, 14). The author's understanding of the victory is summed up in 4:15: 'the LORD routed Sisera and all his chariots'. The song of Deborah celebrates God's triumph over the Canaanites putting the prose account of the previous chapter into an even more clearly supernatural perspective: 'From heaven fought the stars, from their courses they fought against Sisera' (5:20).

For his part Gideon is called by the angel of God himself, who is equivalent to the LORD, is clothed with the Spirit of the LORD, and is reassured by two divine signs (the wet and dry fleece), and a Midianite's dream, which another Midianite explains as follows: 'This is no other than the sword of Gideon . . . into his hand God has given Midian and all his host' (7:14). To emphasise that his victory is a God-given victory Gideon is ordered by God to reduce his army of 32,000 volunteers to a mere 300. Their war-cry was enough to put the Midianites to flight.

Even in stories where divine activity is not highlighted, the author surely sees the hand of God at work and expects his readers to recognise it as well. The account of Ehud's successful assassination of Eglon is not simply very humorous, but it is also characterised by his amazing good luck, in being able to smuggle in a sword, obtain a personal audience with Eglon, and escape without the palace guards realising anything was amiss. But Judges sees Ehud as a deliverer sent by God in answer to Israel's prayer, so his success should not be ascribed to luck but to providence (3:15–30). Similarly Samson's exploits though often motivated by self-interest and revenge are seen by the author as fulfilling God's purposes (14:4, 19; 15:14–15; 16:28–30). The Philistines suppose that it is their god that has delivered Samson into their power, but Samson's prayer and his destruction of the temple of Dagon and his 7,000 worshippers proves the contrary: it is the LORD who is in control. In this way Judges underlines the folly of deserting him, as Israel was so prone to do. So the text's insistence on God's control of Israel's destiny reinforces its central theological and ethical message that total loyalty to Yahweh is indispensable. If the people only recognised which God controlled human affairs, they would not consider giving their allegiance to any other.

But Israel's propensity to desert the LORD shows that they need a wise leader to keep them from going astray. The death of Joshua marks the beginning of national declension, which continues remorselessly downwards throughout the book of Judges. The pace of moral and political decline is halted from time to time by the judges, who inject a degree of national unity and deliver the nation from oppression for a while, but then the situation deteriorates again. The book therefore poses the question: what kind of a leader is required to keep Israel faithful to the LORD, and to give her victory over her enemies? The partial success of different judges in these areas offers glimpses of what a future leader ought to be like, but the book as a whole invites the reader to think about these issues and does not offer pat answers.

The book opens with the post-Joshua era, when there was no institutionalised leadership, and ends with the chaos of an era in which 'there was no king in Israel; every man did what was right in his own eyes'. It would therefore be easy to conclude that the book of Judges is simply presenting an argument for monarchy. The last verse seems to express the hope that a king would solve all the problems. But this is over-simple, for right at the heart of the book is a most unflattering example of kingship, Abimelech. No Israelites in their right mind would want a king like him. So what sort of kingship is being implicitly advocated?

Two terms sum up the activity of the leaders in the book, they deliver (*hošiaʿ*) Israel (3:31; 6:14), or they judge (*šapaṭ*) Israel (10:3; 12:7, 8, 11, 13). A few of them, Othniel, Tola and Samson, do both (3:9–10; 10:1–2; 13:5; 15:20). In the case of Barak and Deborah, the former succeeds in battle and the latter judges (4:4, 15–16). It would seem that the good leader should enjoy military success in war and judge the people in time of peace. As this survey shows, few of the leaders mentioned achieved both feats; in fact only Othniel and Tola, of both of whom very little else is known, delivered and judged. Samson is said only to have begun to deliver Israel. Nevertheless from its accounts of the various leaders, it would appear that the book of Judges is advocating a leadership with the dual function of military leadership and enforcing justice.

But who does the book think may assume such a role? First and foremost they must be divinely appointed; they must be 'raised up' by God (2:16, 18). The first two judges, Othniel and Ehud, are said to have been raised up as deliverers (3:9, 15), though the nature of their call is not specified. Barak is summoned by a prophetess. Gideon and Samson by the angel of the LORD (4:6; 6:11–24; 13:2–24). Nothing is said about the appointment of Tola,[11] Jair, Ibzan, Elon and Abdon. But Abimelech and Jephthah are both appointed as a result of their own efforts. Abimelech asks the Shechemites, '"Which is better for you, that all seventy of the sons of Jerubbaal rule over you, or that one rule over you?" . . . and their hearts inclined to follow Abimelech' (9:2–3). Similarly it is the elders of Gilead who appoint Jephthah. Initially they invite him to be their leader, that is commander of the Gileadites in a war against the Ammonites. But he refuses unless they appoint him 'head', that is permanent chief, as well (11:6–11). Neither Abimelech nor Jephthah are strong recommendations for this way of appointing national leaders.

Jotham's parable provides a powerful internal commentary on the issue of leadership. Superficially it is just an attack on Abimelech's quest for power. The trees want to appoint a king to rule over them. In turn they invite the olive, the fig tree, and the vine to become king, but they all declare they have better things to do. So in desperation the trees invite the bramble to rule over them, who is of course pleased to accept (9:8–15). The comparison is at once unflattering to both Abimelech (the bramble) and to the citizens of Shechem (the trees).

[11] Tola 'arose to deliver Israel' (10:1) echoes the appointment of Othniel and Ehud, perhaps implying God's involvement.

But the parable has a wider relevance. It comes at the point in the book where the quality of leadership even among the God-appointed judges seems to deteriorate markedly. Othniel, Ehud, Barak and Gideon are all portrayed fairly positively, with more good points than bad. But with Jephthah, Samson, and the lack of any leaders in the last few chapters, the inadequacy even of the judges becomes obvious. However the parable of Jotham and the example of Abimelech show that a humanly-appointed leader is no solution: the leader must be raised up by God as the successful judges were.

There may too be a hint in this episode that dynastic succession is not necessarily the best way either. Abimelech was one of Gideon's sons, but his massacre of his brothers shows he was quite unfitted to rule. Now Gideon had been invited to be king over Israel after his victory over the Midianites. The men of Israel said to him 'Rule over us, you and your son and your grandson also'. But he apparently turned down this offer of kingship, insisting, 'I will not rule over you, and my son will not rule over you; the LORD will rule over you' (8:22–23). Now it is not clear whether Gideon's refusal is really a polite way of accepting the kingship,[12] or an outright rejection as most writers suppose. But whatever the case, it is clear that Gideon, and the book of Judges, uphold the principle that God is Israel's real king and any human ruler must be appointed by God and acknowledge God's rule. It is also clear that Gideon's other sons were exercising some sort of rule over Shechem before Abimelech exterminated them. Abimelech bases his claim to kingship on his own descent from Gideon, but despite his claim to dynastic legitimacy the result for the people of Shechem is not a happy one. In this way the story, while demonstrating the need for royal leadership, suggests blind allegiance to dynastic succession may not be the best course.

The exposition

Our preliminary survey of the contents of the book and its use of formulae have indicated the general interests of the writer. Now the individual sections of the book must be examined in greater detail to establish the particular thrust of the author. The prologue or exposition consists of two parts: 1:1 – 2:5, a survey of the tribes' settlement activities, and 2:6 – 3:6, a theological lecture by the implied author setting out his interpretation of the history of the judges' period. We shall examine the two parts of the exposition, and then look at the story of Othniel, who both epitomises the message of the exposition, and as the first of the deliverers introduces the core of the book.

[12] Cf. G. H. Davies, 'Judges 8:22–23', *VT* 13 (1963), 151–7.

The exposition begins by surveying the efforts of the different tribes to capture the territory assigned to them by Joshua (cf. Josh 13–21). Obviously Judges 1 is much shorter than its parallels in Joshua, and it is not clear whether the author of Judges is drawing on the book of Joshua.[13] But comparison of Judges 1 with Joshua indicates it has a different purpose. Whereas the book of Joshua is celebrating the success of the conquest, Judges 1 is highlighting its failures. It is introducing the various peoples, who are going to be such a nuisance to Israel later in the main stories in Judges, the Philistines, the Canaanites, the Sidonians and the Jebusites, to name but a few. The prologue explains how these peoples came to be living in the territory allotted to the tribes and why they failed to drive them out. It shows how the presence of these peoples led to assimilation, intermarriage and disloyalty to Israel's covenant God. It presupposes that Israel had a duty to drive out the indigenous peoples and that their failure to do so led to all sorts of problems subsequently.

The first striking feature about the exposition is the prominence of Judah, a tribe that is rarely mentioned later in the book: more than half chapter 1 is devoted to the activities of Judah, while the other tribes fill the rest of the chapter. It is notable that Judah is not only first but the most successful of the tribes. The Judaeans capture every city they attack, and they fail only with the inhabitants of the plain, and that is excused,[14] 'because they had chariots of iron' (1:19). Judah is said to have sacked Jerusalem (1:8), whereas Joshua 15:63 observes that 'the Jebusites, the inhabitants of Jerusalem, the people of Judah could not drive out; so the Jebusites dwell with the people of Judah at Jerusalem to this day'. Joshua ascribes the capture of Hebron to Caleb (14:13–15; 15:13–14), but Judges simply includes its capture among the successes of Judah (1:10). Other successes of Judah not paralleled in Joshua include the first push against the Canaanites (1:1–2), the defeat of Adoni-bezek (1:4–7), the capture of Gaza, Ashkelon and Ekron (1:18). Another notable achievement is Judah's collaboration with the tribe of Simeon to capture Zephath or Hormah (1:17).

By contrast the other tribes are presented both as half-hearted and unsuccessful in their attempts to claim their territories. It should be noted that the list of tribal actions is arranged according to two principles. First, it begins in the south with the tribe of Benjamin and ends with the tribe that settled in the north, the tribe of Dan. Second, it shows increasing compromise with the Canaanites by the tribes.

[13] Amit, *Judges*, 124–7, thinks it unlikely that Judges knows the present book of Joshua.

[14] O'Connell, *Rhetoric*, 64, thinks the subsequent success of Barak over the chariots of the Canaanites 'retroactively nullifies the legitimacy of Judah's excuse for failing to occupy its allotment'.

This pattern anticipates the arrangement of the book's core, which again begins in the south with deliverers from Judah (Othniel) and Benjamin (Ehud) and ends with the tribe that settled in the north, Dan, and the antics of its deliverer Samson. The pattern of increasing compromise that is evident in the exposition is also plain in the core of the book.

Benjamin's tribal territory was immediately north of Judah's and the city of Jerusalem lay between Judah and Benjamin (Josh 15:8; 18:16). But whereas the Judaeans are credited with taking Jerusalem and setting it on fire (Judg 1:8), the Benjaminites are blamed a few verses later for not driving the Jebusites out of Jerusalem and for allowing the Jebusites to live among them (1:21). The large tribes to the north of Benjamin were the tribes of Ephraim and Manasseh, also known as the house of Joseph. The account of their settlement begins promisingly with an anecdote about the capture of Bethel, which strongly echoes the story of Rahab and the fall of Jericho (Josh 2, 6). However a closer comparison casts a shadow over the achievement. In Joshua the spies make an agreement with Rahab after she has confessed her faith in Yahweh, but the man of Bethel was offered safety solely on the condition that he showed the Israelites into the town. Whereas Rahab became a member of Israel, the man of Bethel and his family went and re-established a new Bethel or Luz somewhere else. This contrasts with Joshua's curse on anyone who rebuilt the city of Jericho (1:22–26; cf. Josh 6:22–26).[15] The picture darkens as we read on. Verses 27–33 do not mention the successes of the northern tribes, but only the towns they failed to take. Each time it is mentioned that the tribe failed to drive out the Canaanites, but made them forced labourers. In the case of Manasseh, Ephraim and Zebulon it is noted that the Canaanites continued to live among them. But with the tribes of Asher and Naphtali it is put the other way round: the Asherites and Naphtalites lived among the Canaanites, suggesting not simply Israelite compromise with, but dominance by, Canaanite culture (1:27–33). But the last comment about the tribe of Dan is the most disturbing of all. 'The Amorites pressed the Danites back into the hill country', but the house of Joseph eventually reduced the Amorites to forced labour. Had they followed the practice of Judah, who helped Simeon to capture Zephath, the tribe of Ephraim should surely have allowed the Danites to return to their tribal land instead of leaving it in Amorite hands. Here we have an adumbration of the intertribal rivalry and self-seeking that will be such a feature of many of the episodes in the core of the book, and more particularly a hint of the pressure on the tribe of Dan that will eventually compel it to migrate to the north

[15] Barry G. Webb, *The Book of the Judges: An Integrated Reading* (JSOTSup 46, Sheffield: JSOT Press, 1987), 91–7.

(Judg 13–18). While the book looks for unity and collaboration between the tribes, it has to relate ever-increasing self-seeking and rivalry between them.

The short paragraph telling of the angel of the LORD rebuking the people for their disloyalty to the covenant (2:1–5), at once comments explicitly on the shortcomings of the tribes listed in chapter 1 and prepares the way for the long analysis offered in 2:6 – 3:6. The LORD had fulfilled his promise to give them the land, but they had ignored his command not to make treaties with its inhabitants but to root out their places of worship. He had warned[16] them that it would be a slow process to expel the Canaanites and that this could prove a trap for them, a trap which they had fallen into. So now they would remain to punish Israel.

The second part of the exposition begins by backtracking to the time of Joshua. His era and that of the subsequent generation, who had experienced God's great deeds in the conquest era, were marked by loyalty to the LORD, but the third generation began the period of apostasy described in Judges (2:6–11). Then the author of Judges gives a short lecture setting out his philosophy of history. It runs in cycles. First, Israel forsakes the LORD to serve other gods, the Baals and the Ashtaroth (2:11–13). This, secondly, provokes God's anger, so he gives them over to plunderers, who defeat Israel because he fights against them (2:14–15). Thirdly, the LORD raises up deliverers, who rescue them from their enemies. Yet despite this God-given salvation the people refuse to obey the commandments of God. Indeed on the judge's death they revert to their sinful ways and behave 'worse than their fathers' (2:16–19). 'Israel is depicted as spiralling downwards into worse and worse apostasy.'[17]

On first reading, this description of the degenerative cycles seems to be the same as the deuteronomic formulae we examined earlier, but there is one important omission: there is no appeal to the LORD. This heightens the feeling that Israel is incorrigible; they do not even pray for salvation. Nevertheless God sends them deliverers, demonstrating his loyalty to them. 'So every deed of salvation is interpreted as an act of divine love to those who do not deserve it.'[18]

The insistent question raised by this cycle of sin and salvation is: how long will the people go on sinning and God go on delivering them? Surprisingly 2:19, 'whenever the judge died, they turned back, and

[16] A. Van der Kooij, '"And I also Said": A New Interpretation of Judges II 3', *VT* 45 (1995), 294–306, makes a good case for the dependence of this passage on Exod 23:23–33 as opposed to Deut 7 (O'Connell, *Rhetoric*, 7) or Josh 23 (Amit, *Judges*, 153) but in context it must be commenting on Judg 1 and consonant with what follows it.

[17] Webb, *Judges*, 112.

[18] Amit, *Judges* (Hebrew), 144 (cf. ET, 155).

behaved worse than their fathers', is not followed by an even more severe punishment. Instead God repeats his earlier decision to leave the Canaanites in the land as a test to see whether they would keep his laws or not, and to train them in the art of warfare. The idea that the Canaanites should serve as a sort of punch-bag to give the Israelites practice in fighting is novel, but that they should serve as a test for Israel's loyalty to Yahweh is not. That has already been stated by the angel in 2:3. Yet the repetition of the same idea here after the long reflection on Israel's repeated cycles of disobedience in 2:11–19 is profoundly discouraging. Judges is not going to relate a series of apostasies followed by a climactic judgement and a new start, but a tale of repeated conflicts which show the nation becoming ever more negligent of its covenant obligations and hence becoming totally frustrated as it is unable to escape the consequences of its own incorrigibility.

This gloomy introduction prefaces a book which is largely devoted to recalling the triumphs of Israel's leaders against overwhelming odds, Barak against Sisera, Gideon against the Midianites, often achieved by daring, bizarre and comic means (Ehud, Samson). The core of the book makes exciting reading and the victories of the judges enthral and encourage the reader. Yet 'the anticipatory description of the period as a series of repeated sins directs the reader to focus upon the lesson of its negative features, notwithstanding that the vast bulk of the book is dedicated to description of acts of deliverance'.[19]

So how should this tension between the author's declared didactic purpose and the apparently up-beat message of the judges' victories be explained? Amit has rightly emphasised the book's interest in drawing out God's control of events: he is responsible both for punishing Israel for its disobedience and for answering their prayers and giving their leaders victory. That salvation comes from the LORD is reiterated often. He hears his people's prayers however great their folly (cf. Jephthah 11:30–36; Samson 16:28) or grave their sin (20:18, 23, 28). As in Genesis human sinfulness does not nullify God's graciousness. Israel may break the covenant, and suffer for it, but God will still hear their prayer when they repent. God's readiness to answer prayer runs through the book of Judges and relieves its otherwise gloomy message. Nevertheless the abysmal state of the nation portrayed in the closing chapters is unresolved. It leaves the reader asking what can be done to put the nation on to a better footing. The last verse of the book, while underlining the critical situation, also hints at a way forward: 'In those days there was no king in Israel; every man did what was right in his own eyes' (21:25).

[19] Amit, *Judges*, 159.

The core (3:7 – 16:31)

We have already discussed many aspects of the main stories, so that it is not necessary to review them all here. They do show God's intervention in Israel's affairs, often in a spectacular way. They do begin with a judge from the tribe of Judah, Othniel, and end with a judge from the tribe of Dan. They do show a progressive deterioration in both the nation's behaviour and that of the judges who deliver them. As a whole the book of Judges appears to be implicitly commending a different kind of leadership: through its portrayal of the inadequacies of the judges it is implying that a king could lead to more fidelity to the covenant within the nation and offer more security from external threats. Nowhere though does it give its perfect model for kingship; rather by painting a variety of judges it encourages its readers to reflect for themselves on what the best kind of leader would be.

The major judges are said both to 'judge' Israel and to 'deliver' the nation (3:9–10; 10:1–2; 13:5; 15:20), that is, they promote obedience to covenant standards by administering the law[20] and they act as military leaders in time of war. Interestingly the book looks back to the era of Joshua as a period before things went wrong (1:1; 2:7). He of course was the military leader *par excellence* under whose leadership important victories over the Canaanites were achieved and through whom the land was allocated. He was moreover a punctilious observer of the law of Moses. When he was commissioned by the LORD as Moses' successor, he was told, 'This book of the law shall not depart out of your mouth, but you shall meditate on it day and night, that you may be careful to do according to all that is written in it: for then you shall make your way prosperous, and then you shall have good success' (Josh 1:8). The book of Joshua witnesses to Joshua's total commitment to these principles; he is shown to be concerned not only with carrying out the major demands of Deuteronomy, but with its detailed injunctions.[21] So too are the people, apart from an occasional blip at Ai and Gibeon (chs 7 and 9). Consequently the campaign of conquest led by Joshua is a great success. By alluding back to Joshua right at the start of its narrative the book of Judges suggests that the ideal leader of the nation should emulate his qualities.

[20] It is unlikely that judges quoted from written codes in Israel, as this was not the practice elsewhere in the ancient Near East, cf. Eckhart Otto, 'Aspects of Legal Reforms and Reformulations in Ancient Cuneiform and Israelite Law', in *Theory and Method in Biblical and Cuneiform Law* (ed. Bernard M. Levinson; JSOTSup 181, Sheffield: JSOT Press, 1994), 160–1, rather they made decisions on the basis of justice and precedent; cf. Ps 72:1–2.

[21] Cf. G. J. Wenham, 'The Deuteronomic Theology of the Book of Joshua', *JBL* 90 (1971), 140–8.

The first of the judges, Othniel, is described very briefly and formulaicly: the account of his career is largely made up of deuteronomic phrases that typically frame the account of each judge, (*a*) sin, (*b*) punishment, (*c*) crying out, (*d*) deliverance and (*e*) quiet. He is said both to have judged Israel and to have delivered them. His deeds are said to have been inspired by the Spirit of the LORD (3:7–11). Earlier in his career he had participated in the conquest of Kiriath-Sepher (1:13).

> Othniel thus constitutes a transitional figure, bringing out the characteristic feature of all the heroes of the book of Judges: they all act first and foremost by the strength of God and his will. Othniel set out to deliver his people because the hand of the Lord was upon him, and he prevailed over Cushan-Rishathaim because God gave him into his hand.[22]

Othniel is not only the first judge, but he is also the only one who is not criticised implicitly or explicitly by the author. He also came from the tribe of Judah, and fought with king Cushan from Aram-Naharaim far outside Israel's borders, whereas later judges were concerned only with Israel's near neighbours such as the Moabites, Philistines and Canaanites. This clothes Othniel with an aura suggestive of the later Davidic dynasty.

By contrast Othniel's successors are more parochial in their military operations, and none escape censure in some regard or other for their actions. Ehud, the left-handed Benjaminite, showed his mettle in his daring assassination of Eglon, king of Moab, and his rallying of the Ephraimites to slaughter the Moabites at the fords of the Jordan. The author tells us explicitly that the LORD raised up Ehud as deliverer (3:15), and the remarkable sequence of coincidences whereby Ehud obtained a private audience with Eglon, killed him, and escaped without arousing suspicion witness to the effectiveness of divine providence protecting him. Nevertheless his association with the idols at Gilgal, (RSV 'sculptured stones') (3:19, 26) casts a shadow over Ehud's victory.

Barak's victory over Sisera is another occasion where God's intervention on Israel's behalf was obvious. Many of the tribes rallied to his call and the natural elements swept the Canaanite chariots away. There was no doubt in the Israelites' minds that 'From heaven fought the stars, from their courses they fought against Sisera' (5:20). This is one of the most dramatic demonstrations of divine power to save his people, and of course it reflects well on Barak and Deborah who lead the Israelite tribes. But in her song Deborah bemoans the unwillingness of four of the tribes, Reuben, Gilead (Manasseh), Dan and Asher to support the campaign (5:15–17); evidently national unity was not as solid as it should have been. However while the absent tribes are

[22] Amit, *Judges*, 164.

condemned outright, Barak himself also suffers a mild rebuke from Deborah. She tells him: 'The LORD, the God of Israel, commands you, "Go".' But he replies: 'if you will not go with me, I will not go' (4:6, 8). Such wimpishness in Israel's supreme commander ill becomes one who should be emulating Joshua, who was told to 'be strong and very courageous' (Josh 1:7). The book of Deuteronomy insists that ordinary soldiers who are fearful and fainthearted should return home, not participate in the battle (20:8). If this was the attitude required of the soldier, how much more of their commanders! Little wonder then that Deborah scolds Barak with the words: 'I will surely go with you; nevertheless, the road on which you are going will not lead to your glory, for the LORD will sell Sisera into the hand of a woman' (4:9). Nevertheless Barak, like Othniel and Ehud before him, brings a long period of peace to the nation (forty years, 5:31; cf. 3:11, 30).

Hesitation and fearfulness are even more characteristic of Gideon than they are of Barak, despite the fact that he is commissioned by the angel of the LORD and not just a prophetess. He demands a series of signs before he accepts his commission to lead Israel (6:17, 36, 39). His fearfulness is explicitly mentioned in 6:27 and 7:10, and that is after he has sent 22,000 home because they were 'fearful and trembling' (7:3)! Despite this inappropriate attitude, Gideon achieves a spectacular victory with just 300 men demonstrating that it was God that gave Midian into his hand (7:14).

This is followed by the call to the tribes of Naphtali, Asher, Manasseh and Ephraim to pursue the Midianites, to which they duly respond. A row with the Ephraimites is defused by Gideon, but a much more serious dispute with Succoth and Penuel leads to him taking savage revenge on these Israelite towns. This is the first occasion of civil war in Judges, which breaks out even more seriously under Gideon's son, Abimelech. Deborah and Barak simply rebuked the other tribes for their lack of support: Gideon tortures his opposition, damages their city, and kills some of them.

Furthermore, despite his professed piety, he sits loose to covenant fundamentals. Out of Midianite gold earrings he makes an ephod. Ephods did have a legitimate role in worship, so a benevolent reader[23] may suppose there was nothing wrong with this act. However the echoes of the similar production out of Egyptian earrings of Aaron's golden calf makes Gideon's action suspect.[24] This at least is the writer's view for he comments: 'and all Israel played the harlot after it there, and it became a snare to Gideon and his family' (8:27). Furthermore, Gideon is the first judge to commit the ultimate sin of intermarriage with the Canaanites (3:6) by taking a concubine from Shechem, who appears to

[23] E.g. Amit, *Judges*, 260–2.

[24] O'Connell, *Rhetoric*, 163.

have been a Canaanite (8:31). Abimelech, the son of this liaison, becomes a real thorn in the nation's side.

> Thus, Gideon, like Barak, is a microcosm of Israel's reluctance to follow YHWH wholeheartedly . . . The irony of this characterisation is that YHWH raises up a deliverer for Israel who is none other than Israel in miniature. So it is little wonder that the outcome of the Gideon story is hardly better than its beginning. A deliverer who acts like Israel can hardly be expected to save Israel from the inclinations that lead them to return to evil.[25]

With Abimelech, one of Gideon's seventy sons, we are presented with a picture of the horrors of the wrong sort of kingship. He is vicious, showing no loyalty to his brothers, whom he massacres. He manipulates the people of Shechem and provokes civil war. But ultimately he meets his just deserts. He slew his brothers on one stone, and was himself mortally wounded by a millstone dropped on his head (ch. 9).

We have already noted that the book of Judges, by describing different leaders, is implicitly inviting the reader to decide what the ideal sort of leader would be like. The closing chapters suggest that what Israel needs is a king, who would unite the nation, judge them fairly, and bring them peace. But the one Israelite king in Judges cannot be anyone's ideal. The closing chapters appear to castigate the tribe of Benjamin and the town of Gibeah in particular as a means of discrediting Saul and his sons, who came from that town. Already in the depiction of Gideon and more particularly his son Abimelech there are features that could be thought to foreshadow Saul's career (1 Sam 17:11; 28:5; 16:14; 18:1 – 26:25; 31:4–6). In particular Gideon's fearfulness in battle is a notable trait of Saul. The evil spirit of Abimelech, the relentlessness with which he pursues civil war, and the manner of his death at his armour bearer's hand are also suggestive of Saul. Admittedly these points of comparison are not as obvious as in the last three chapters of the book, but this could be a mark of the writer's rhetorical skill. Too sharp an attack on Saul too early would not be as effective as one that developed gradually.

Between the story of Abimelech and that of Jephthah comes an extended editorial reflection on the state of the nation. It is not simply suggesting that sin, punishment and salvation are cyclical, but that the cycles are really a downward spiral with the nation's sins becoming ever graver resulting in God becoming more reluctant to help. The LORD reminds Israel of his past interventions on their behalf against the Egyptians, Midianites and Amalekites among others, 'Yet you have forsaken me and served other gods: therefore I will deliver you no more. Go and cry to the gods whom you have chosen; let them deliver you in the time of your distress' (10:13–15).

[25] O'Connell, *Rhetoric*, 163.

Israel's subsequent repentance looks superficial, though it does lead to God becoming indignant over Israel's suffering. But the choice of Jephthah that follows is not ascribed to Yahweh's election at all, but it appears to be the outcome of grubby bargaining between the leaders of Gilead and Jephthah. The Gileadites appeal for any military leader who can throw out the Ammonites and say they are willing to make him their permanent head. However, when the disreputable Jephthah is the only one they can find, they promptly lower their offer to being merely temporary military leader (11:6). But he insists that if he is victorious in battle, he must become their permanent head. Eventually the Gileadites agree to Jephthah being appointed both head and leader (11:11).

There then follows a long negotiation between Jephthah and the king of the Ammonites about their territorial claims. Jephthah apparently lays great store by the fact that the Israelite territory had been given them by the LORD, and he concludes with an appeal to God to vindicate his cause (11:27). Then, inspired by the Spirit of the LORD, he rallies the tribe of Manasseh and the Gileadites to enlist in his army. Then he makes a vow to the LORD that if he is successful in battle, 'whoever comes forth from the doors of my house to meet me . . . I will offer him up for a burnt offering' (11:31). This translation reflects the consensus of most commentators ancient and modern that Jephthah was promising human sacrifice if he was victorious. Vows, which often involved the offering of sacrifice, were quite legitimate in desperate situations in biblical times. Human sacrifice was practised by Israel's neighbours, but many Old Testament books regard it as abominable.[26] That this is Judges' stance too is shown by the way the sacrifice of Jephthah's daughter quite overshadows his victory over the Ammonites. In other episodes in Judges the victories are described at length. Here a mere two verses are devoted to a tremendous victory, as opposed to nine pathos-filled verses about the sacrifice of Jephthah's only daughter (11:30–40).

This shameful event in Jephthah's personal life is then followed by a civil war in which the Gileadites slaughter some 42,000 Ephraimites. But it is not just the scale of the casualties that show the author's abhorrence of this warfare, it is the way he sets Jephthah's provocative response to the complaints of the Ephraimites over against Gideon's quiet reply to them which had on an earlier occasion calmed them down (8:1–3; 12:1–6). It was at the fords of the Jordan that Ehud had killed 10,000 Moabites, but Jephthah slew there 42,000 Ephraimites. These comparisons all tend to put Jephthah in a quite unfavourable light as a person. They also tend to discredit the elders of Gilead who chose him

[26] Lev 18:21; 20:2–5; Deut 12:31; 18:10; 2 Kgs 16:3; 17:31; 21:6; Jer 7:31; 19:5; 32:35; Ezek 20:25–26.

as their leader, instead of waiting for the LORD to raise up a more suitable leader. In this respect the story of Jephthah parallels that of Abimelech, who was also elected by the citizens of Shechem and was backed by a gang of 'worthless and reckless' henchmen (9:4; 11:3). Once again one must ask whether this may also be an oblique criticism of Saul, whose election was also in response to popular demand. Saul nearly made the same mistake as Jephthah too, when he cursed anyone who ate during the battle. Like Jephthah's daughter Saul's son, Jonathan, unwittingly fulfilled his father's vow, and Saul would have executed him too, had not the people intervened to save Jonathan (1 Sam 14). The parallels between Saul and Jephthah do not enhance the former's moral standing.

Samson is the only judge whose life-story is told from birth to death. Unlike Jephthah's exploits which are recounted quite briefly, Samson's are related in detail and with relish. Nevertheless many of them are bizarre, setting fields alight with foxes, carrying off the gates of Gaza, killing a thousand with the jawbone of an ass and so on. Judged by the standards of his predecessors he achieved relatively little at the national level. Samson is not said to have delivered Israel, indeed the angel promises only that 'he shall begin to deliver Israel from the hand of the Philistines' (13:5). Furthermore though the narratives about Samson begin with the usual formulae about Israel sinning and being punished by being given into the hand of the Philistines, it is not said that they cried to the LORD (13:1). This seems one stage worse than the time of Jephthah where Israel's cries are met with divine rebuke for the superficiality of their repentance (10:10–16). Yet despite Israel's increasing apostasy and failure to call on the LORD, he still intervenes to demonstrate his power to save and his superiority over the gods of the Philistines.

The excitement and humour of the Samson stories may easily prevent the reader from appreciating the true state of play as the author sees it. He wanted 'to emphasise the tremendous redemptive powers available to Samson, contrasted with the utter failure of his leadership'.[27] His miraculous conception by a barren couple and his life-long Naziriteship make him unique among the judges. In his youth the Spirit of the LORD begins to stir him. But after this most promising start in chapter 13, he decides to marry a Philistine, which even his parents disapprove of, let alone the author of Judges (14:3; cf. 3:6), for whom intermarriage represents the ultimate compromise with Yahweh's enemies. Nevertheless as the author points out, the Spirit of the LORD does not forsake Samson because of his infidelity to the covenant, rather the LORD uses the anger generated through Samson's contact with the Philistines to inflict damage on them (14:4). Basically all Samson's

[27] Amit, *Judges*, 275.

skirmishes with the Philistines are individualistic personal acts of revenge. He makes no attempt to mobilise his own tribe against the Philistines, let alone the other tribes. Indeed the tribe of Judah find him such a liability that they send 3,000 men to capture Samson and deliver him bound to the Philistines (15:9–13)! What a parody of the proper relationship of judge, people and their enemies. Instead of co-operation and mutual support between the tribes, there is conflict and treachery. The anarchy of the closing chapters of the book is not far away. Nowhere in fact is Samson portrayed as a leader. He is the deliverer, who in the final analysis did not deliver. He is the last judge, who died in enemy captivity, 'leaving the people under the yoke of the Philistines and strengthening the impression that the judges' leadership is unable to confront the problems of the period'.[28]

The epilogue 17:1 – 21:25

It used to be received critical wisdom that the last five chapters of Judges were a later appendix to the book coming from a different hand and a different era from the rest of the work. It is set off from the preceding chapters by the refrain 'In those days there was no king in Israel; every man did what was right in his own eyes' (17:6; 21:25; cf. 19:1) and by its contents. Instead of stories focused on a particular judge and his saving exploits, we have two longish narratives about tribes misbehaving and achieving little except mayhem. Nearly everything they do seems to be irregular by the standards of the rest of the Old Testament.

But are the distinctive features of these closing chapters proof that they do not belong with the rest of the book? A number of recent studies of the book have argued to the contrary that the two extended narratives with which the book closes are integral to the editor's scheme and indeed give the greatest insight into his purpose in composing the book.[29] Whatever the origins of the stories in these closing chapters, they now do form its conclusion. And whether we posit a series of sources and editorial hands or just one principal author, it is clear that the final

[28] Amit, *Judges*, 289.

[29] E.g. Webb, *Judges*; O'Connell, *Rhetoric*; M. K. Wilson, '"As You Like It": The Idolatry of Micah and the Danites (Judg 17–18)', *Reformed Theological Review* 54 (1995), 73–85; Marvin A. Sweeney, 'Davidic Polemics in the Book of Judges', *VT* 47 (1997), 517–29; Daniel I. Block, 'Will the Real Gideon Please Stand Up?' *JETS* 40 (1997), 353–66; Amit, *Judges*. Amit unusually holds that the book of Judges properly consists of chs 1–18, and that chs 19–21 are from a different later hand. Though they have been spliced on to chs 17–18 by the 'no-king-in-those-days' formula, their assumptions about tribal unity and moral concern do not in Amit's opinion fit with the rest of the book. However she does regard these chapters as anti-Saulide polemic, which makes her interpretation of them similar to those who see them as integral.

author or editor of Judges thought chapters 17–21 belonged with what preceded. This means that an interpretation from a canonical perspective must read the whole book together. So in what follows we shall endeavour to read the epilogue as a coherent ending to the whole book.

The first story in the epilogue concerns the tribe of Dan. Unable to establish themselves in their tribal allotment adjacent to Judah in the south of Canaan, they decide to move north. On the way they come across an irregular shrine in Ephraim manned by a Levite, so they conscript him and make off with the shrine and its sacred furnishings despite the owner's protest. Arriving at a 'quiet unsuspecting' city in the north called Laish, they kill its citizens and burn it down. When they rebuild it, they establish a shrine there with its graven image served by the hijacked Levite. Readers attuned to the religious and moral norms will be shocked by the behaviour described here, but to underline his disapproval the editor twice comments about the absence of a king which allowed such things to occur (17:6; 18:1).

These comments could be taken positively if the behaviour being described was admirable, but 'none of the characters are portrayed in a positive light'.[30] Micah was a thief, who returned the stolen money to his mother only because he feared her curse, not for more conscientious reasons. The Levite is quite prepared to work in an irregular shrine with graven images, and Micah even imagines that God will prosper him because he has set up this idolatrous cult.

> Precisely the fact that all of the parties acted in innocence and with the intention of doing what is right in the eyes of God, rather than out of wickedness or contempt, reveals the distorted values of the period. The author's barbs of criticism are thus not directed against Micah or the Levite, but against the circumstances that facilitated the existence of situations and phenomena of this type.[31]

Wilson[32] points out that the epilogue's phrase about 'every man doing what was right in his own eyes' mirrors the refrain earlier in the book about Israel doing what was 'evil in the eyes of the LORD'. Each of the major judges in chapters 3–16 is sent to rescue the people from their addiction to idolatry; but they all ultimately fail, for Israel reverts to the worship of idols. The epilogue, particularly chapters 17–18, shows how the Israelites viewed idols at that time. Micah, the Levite, and the Danites all approve irregular shrines with their idols. Indeed they hope to prosper as a result of them. They are doing what is right in their own eyes, quite unaware apparently that it was evil in the LORD's eyes.

30 Amit, *Judges*, 326.
31 Amit, *Judges*, 328.
32 Wilson, '"As You Like It"', 74–5.

There are a number of parallels between the behaviour of the Danites in chapter 18 and Micah in chapter 17 which serve to put them into an even worse light than him. Both stole, both used the stolen goods in their shrine, both employed a Levite, both justified their own behaviour, and eventually both saw their shrine destroyed. But the Danites used violence to achieve their ends, threatening armed intervention against Micah, press-ganging the Levite, and conquering a peaceful unsuspecting town. Implicitly 'the author criticises everything done by the Danites: they are greedy, attack the weak, and serve stolen gods'.[33] Yet he does not blame it on their character, rather it reflects the era in which they live, 'in which each man did what was right in his own eyes'.

The same point is made right at the beginning and right at the end of the next narrative (19:1; 21:25), which is surely one of the most horrifying stories in the Bible. This time the arch villains are the tribe of Benjamin and particularly the town of Gibeah. However, in reacting to the crime of Gibeah none of the tribes come out with any credit: full-scale civil war leads to the near-extinction of the tribe of Benjamin, which is rescued only by treating the citizens of Jabesh-Gilead and the girls of Shiloh with extraordinary barbarity.

Once again a wandering Levite sets in train the catastrophic chain of events, which lead this time not to the destruction of one small Canaanite village, but to the death of tens of thousands of Israelites in a civil war. To appreciate the author's viewpoint this tale needs to be read in the light of Genesis 19 and 1 Samuel 11 (Saul's rescue of Jabesh-Gilead). At every point the principal figures in Judges 19 are portrayed as behaving worse than their parallels in Genesis and 1 Samuel. The action starts with the Levite and his slave wife arriving in Gibeah and only the non-local Ephraimite offering hospitality, just as Lot the foreigner was the only one to entertain the angels in Sodom. The Ephraimite's peremptory 'Only, do not spend the night in the square', reminds us of Lot's concern that the angels should stay with him, not stay in the streets of Sodom all night (Judg 19:20; Gen 19:2–3). And rapidly the Benjaminites of Gibeah are shown to be even worse than the men of Sodom. The latter were at least frustrated in their plan to rape the angels; the Gibeathites gang-raped the Levite's concubine all night and she died in the morning.

The impression of the Levite's callousness in thrusting out his concubine to save his own skin is confirmed by his reaction to finding her dead on the doorstep next morning. His dramatic gesture of dismembering her corpse and sending a part to every tribe is even more shocking, for prompt and proper burial was the accepted way of

[33] Amit, *Judges*, 334.

honouring the dead.[34] Comparison with Saul's gesture of cutting up oxen and sending the parts throughout Israel as a warning to the tribes also reflects discreditably on the Levite. But most damning of all is his distorted account of what happened at Gibeah, which fails to mention his responsibility for handing his concubine over to the mob and his assertion that it was the lords (leading citizens) of Gibeah not 'men of Belial' who were responsible for the outrage. The misrepresentation doubtless exacerbated the assembly's reaction to the awful events.[35] A straightforward account of the crime should have been sufficient in itself to provoke a national response.

The author does not make it clear what should have been done in this case. The LORD destroyed the city of Sodom for their actions, which as described in Genesis 19, were less serious than Gibeah's. Deuteronomy 13 prescribes that in the case of a village apostatising and serving other gods at the instigation of 'base fellows' (sons of Belial), an enquiry should be held, and if guilt is proved, all the inhabitants should be killed, the village burnt down and never rebuilt (Deut 13:12–18). Echoes of Deuteronomy 13 in Judges 20 lead O'Connell to argue that this is what the author of Judges held should have been done in this case.[36] However the Benjaminites refuse to hand over even the 'base fellows' of Gibeah for punishment. It is the Benjaminites' solidarity with the Gibeathites which triggers off the disastrous civil war that follows. Both sides suffer heavy casualties, but the Benjaminites lose so many that the other tribes resort to drastic measures to preserve the tribe. There are three major battles between Benjamin and the other Israelite tribes. Strangely, although God sanctions all the attacks of Israel, they lose the first two and defeat Benjamin only at the third attempt. This and the ambush tactic used at the end resemble Joshua's assault on Ai: there too a defeat was followed by a successful assault on the city. The defeat at Ai is explained in Joshua as the consequence of Achan's breaking the ban on taking plunder from Jericho. No such reason is offered in Judges for the two initial defeats of Israel by the Benjaminites, though divine displeasure at the operation is surely implied.

This prompts serious soul-searching by the Israelites, who fasted, offered sacrifice and prayed. Eventually the LORD said, 'Go up; for tomorrow I will give them into your hand' (20:28). So this time the Benjaminites are defeated and Gibeah is sacked. This should have been the end of the affair, but dismayed by the Benjaminite losses, which

[34] According to Deut 21:23 even executed criminals must be buried promptly; cf. 1 Sam 31:8–13. In Homer 'the ultimate evil is death followed by desecration of the body' (MacIntyre, *After Virtue*, 120).

[35] S. Lasine, 'Guest and Host in Judges 19: Lot's Hospitality in an Inverted World', *JSOT* 29 (1984), 37–59.

[36] O'Connell, *Rhetoric*, 256–8.

they fear will lead to the extinction of the tribe of Benjamin, the Israelites sack Jabesh-Gilead and hand over the unmarried girls of the town to be wives of the Benjaminites. As this still does not make up the deficit of Benjaminite women, the Benjaminite men are encouraged to seize girls from Shiloh during the annual feast of the LORD and take them home, even if their fathers or brothers protest (21:1–23).

The bitter irony of the conclusion is evident. The civil war had been triggered by the rape of a solitary Bethlehemite concubine at the hands of the Benjaminite town of Gibeah. It is concluded by all the tribes of Israel encouraging the surviving Benjaminite men to ravish the girls of Jabesh-Gilead and Shiloh. Had the episode in Gibeah just been ignored, many lives would have been saved and many women saved from brutal treatment. Instead it has led to one last twist of the spiral as the nation descends into darkness and barbarity.[37]

To sum up: the book of Judges portrays Israel becoming progressively more lax in its religious practice, and ever more prone to disunity between the tribes, and in the epilogue both trends reach a climax with outright idolatry among the Danites and a civil war that could have destroyed the nation. The reader is driven to conclude: this must not continue, if the nation is to enjoy harmony at home and peace abroad. A new way of life under new leadership is required, if Israel is to survive in Canaan.

A setting for Judges

Theories about the composition of Judges have ebbed and flowed. At the beginning of the twentieth century it was commonly held that the pentateuchal sources J, E and D were present in Judges.[38] Great efforts were made to define the extent of these sources, but little attention was paid to the final form of the book and its significance.

A similar failure to focus on the final form of Judges is apparent in the dominant view in the second half of the century. Since M. Noth (1943) Judges has widely been perceived to form part of the deuteronomistic history, which relates Israel's history from the conquest to the exile. The major unifying theological idea of this work is that Israel's fortunes depend on its fidelity to the covenant: disloyalty brings distress, whereas faithfulness brings prosperity. This approach, like the earlier source-critical approach, sees the message of Judges as directed to the exiles, explaining to them the reason for their plight.

[37] 'The Book of Judges draws to a close . . . with Israelite men repeating on a mass scale the crimes of the men of Gibeah.' J. C. Exum in *Judges and Method* (ed. Gale A. Yee, Minneapolis: Fortress Press, 1995), 86.

[38] E.g. George F. Moore, *A Critical and Exegetical Commentary on Judges* (ICC, Edinburgh: T&T Clark, 1895), xxxiii–xxxvii.

The most recent phase of study has recognised that both these earlier approaches do not pay sufficient attention to the particular features of Judges. While not denying the connections between Judges and other historical books, recent scholarship has focused on the special interests of the book. However, while there is broad agreement among recent writers that the book as a whole is coherent and aims to commend the interests of the tribe of Judah and its right to lead the other tribes, there is less consensus about the period it is addressing.

Much of the evidence is compatible with the book's composition at a wide variety of dates in Israel's history from the early monarchy to the post-exilic era. But there are two strong pieces of evidence which suggest very different dates. In 18:30 it says: 'The Danites set up the graven image for themselves . . . until the day of the captivity of the land.' The simplest way to take this unusual phrase 'captivity of the land' is until the destruction of the northern kingdom of Israel by the Assyrians in 722 B.C. This would imply that Judges was written some-time after 722. For this reason Amit constructs a scenario in which the message of Judges would make sense in the time of Hezekiah. After the fall of Samaria there was a need to explain the survival of the southern kingdom and the destruction of the northern kingdom. A school of historiography came into being that reflected on Israel's past and traced back the faults of the northerners to the judges' period and justified Judaean leadership.

This reading of the book is plausible if little weight is attached to chapters 19–21. These chapters contain sharp polemic against the Benjaminites in general and the towns of Gibeah and Jabesh-Gilead in particular. The first was Saul's home town, and the second his burial place (1 Sam 11:4; 31:11–13). There are hints of anti-Saul polemic too in the characterisation of some of the judges. On the other hand the positive portrayal of the tribe of Judah in chapter 1 and the exemplary role of Othniel give the story a pro-Davidic spin. For O'Connell these are indications that the book was written in the early days of David's reign before Jerusalem had been captured while the supporters of Saul were still a threat. The book was, he suggests, particularly addressed to the Ephraimites, who are often mentioned in Judges. By discrediting Saul and praising Judaean leadership, the author hoped to swing his Ephraimite readers behind David.[39] As for the phrase 'until the day of the captivity of the land' O'Connell suggests it either refers to a deportation carried out by the Philistines or the text may be slightly corrupt and should read 'until the day of the captivity of the ark'.[40]

[39] O'Connell, *Rhetoric*, 305–29.

[40] This idea has been proposed by a number of very different scholars (see O'Connell *Rhetoric*, 337 n. 61), simply on the ground that a reference to an Assyrian deportation seems out of place here.

The diversity of settings proposed by Amit and O'Connell cannot disguise the fact that the two fullest and most recent studies of Judges, despite their very different critical starting points, read the message of the book in a similar way. They both see it as showing God's control of Israel's destiny, as prescribing the kind of leadership required, as criticising Israel's failure to conquer the land fully and its acceptance of intermarriage and idolatry. They also agree that it is promoting Judaean leadership, not that of the other tribes. They also read Judges as portraying a progressive decline into greater and greater sin. But this does not mean the end of divine involvement with Israel: throughout the story judges are raised up and filled with the Spirit and carry out saving deeds on the nation's behalf. The later judges, such as Jephthah and Samson, are notably defective in piety and morality from the author's point of view, but nevertheless God uses them despite their deficiencies to advance his glory and demonstrate his power over the gods of surrounding peoples and to encourage the faith of Israel. As in the book of Genesis the heroes of Judges are by no means sinless: yet despite the book's portrayal of their many faults it still affirms that God in his grace may use them to fulfil his purpose.

5

ETHICAL IDEALS AND LEGAL REQUIREMENTS

So far we have been concerned with general principles of the ethical interpretation of narrative and looked at the broad concerns of two particular books, Genesis and Judges. We have argued that ethical readers should aim to discover the views of the implied author and this requires them to engage with his ideas and to share his stance on many issues. To become a sensitive reader involves understanding the implied author's outlook and to approximate oneself to the implied reader, that is the sort of reader the implied author had in mind when he was writing his book. From this perspective it matters little whether the narratives are historical or fictional, whether they are composed from a multitude of sources or were entirely the creation of a single writer. We are not concerned with the process of composition, which may be hard to reconstruct, but with what the implied author is communicating by telling the narrative. This involves careful study of the final form of the different books to determine the message that they were attempting to communicate to their implied readers.

In the case of Genesis we argued that the book focuses on the issues that were alive in the period of the united monarchy, intertribal jealousies, particularly the right of the tribe of Judah to leadership, and relations with the Canaanites and surrounding nations, particularly the Aramaeans, Edomites, Philistines, Ammonites and Moabites. In response to these disputes Genesis breathes a spirit of peace and reconciliation. Their forefather Jacob made peace with his uncle Laban the Aramaean and his brother Esau. Abraham and Isaac cultivated good relationships with the Philistines, while Joseph forgave his brothers despite the years of suffering which they had inflicted on him. Though Genesis does not allow intermarriage with the Canaanites,[1] it definitely appears to encourage good relations between Israel and its other neighbours and between the Israelite tribes.

Judges appears to be dealing with similar issues to Genesis: disputes between the tribes leading to civil war, oppression by neighbouring peoples such as the Moabites, Midianites, Ammonites and Philistines. The issue of leadership is again to the forefront in Judges, with its closing lament about there being no king in Israel and its positive

[1] Indeed passages such as 9:25; 12:6; 15:16 look forward to their subjugation at least.

approach to the tribe of Judah's achievements. But its approach to both external and internal problems is very different from Genesis. Whereas Genesis portrays the patriarchs endeavouring to live at peace with these peoples, Judges describes battles with them in which a heroic judge usually leads Israel to victory. On the leadership issue Genesis is quite open about commending Judah's claims (e.g. 49:8–12), whereas Judges is much more circumspect about endorsing Judah though it knocks the claims of Benjamin and particularly Gibeah, Saul's home town, very hard indeed. Finally, whereas Genesis ends on an up-beat note looking forward to the tribes happily settled in Canaan, Judges paints a picture of catastrophic decline into anarchy and chaos. As with the book of Genesis various settings have been proposed for Judges. If O'Connell's date in the early reign of David before the house of Saul had given up fighting for the throne is correct, the negative attitudes towards Gibeah and Benjamin are readily explicable. The shrillness of Judges' polemic reflects the uncertainty of the supporters of David that his side will prevail. However this historical setting is by no means certain, and the message of the book does not depend on an early dating.

Despite their very different approaches to war and peace and national leadership Judges and Genesis do share a number of common assumptions. The first is that the land has been given by God to Israel. Throughout Genesis the LORD appears to the patriarchs promising the land, and the book climaxes with Jacob's poetic vision of the tribes settled in the land enjoying its God-given territory (e.g. 12:1, 7; 49:2–27). Judges discusses Israel's right to the land and the failure of most of the tribes to exercise that right throughout the prologue (1:1 – 3:6). It is again referred to by Jephthah as a well-known fact in his abortive attempt to make peace with the Ammonites (11:21–27) and the presupposition of all the judges' victories is the LORD's gift of the land to Israel.

The second feature common to both books is the conviction that in the land Israel is meant to enjoy peace. Genesis portrays the whole world, God, mankind and the animals, initially at peace with each other. Then of course human disobedience leads to conflict between all the parties, tearing apart even such fundamental institutions as marriage and the family and leading to nations at war with each other. Nevertheless the patriarchs, at least in their mature old age, work for peace and reconciliation within their families and with their neighbours. Judges too reflects a yearning for peace. The first four judges brought the nation 200 years of rest, but later judges despite their divine call and endowment with the Spirit failed to bring any. Indeed the book closes with all the tribes at war, in danger of annihilating each other.

The third assumption common to both books is that the deeds of their heroes are not always praiseworthy. This is most obvious in the book of Judges, which portrays its leading figures as being increasingly compromised by their involvement in idolatrous practices and inter-marriage with the people of the land. Nevertheless the LORD uses the judges to deliver Israel. Ehud and Gideon dabble with idolatry. Jephthah's vow of human sacrifice does not prevent him from enjoying the Spirit's power to achieve a great victory. Even Samson, slave to passion that he was, is endowed with the Spirit of God on several occasions to check the Philistine oppression. The book of Judges shows God saving Israel despite the moral and religious shortcomings of the judges, not because of their righteousness. It illustrates tellingly the reflections of Deuteronomy:

> Not because of your righteousness or the uprightness of your heart are you going in to possess their land; but because of the wickedness of these nations the LORD your God is driving them out from before you, and that he may confirm the word which the LORD swore to your fathers, to Abraham, to Isaac, and to Jacob. (Deut 9:5)

It is God's grace and his faithfulness to his promises, not Israel's merits, that lies behind what successes the judges do achieve. The same holds true in Genesis to a large extent. Admittedly none of the patriarchs is as dissolute as Samson, and on some occasions, just like the judges, their behaviour is admirable. Nevertheless Jacob's reparations to Esau and his sons' plea for forgiveness from Joseph are admissions of their past sins. Similarly Abraham's silence when his actions are castigated by the Pharaoh (12:20), and in a similar situation Isaac's failure to answer Abimelech (26:10), are tacit admissions of guilt. It is evident that neither Genesis nor Judges holds up all the actions of its actors as admirable, but that God acts in grace towards his fallible people.

But can we be any more precise? In recounting these stories was the implied author really expecting his readers to be in doubt about the fitness or otherwise of much of his heroes' behaviour? What was the standard he expected his implied readers to bring with them when they read the text? If we can answer these questions, we shall be in a better position to decide what message he was imparting to his readers.

Much confusion has been generated by a failure to keep the perspective of the implied author to the front of the discussion. The source-critical and tradition-historical approaches have focused on earlier putative stages of the stories in Judges and Genesis when perhaps they were told in quite different contexts in order to make quite different points. Thus it is argued that some morally questionable deeds were supposedly related to glorify the patriarchs: they show how smart the patriarchs or matriarchs were in overcoming opposition. For example Vawter holds that 12:10–20, in which Abraham deceives the Pharaoh by telling him that Sarah is his sister, portrays 'Abraham as a man of shrewdness and sagacity'.[2] Skinner states: "It is assumed that in the

[2] Bruce Vawter, *On Genesis: A New Reading* (New York: Doubleday, 1977), 181–2.

circumstances lying is excusable. There is no suggestion that either the untruthfulness or the selfish cowardice of the request was severely reprobated by the ethical code to which the narrative appealed.'[3] According to Gunkel, 12:10–20 celebrates the beauty of the tribal mother and her loyalty.[4] The narrator is not troubled by Abraham's lies: he 'silently rejoices that Abraham had lied so extraordinarily well and made a virtue out of a necessity'.[5] As for the danger Abraham placed his wife in, Gunkel remarks: 'The ancient Israelite did not know the chivalrous duty of protecting his wife or daughter even to death.'[6] Discussing chapter 27 he says: 'We are meant to be pleased about the cleverness of son and mother. Jacob is clever in that he foresees that his father will touch him; but his mother is even cleverer in knowing a way of deceiving him nevertheless.'[7] When Jacob takes God's name in a lie, 'the old saga does not regard it as especially evil, but thinks, "that was a good lie".'[8] Prouser writes: 'Throughout biblical narrative, deception is considered a legitimate tool for less powerful people to use in order to succeed. In addition to not being punished for their actions, tricksters are often rewarded and applauded for their cleverness.'[9] 'It is more likely that the ancient Israelite audience would cheer Rebecca's quick thinking and clever antics than condemn them.'[10]

Witty and perceptive as these observations may be about early Israelite attitudes, they do not represent those of the implied author of Genesis, who sets these episodes in contexts which make clear both his own and God's displeasure at these lies. We have already noted Jacob's attempts to make amends to Esau when they meet again, showing his own penitence as well as fear of his brother.[11] Furthermore, after deceiving his father and cheating his brother, Jacob lives under a cloud of divine displeasure for most of the rest of his life. He is not simply

[3] John Skinner, *A Critical and Exegetical Commentary on Genesis*[2] (ICC, Edinburgh: T&T Clark, 1930), 249.

[4] Hermann Gunkel, *Genesis*[9] (Göttingen: Vandenhoeck & Ruprecht, 1977), 169.

[5] Gunkel, *Genesis*, 170.

[6] Gunkel, *Genesis*, 170.

[7] Gunkel, *Genesis*, 310.

[8] Gunkel, *Genesis*, 311.

[9] O. H. Prouser, 'The Truth about Women and Lying', *JSOT* 61 (1994), 15–28, quote p. 16.

[10] Prouser 'Truth', 17.

[11] That Jacob is motivated by sincere remorse not just fear is shown by the term he uses to describe his gifts to Esau. 'Jacob said ". . . if I have found favour in your sight, then accept my present from my hand; for truly to see your face is like seeing the face of God, with such favour have you received me. Accept, I pray you my *blessing* that is brought to you"' (Gen 33:10–11). The use of the word 'blessing' is especially significant. His father Isaac had condemned Jacob with the words 'Your brother came with guile, and he has taken away your blessing' (Gen 27:35). But in ch. 33 Jacob confesses his guilt by using this key word and tries to make amends.

forced to flee for his life and leave home, but in exile he suffers deception from his father-in-law by being forced to marry Leah. When Jacob protests at this, Laban comments sarcastically, 'It is not done in our country, to put the younger before the first-born.' Unspoken but doubtless understood by Jacob Laban might have continued 'as you Jacob the younger brother put yourself before your elder brother' (Gen 29:26).[12] The unhappiness of his bigamous marriage to Leah and Rachel stalks Jacob for the rest of his life and spills over into the next generation as the sons of Leah gang up against the sons of Rachel, Joseph and Benjamin. To rub the point in that Jacob's sadness at the apparent death of Joseph is in fact a consequence of his deception of his father, Leah's sons use a dead goat to deceive Jacob about Joseph's apparent death (37:31–35), just as Jacob used a goat to convince his father Isaac that he was really Esau. It is not until Jacob goes down to Egypt and meets Joseph alive and well that the cloud caused by his original deception of his father lifts. Thus if we read the story of Jacob's deception of his father within the context of the whole book of Genesis it becomes very difficult, if not impossible, to suppose the implied author is commending this action. It would be to read the story against the grain and impose on it a sense that is quite foreign to the writer's purpose.

Reading against the grain is not always the product of source-critical dissection of biblical books: it may be the result of the reader's own prejudice. Older commentators sometimes imply that the modern reader cannot take such outdated moral ideas seriously, for we know better. S. R. Driver, while generally very sympathetic to Genesis, observed that it was 'addressed to men who, though far from uncivilised . . . were nevertheless in many respects spiritually immature.'[13] Recently commentators have become much more aware of their own ideology and how it impacts their reading of the Bible. Judges naturally has attracted numerous gibes for its ghastly outlook. Deist, for example, berates its editors for endorsing 'ethnocentrism and cultural anxiety'.[14] Feminists frequently challenge what they perceive as the misogynist attitudes of Bible times, and Judges furnishes plenty of examples for them. But Alice Bach complains that traditional and feminist readers alike seem to have ignored the rape of the women of Shiloh in Judges 21. 'Male and female commentators alike seem to identify deeply with the portrait of female victimisation expressed in the narratives of violence to one woman, but silence greets the genocidal brutalization of the women of Shiloh.'[15]

[12] J. P. Fokkelman, *Narrative Art in Genesis* (Assen: Van Gorcum, 1975), 115–28.

[13] S. R. Driver, *The Book of Genesis*[3] (London: Methuen, 1904), lxxiii.

[14] F. E. Deist, '"Murder in the Toilet" (Judgs 3:12–20)', *Scriptura* 58 (1996), 263–72, quote 269.

[15] Alice Bach, 'Rereading the Body Politic: Women and Violence in Judges 21', *Bib Int* 6 (1998), 1–19, quote 15–16.

Ideological critiques like these, while they do not always clarify the perspective of the implied author, do have value in raising questions and encouraging a more careful reading of the text. The same is true of those driven by source-critical concerns and they remind us of the difficulty of reading. As Booth puts it:

> The problem for the reader is thus really that of discovering which values are in abeyance and which are genuinely, though in modern works often surreptitiously, at work. To pass judgement where the author intends neutrality is to misread. But to be neutral or objective where the author requires commitment is equally to misread, though the effect is likely to be less obvious and may even be overlooked except as a feeling of boredom.[16]

It clearly makes a great difference to our interpretation of Judges 21 whether we read it as the horrifying climax to an appalling tale[17] or as an example of God bringing good out of evil.[18]

So how do we discover the author's commitments when we read individual episodes within a particular book? The techniques of rhetorical criticism may allow us some insight into the central message of particular books, but it still leaves considerable doubt about the author's attitudes on particular points. In so far as there has been explicit discussion of this issue it has been asserted that the laws of the Pentateuch give the best insight into the writers' outlook. Thus Joshua to 2 Kings are regularly described as the deuteronomistic history because their interpretation of events is strongly coloured by ideas found in Deuteronomy. Similarly Sternberg suggests that the author of Genesis evaluated actions by the standards enshrined in the later law books. Discussing the rape of Dinah, he cites Deuteronomy 7:1–4 'Thou shalt make no covenant with them and show no mercy to them; thou shalt not make marriages with them: thy daughter thou shalt not give to his son': 'Deuteronomy would seem to look back with the highest approval on the brothers, who have practiced in exemplary fashion, and to the letter, what it now preaches against exogamy to the nation at large on the eve of resumed dealings with the Canaanites.'[19]

Similarly in discussing Judges' attitude to Micah's image, Amit notes how the terminology of the narrative echoes the decalogue and kindred passages (Exod 20:3, 23; 32:4, 8; 34:17). Micah makes for himself a graven and a molten image (17:4), indeed later he says 'you take my gods which I have made' (18:24). This shows to the alert reader both

[16] W. Booth, *Rhetoric of Fiction*, 144.

[17] Cf. our reading of Judges 19–21 in the preceding chapter.

[18] 'Even the evil that men do, the reactor [*sic*] seems to be saying, could be providentially exploited on that occasion, thanks to the quick-witted reasoning of Israel's elders.' R. G. Boling, *Judges* (AB, Garden City: Doubleday, 1975), 294.

[19] M. Sternberg, 'Biblical Poetics and Sexual Politics: From Reading to Counterreading', *JBL* 111 (1992), 463–88, quote 483.

how blatant his sin is and how oblivious Micah is to his own guilt, for 'none of the protagonists see anything wrong in the worship of graven and molten images'.[20]

Clearly Micah falls far short of the law's standards: he breaks the first two commandments and does not realise he is doing wrong. But would a halachic conformity to the letter of the law have made him a good person in the eyes of the author of Judges? Is it sufficient just to avoid breaking the law? Are the narratives simply written to encourage their readers to be law-abiding citizens? These questions bring us to the heart of Old Testament narrative ethics. While an obedience-to-the-law ethic is central to most books of the Old Testament,[21] including the narrative works, it is not the only strand: the Bible is also interested in the character of individuals and the virtue or otherwise of their actions, in the communal dimension of behaviour, and in the call to imitate God. I shall therefore first argue that obedience to the rules is not a sufficient definition of Old Testament ethics, but that much more is looked for from members of the covenant people than this. Then I shall sketch briefly the importance of virtue, community values, and the imitation of God for an understanding of the values of the biblical narrators.

The inadequacy of law as a definition of Old Testament ethics

Otto's *Theologische Ethik des Alten Testaments* (1994) is the most comprehensive discussion of Old Testament ethics available and is devoted almost entirely to discussing the legal material in the Pentateuch and the ethics of wisdom. In it he pays no attention to the narratives of the Old Testament and their implications for ethics. Elsewhere he has stated: 'In my view, the primary subject of an ethics of the Hebrew Bible . . . is the system of legal and ethical rules in the Covenant Code, Deuteronomy, Decalogue, and the post-priestly Holiness Code.'[22] But this gives much too narrow a focus to biblical ethics. Law as it is conventionally understood, and certainly in the biblical texts just mentioned, may be defined as 'the norms, structures and procedures which regulate the lives of individuals and groups within a given political society'.[23] Law is expressed in rules, which prescribe how people should act in certain circumstances and what will happen if they do not. Obedience to it is generally enforced by the state. 'In

[20] Amit, *Judges*, 328.

[21] 'Obedience to the declared will of God is probably the strongest model for ethical obligation in most of the books of the Hebrew Scriptures.' J. Barton, 'The Basis of Ethics in the Hebrew Bible', *Semeia* 66 (1994), 11–22, quote 13.

[22] *Semeia* 66 (1994), 162.

[23] Z. W. Falk, *Religious Law and Ethics: Studies in Biblical and Rabbinical Theonomy* (Jerusalem: Mesharim, 1991), 4.

general, the law prescribes external behaviour rather than states of mind and intentions.'[24]

The law sets a minimum standard of behaviour, which if transgressed attracts sanction. It regulates institutions like marriage or slavery, but it does not prescribe ideals of behaviour within marriage. Does the regulation of slavery or bigamy mean that the Old Testament endorses these institutions and regards them as ethically desirable? If the law punished adulterers with death only where the woman involved was married, does that mean affairs by husbands with unattached girls or prostitutes were permissible? If false testimony in court was subject to the *lex talionis* (Deut 19:16–21), does that mean that in other circumstances flexibility with truth was allowed: that slander, boasting, exaggeration, gossip could be indulged in with an easy conscience?

To pose the questions is to suggest their answer. In most societies what the law enforces is not the same as what upright members of that society feel is socially desirable let alone ideal. There is a link between moral ideals and law, but law tends to be a pragmatic compromise between the legislators' ideals and what can be enforced in practice. The law enforces a minimum standard of behaviour. Those who fail to live up to this standard are punished. But though I may not have stolen my neighbour's car or had an affair with his wife, I may be far from being a model citizen. I may have kept every law of the land to the letter yet be an obnoxious person to live with. To put it another way, ethics is much more than keeping the law. Or to put it in biblical terms righteousness involves more than living by the decalogue and the other laws in the Pentateuch.[25]

On reflection these points seem self-evident. What legislators and judges tolerate may not be what they approve. Laws generally set a floor for behaviour within society, they do not prescribe an ethical ceiling. Thus a study of the legal codes within the Bible is unlikely to disclose the ideals of the law-givers, but only the limits of their tolerance: if you do such and such, you will be punished. The laws thus tend to express the limits of socially acceptable behaviour: they do not describe ideal behaviour. If this is the case with the laws, may this not also be the case with the authors of biblical narrative? We may well agree with Amit that the author of Judges did not favour Micah's transgression of

[24] Falk, *Religious Law*, 4.

[25] Z. W. Falk, 'Law and Ethics in the Hebrew Bible' in *Justice and Righteousness* ed. Henning G. Reventlow and Yair Hoffmann (JSOTSup 137, Sheffield: JSOT Press, 1992), 82–90. This contrast between law and ethics is of course not clear-cut within the pentateuchal legal collections. Whereas they are mostly concerned with what could be enforced by the courts, they are sprinkled with exhortations to kindness and generosity (e.g. Exod 22:21–27; Lev 19:14–18; Deut 15:10–15) which indicate that the legislators' ethical ideals are higher than the letter of their laws.

the Ten Commandments, but if he had sinned less blatantly would his behaviour have met with our implied author's approval?

Before we can attempt to answer these questions, we need to explore the discrepancy between the ethical ideals of the Old Testament and its legal requirements more broadly. For example the law proscribes the worship of gods other than Yahweh. 'You shall have no other gods before me' is the first commandment (Exod 20:3). Other texts insist on the death of the individual or group which breaks this rule (Exod 32; Lev 20:2; Deut 13:7–19). This is the minimum legal requirement for belonging to the Israelite community. In the case of secret idolatry extirpation[26] and divine curse are invoked (Lev 20:3–5; Deut 27:15). This is why intermarriage with Canaanites is forbidden: 'for they would turn away your sons from following me to serve other gods' (Deut 7:4; cf. Exod 34:12–16).

But the Bible goes beyond legal sanctions and negative commands: its ethico-religious ideal is wholly positive. Israel is enjoined to love the LORD with all her heart, soul and strength. To walk after, cleave to, and to love him. Though it has been correctly pointed out that these are the actions required of loyal treaty partners,[27] and that love and fear of God is expressed chiefly through keeping his commandments, it is wrong to reduce love to obedience. It is obedience, but more than obedience. This covenantal loyalty is also the attitude looked for within a family, between children and parents, and between spouses. Israel's loyalty to and affection for her God should mirror his love for her. In the psalms there are glimpses of the human spirit reaching out towards this goal.

> My soul longs, yea faints for the courts of the LORD,
> my heart and flesh sing for joy to the living God. (Ps 84:2)

Genesis implies that mankind was intended to enjoy such intimacy with God. In the garden of Eden story Adam and Eve and their creator seem to be on the friendliest terms until the serpent upsets it. The LORD worries about Adam's loneliness. He brings the animals to him, and then having created Eve out of a rib, presents her to him as a benevolent father-in-law would. Their intimacy is perpetuated by them all walking together in the cool of the day. Expulsion from Eden ends this age of intimacy. Cain remarks that his sentence to be a perpetual nomad is unbearable, for 'from thy face shall I be hidden' (Gen 4:13–14). For

[26] This probably denotes a sudden and mysterious death at the hand of God, so H. H. Cohn, *Israel Law Review* 5 (1970), 70. J. Milgrom, *The JPS Torah Commentary: Numbers* (Philadelphia: JPS, 1990), 405–8, prefers to think the punishment involves death of the offender's descendants or his extinction in the afterlife.

[27] E.g. W. L. Moran, 'The Ancient Near Eastern Background of the Love of God in Deuteronomy', *CBQ* 25 (1963), 77–87. M. Weinfeld, *Deuteronomy and the Deuteronomic School* (Oxford: Clarendon Press, 1972).

him, like many a later psalmist, banishment from God's presence was the ultimate calamity.

By painting a picture of this intimacy between God and man in its opening chapters Genesis invites us to read all the subsequent stories, whether it be Jacob at Bethel (Gen 28:10–22) or Joseph in prison (Gen 39), with this picture in mind to guide our evaluation of the subsequent narrative. Within this framework the LORD's appearances to the patriarchs become extraordinarily significant. The narrator is generally quite coy about what this meant in practice, but within the larger context it was clearly an immense privilege that was rarely granted. Moses of course is described by the LORD in the following terms: 'With him I speak mouth to mouth, clearly, and not in dark speech; and he beholds the form of God' (Num 12:8; cf. Deut 34:10). Nevertheless even he is barred from the perfect vision of God, for though he met the LORD in the cloud on mount Sinai, he was not allowed to seek God's face, but only his back (Exod 33:23). Similarly in the later sanctuaries, where the LORD walked as in Eden (Gen 3:8; cf. Lev 26:12; 2 Sam 7:6–7), only the high priest was allowed to enter the holy of holies once a year wreathed in a cloud of incense lest he should see God (Lev 16:13). Yet to see God in his sanctuary remained the ultimate goal of every worshipper (cf. Ps 42).

This discussion of the first commandment illustrates the gap between law and ethics. The law merely punished extreme forms of disloyalty to God, i.e. religious apostasy and idolatry, and prohibited actions such as intermarriage that might lead to the ultimate religious disloyalty. But fearing, loving, cleaving to the LORD was not fulfilled just by avoiding the worship of other gods. The ethico-religious goal was far deeper and more embracing: it involved both loyalty to God and an enjoyment of his presence.

The laws on homicide and the biblical attitude to life also illustrate the gap between law and ethics. At the level of wilful homicide the principle of talion is strictly applied: 'life for life' is the basic principle governing the punishment of those who take human life deliberately[28] (Exod 21:23; Lev 24:19–21; Deut 19:19–21). Numbers 35 and Deuteronomy 19 give a number of examples to show how different types of homicide are to be categorised and dealt with. These passages illustrate the law's concern to keep the land free from blood guilt, but otherwise only hint at the wider implications of preserving human life.[29]

[28] Culpable homicide (murder), and non-culpable (manslaughter) are probably distinguished by the fact of premeditation in murder, so B. S. Jackson, *Essays in Jewish and Comparative Legal History* (Leiden: Brill, 1975), 91.

[29] For a valuable discussion of the religious principles informing these laws see P. Haas, '"Die he shall surely die": The Structure of Homicide in Biblical Law', *Semeia* 45 (1989), 67–87.

Much more revealing for the relationship between law and ethics is Genesis 9:1–7. Here we have the only quasi-legal statement within the opening chapters of the Torah. 'For your lifeblood I will surely require a reckoning, of every beast I will require it and of man; of every man's brother I will require the life of man. Whoever sheds the blood of man, by man shall his blood be shed; for God made man in his own image' (9:5–6). Here a statement of legal principle is backed up by theology: 'for God made man in his own image'. This alone suffices to demonstrate that the writer of Genesis sets law within a much broader framework of ethical and theological principle. And the context makes this even plainer. The judicial sentence 'by man shall his blood be shed' (v. 6) is framed by the comment 'be fruitful and multiply and fill the earth' (v. 1), which is repeated in v. 7 with some expansion. The creator wants the world to be filled with God-shaped creatures, with human beings. Those who oppose the divine plan to populate the earth with men in the divine likeness, who take the life of their fellow men, must themselves be eliminated. Capital punishment for murder thus paradoxically reflects the pro-life ethos of the Bible.

Moreover the position of this sentence on murder immediately after the flood story gives it a special prominence. Within Genesis the flood divides history into two eras: the old world was destroyed in the flood, and a new world was created after it. God's original mandates to mankind are now reaffirmed and to some extent modified.[30] The single command to Adam to be fruitful is repeated to Noah no less than four times, perhaps to counteract the idea that God was opposed to the human race *per se*, an easy conclusion to draw from the flood story. In the parallel Babylonian version of the flood story, the Atrahasis epic,[31] such a conclusion would be quite warranted. There the flood was sent to stop the population explosion, because the noise of man on earth was spoiling the repose of the gods in heaven! And after the flood's failure to deal with the problem completely, the gods decreed that infertility, miscarriage, and childhood ills would curtail population growth. Genesis by contrast insists that God wants the earth populated by mankind: he encourages it once before the flood and repeatedly afterwards. It was not the population explosion, but human sin that prompted the flood.

These considerations make it highly likely that in the realm of piety and respect for human life the author of Genesis at least would not have described his ethical ideals simply in terms of the prohibitions of the decalogue and the punishments of the law. But when it comes to

[30] E.g. about food. The vegetarianism of 1:29 is now replaced by limited consumption of meat (9:3).

[31] For a modern translation see Stephanie Dalley, *Myths from Mesopotamia* (Oxford: Oxford University Press, 1990).

sexual ethics many writers take such a position.[32] It therefore warrants a fuller discussion.

It is generally accepted that at the legal and social level ancient Israel, like the surrounding nations and many cultures since, operated on the double standard.[33] This meant that men had more sexual freedom than women. Thus a man could have several wives, but a woman only one husband. If a wife or a betrothed girl had intercourse with a man who was not her husband or fiancé, that was adultery, and both parties involved were liable to the death penalty.[34] On the other hand if a married man had sexual intercourse with an unattached woman, that was not regarded as adultery against his wife, though he might face heavy damages. Within this framework also divorce was more easily available to husbands than to wives.

Stated thus crudely it seems that the law discriminated harshly against women and created an environment in which marriages were easily terminated. However, just looking at the law gives a misleading view of what actually went on in ancient Israel and it does not show how the biblical writers, who incorporated these laws on sex within their works, in fact hoped for a much higher standard of sexual ethics than the law insisted on.[35]

In reality social custom and pressures greatly curtailed the sexual freedom of men in Bible times. First, marriages[36] were customarily arranged by parents, as soon as children passed puberty. This meant that there were few unattached girls: most females of marriageable age were either married or betrothed, with whom third-party intercourse

[32] E.g. Eckart Otto, *Theologische Ethik des Alten Testaments* (Stuttgart: Kohlhammer, 1994), 39–64. At the end of his section on Old Testament marriage ethics Otto does briefly discuss Genesis 2–3 with a view to suggesting that it aims to question male headship, but he does not comment on other aspects of the marriage relationship that this passage addresses.

[33] At some points Israel's laws on sexual behaviour, notably on incest and homosexuality, were markedly stricter than her neighbours. See G. J. Wenham, *The Book of Leviticus* (Grand Rapids: Eerdmans, 1979), 249–61 and idem, 'Attitudes to Homosexuality in the OT', *Exp Tim* 102 (1991), 359–63.

[34] For a discussion of when the death penalty might be commuted see R. Westbrook, *Studies in Biblical and Cuneiform Law* (Paris: Gabalda, 1988), 39–88.

[35] This is implied by the Damascus Rule and some rabbinic texts. D. Daube develops this theme in 'Concessions to Sinfulness in Jewish Law', *JJS* 10 (1959), 1–13. On p. 6 he writes: 'Polygamy was widely rejected as below the standard set for man by his creator. But there are nuances. For the Rabbis, it is legally correct, though against what is naturally fitting as manifested in the first union between Adam and Eve . . . It is probable that divorce was judged on similar lines.' But L. M. Epstein, *Marriage Laws in the Bible and the Talmud* (Cambridge, Mass.: Harvard University Press, 1942), 12–25, paints a rather different picture of rabbinic attitudes suggesting dissent from Daube's view.

[36] For a fuller review of marriage customs in Bible times see de Vaux, *Ancient Israel*, 24–38; M. Burrows, *The Basis of Israelite Marriage* (New Haven: American Oriental Society, 1938).

was adulterous. Second, intercourse with a single girl was liable to severe punishment, as the damages prescribed in the law witness.[37] Third, the size of the marriage present (*mohar*) meant very few men apart from wealthy patriarchs and kings could afford to marry more than one wife. Finally the dowry system would have discouraged capricious divorce. These factors would have meant that lifelong monogamy was the normal pattern for marriage.

If this was the case, we should expect the literature to reflect a positive attitude towards monogamy. Certainly the wisdom and prophetic literature seems to presuppose that monogamy was normal. Occasional mentions of divorcees show that their situation was viewed as less than ideal.[38] Furthermore the comment in Genesis 2:24 that 'they become one flesh' suggests that a kinship-like bond is created in marriage. This concept explains some of the rules on affinity found in Leviticus 18 and 20.[39] In other words Genesis 2 is implying that the creator intends marriage to be permanent.

Even more clearly Genesis sets out monogamy as the divine plan. It does this both positively by telling how God created one Eve for Adam, and negatively by showing the misery of bigamy. To start with God created all the animals as potential companions for Adam, but none were satisfactory. But one Eve delighted him, as his exclamation of joy demonstrates. Given God's generosity he doubtless could have created any number of Eves to satisfy Adam, but one wife was enough. And the narrator draws a general principle from this story, 'Therefore a man leaves his father and his mother and cleaves to his wife' (2:24). Note the singular 'wife': the writer implies that having one wife is as natural as having one father and mother.

However, it is not long before bigamy appears in human history. Lamech marries Adah and Zillah (Gen 4:19–24), whose names suggest that one has a pretty face and the other a sweet voice.[40] But the portrait of Lamech is by no means flattering. Not only has he succumbed to sensuality,[41] but he is a vicious thug, who boasts of killing anyone who tangles with him. Abraham's taking of Hagar as second partner is, as we have noted, discreetly condemned by the narrator, who implies that the birth of Ishmael slowed down the fulfilment of the promise of a real son to Abraham by his true wife. Then there is Jacob. What could have

[37] Exod 22:15–16; Deut 22:29.

[38] They are banned from marrying priests and high priests (Lev 21:7, 14), while Prov 30:23 comments unfavourably on the remarriage of divorcees; so R. Yaron, 'On Divorce in OT Times', *RIDA* 3 (1957), 117–28.

[39] See Wenham, *Leviticus*, 255–6, cf. idem, 'The Restoration of Marriage Reconsidered', *JJS* 30 (1979), 36–40.

[40] So Umberto Cassuto, *A Commentary on the Book of Genesis Vol. 1* (Jerusalem: Magnes Press, 1961), 234.

[41] J. Gabriel, 'Die Kainitengenealogie', 417.

been the perfect marriage was ruined by Laban imposing Leah on Jacob. This not only displeased Jacob (indeed he never really regarded Leah as his wife or her children as his; cf. Gen 44:27), but ensured a life of misery for Leah and Rachel, and for their children. Genesis 29–50 is a graphic portrayal of the tensions and sorrows caused by bigamy.

Legal texts, while allowing for the existence of bigamy, again by implication draw attention to its undesirability. 'You shall not take a woman as a rival wife to her sister' urges Leviticus 18:18.[42] Deuteronomy's dislike of polygamy is apparent from 17:17, when it advises the man most likely to be polygamous, the king, 'not to multiply wives for himself'. Then again 21:15–17, the law on distributing inheritance among sons of different wives, while it demonstrates the legitimacy of polygamy, actually shows up its problems.

Thus, though the law does not require monogamy of Israelite husbands, perhaps because it would have been difficult to enforce, it is clear that the biblical writers did not expect people just to live by the law. They hoped for better behaviour. Life-long monogamy was the creator's intention, and those who do not follow this pattern may well face difficulties.

Similarly, though a married man may not face the charge of adultery for extramarital affairs, this does not mean the Bible condones male infidelity, any more than the legality of bigamy means it was approved ethically. There are various texts which imply that husbands were expected to be faithful to their wives. In biblical times the only kind of unattached women with whom men could consort without risking enormous financial loss were prostitutes. The historical books never speak approvingly of prostitutes.[43] Judah's secretive manoeuvrings after consorting with Tamar are eloquent testimony to the disreputability of his conduct (Gen 38:20–23). The Book of Proverbs devotes nearly three chapters (5–7) to persuading young men about the inappropriateness and folly of resorting to prostitutes. Job goes even further claiming he has been totally loyal to his wife: 'I have made a covenant with my eyes, how then could I look on a virgin?' (Job 31:1). To underline his commitment, he says that if he had been unfaithful to his wife, he would be justly punished by someone having intercourse with her (31:10).

Job witnesses to a mutuality in relations between husband and wife. He ought to be as faithful to her, as he expects her to be to him. How far was this a general view in the Bible, or was Job exceptionally upright

[42] Though this is usually taken as a prohibition against marrying two sisters, as Jacob did, it may be forbidding any bigamous union. So A. Tosato, 'The Law of Lev 18:18: A Reexamination', *CBQ* 46 (1984), 199–214, and G. P. Hugenberger, *Marriage as a Covenant* (VTSup 52, Leiden: Brill, 1994), 115–18.

[43] For a discussion of biblical attitudes to prostitution see P. A. Bird, 'The Harlot as Heroine: Narrative Art and Social Presupposition in Three OT Texts', *Semeia* 46 (1989), 119–39.

in this area? This depends on the Israelite view of marriage. If it was regarded as a covenant, which is the usual view,[44] mutual loyalty would have been a key element within matrimony. Unfortunately we have no wedding rites from Bible times, so we do not know quite what bride and groom said to each other when they married. However the essence of a covenant is the pledge of mutual loyalty under oath, so it seems likely that something to this effect was promised in Israelite weddings. That prophets like Hosea, Jeremiah and Malachi could liken God's covenant with Israel to a marriage shows that total loyalty was expected between married couples. God's faithfulness to Israel, despite her waywardness, implies that good husbands were faithful to their wives. Indeed the divine parallel suggests that they should have been more than faithful, they should have cared supremely for their wives' welfare.[45]

This evidence makes it probable that in the realm of marriage, just as in respect to worship and homicide, there was a gap between the ideals or hopes of the implied writers and the lesser demands of the law. This gap seems to be clearer in the case of Genesis and the wisdom books than elsewhere in the Old Testament. This is not because the implied authors of, say, Judges or Samuel did not have ethical ideals, but because unlike Genesis they do not include a description of life before the fall. In Genesis this gives us a window into the creator's intentions for the human race, with which we presume the writer identified, but in the case of the book of Judges there is no golden age to look back to and therefore it is more difficult to know where the author stands. All that is apparent is that the earlier judges are not so decadent as the later ones, so that it is likely that Othniel and Barak come closer to his ethical ideals than, say, Jephthah or Samson.

Character and virtue

Ethical discussions of the Old Testament have been very much dominated by the law. This is true both of modern scholarship and the older Jewish tradition of halacha, Jewish casuistry, which is preserved and hallowed in works such as the Mishnah and Talmud. Within this tradition obedience to the declared will of God is the cardinal religious and ethical virtue. Thus the only perfect man in Genesis is Noah, of whom it is said four times, 'Noah did all that the LORD had commanded him' (7:5; cf. 6:22; 7:9, 16). Similarly Abraham's career begins and ends with

[44] See Hugenberger, *Marriage*.

[45] This is probably the implication of Gen 2:24 with its stress on a man leaving his parents and cleaving to his wife. A literal leaving is unlikely, given that Israelite marriage was patrilocal. Rather a husband should put his care for his wife above even his filial duty. See Wenham, *Genesis 1–15, ad loc.*

two dramatic and costly examples of his absolute obedience to God's commands, his leaving home and his sacrifice of his only son (12:1–4; 22:1–19).

Now very many aspects of behaviour may be subsumed under the rubric, 'obedience to the declared will of God', but an alternative approach to ethics was taken by the Greek tradition which tended to focus on defining virtue and character. Some studies of the biblical wisdom literature have endeavoured to build up pictures of the ideal person by putting together all the remarks in Proverbs about the wise man and the fool.[46] It has been suggested that these wisdom stereotypes may lie behind the characterisation of Joseph in Genesis and David and Solomon in Samuel–Kings.[47] Modern literary critics, such as Alter and Sternberg, have done brilliant work on the way actors in the narrative works are characterised, but they have only incidentally suggested what sort of ethical model the authors are working with.

Obviously within Old Testament narrative we have all kinds of virtues and vices depicted. In some cases it is obvious whether the implied author approves or disapproves of the behaviour described. Clearly Abraham's hospitality towards the three angels in Genesis 18 is viewed as a very positive trait, whereas Lamech's vicious boasting in 4:23–24 is not. But this does not take us very far. Apart from such obvious cases and some universal values that are exemplified throughout world literature, it is not easy to be sure what stance the implied author is adopting to the character traits depicted. How then can we determine what traits are seen as virtues by the author?

I suggest three main criteria for supposing that an actor's behaviour in a particular situation is regarded as virtuous by the implied author. First, the behaviour pattern[48] should be repeated in a number of different contexts. It is more likely that a repeated pattern is intended to be imitated than one that is described just once. This is especially the case in the Bible, which tends to enlarge on heroic deeds and describe sins quite tersely (e.g. Gen 9:22). Thus the readiness of the patriarchs Abraham, Isaac and Jacob to live at peace with the Canaanites and

[46] William P. Brown, *Character in Crisis* (Grand Rapids: Eerdmans, 1996), 22–49.

[47] For a recent review of such suggestions see Robert P. Gordon, 'A house divided: wisdom in OT narrative traditions', in *Wisdom in Ancient Israel* (ed. John Day, Robert P. Gordon, Hugh G. M. Williamson, Cambridge: Cambridge University Press, 1995), 94–105.

[48] The exact definition of virtue is controversial. Virtues are not simply patterns of behaviour, they also include appropriate attitudes and facets of character. For further discussion see Robert B. Kruschwitz and Robert C. Roberts, *The Virtues: Contemporary Essays on Moral Character* (Belmont: Wadsworth, 1987); Romanus Cessario, *The Moral Virtues and Theological Ethics* (Notre Dame: University of Notre Dame Press, 1991); Stanley Hauerwas and Charles R. Pinches, *Christians among the Virtues* (Notre Dame: University of Notre Dame Press, 1997).

others seems to indicate that the writer regards this as virtuous even though intermarriage with them is not allowed (cf. 24:3; 27:46).

Second, to suppose that the implied author regards a character trait as a virtue, it should be exhibited in a positive context. The book of Judges depicts the nation of Israel spiralling down into moral and political anarchy so we need to be cautious about supposing that any action it describes exemplifies virtue. On the other hand Genesis' more positive presentation of the patriarchal era makes it easier to assume their deeds are virtuous. But there are of course exceptions to both generalisations. The courage of the judges is doubtless viewed positively, while the propensity of the patriarchs to pass their wives off as their sister always ends with a just rebuke from a foreign king, with which the author may be assumed to concur. Jacob's life-long suffering as a result of him deceiving his father and cheating his brother indicates he has not acted properly.

Third, remarks in the legal codes, psalms and wisdom books often shed light on Old Testament attitudes to different virtues and vices. These comments may confirm the conclusions arrived at by studying the narratives themselves. However, caution is needed in that the wisdom books may not have originated in the same period and circles as the story books, so their authors may not have seen things the same way. For example, Genesis stresses the beauty of Sarah, Rebekah and Rachel implying that it was one of their great virtues, whereas Proverbs seems to relativise female beauty saying 'Charm is deceitful, and beauty is vain, but a woman who fears the LORD is to be praised' (Prov 31:30). Nevertheless it seems likely that wisdom writers and storytellers from biblical times were closer to each other in outlook than either are to modern readers, so that one may helpfully shed light on the other.

Using these criteria I shall now try to sketch some of the virtues that Genesis seems keen to commend to its readers. We have noted that obedience to the declared will of God is central to the biblical writers' vision of the moral life, but more broadly speaking we could say that piety is a virtue that is conspicuous in many a story. Piety involves 'habitual reverence and obedience to God', but also 'godliness, devoutness, religiousness'.[49] In several incidents the piety of the hero is obvious. Noah offers a sacrifice as soon as he emerges from the ark, and so do the patriarchs at key points in their wanderings (8:20; 12:7, 8; 13:18; 26:25; 33:20; 31:54; 35:7; 46:1). But their piety is even more evident in their prayers. Abraham's plea for Sodom exhibits both deference towards God on the one hand and intimacy on the other (18:23–32). Near the beginning of his prayer he says: 'I have taken upon myself to speak to the LORD, I who am but dust and ashes' and he completes his prayer with the words 'Oh let not the LORD be angry, and

[49] *Shorter Oxford English Dictionary*, 1499.

I will speak again but this once' (vv. 27, 32). The sequel makes plain that God approved of Abraham's intercession, for although the city was not spared, because it contained less than ten righteous citizens, 'when God destroyed the cities, God remembered Abraham, and sent Lot out of the midst of the overthrow' (19:29). Abraham's servant who is sent to find a wife for Isaac is not just a paradigm of loyalty but of piety. His prayerfulness and dependence on God is highlighted not merely in the narrator's first telling of the events at the well, but in the servant's own retelling of them. He appeals to the prompt answer to his prayer, 'Let the maiden to whom I say "Pray let down your jar that I may drink" . . . be the one thou hast appointed for thy servant Isaac' as proof that the LORD had prospered his journey (24:12–48). Similarly Jacob is portrayed at Bethel and at Mahanaim as expressing his total dependence on God as he prays for his safety (28:20–22; 32:9–12). Joseph's piety is apparent not so much in his prayers, which are hinted at rather than recorded, but in his ascription to God of his gift of dream interpretation, his loyal service of Potiphar and his repeated assertion that he saw God's hand controlling his destiny: 'God sent me before you to preserve life' (45:7; cf. 50:20; 39:1–9; 40:8; 41:16, 25, 32). The typical wisdom phrase for piety is 'the fear of the LORD' which 'is the beginning of knowledge' (Prov 1:7). Abraham's willingness to sacrifice Isaac showed that he feared God (Gen 22:12), but this phrase is also used in Genesis of a more general piety that is not confined to Israelites (20:11; 42:18).[50]

In modern popular thought piety is often associated with gentleness, if not weakness or even effeminacy. But this is certainly not the association apparent in the patriarchal narratives: they are portrayed as strong and courageous[51] with often a touch of dogged persistence too. It is clear that physical and mental toughness is admired by the biblical authors. Jacob's wrestling with the angel at the Jabbok and his refusal to let him go shows both strength and persistence, and after this bruising encounter he goes ahead of his family to be the first to meet Esau. Yet just the day before Jacob had been greatly afraid and distressed (32:7 – 33:3). This dramatic transformation coincides with the change of name from Jacob, 'deceiver', to 'striver with God'. God's giving of this new name is not merely an acknowledgement of Jacob's strength but an endorsement of it. Perhaps the most striking military victory in Genesis is Abram's defeat of the four kings of the north, who had conquered various peoples in Canaan before defeating a coalition of towns from the Dead Sea valley. But Abram with just 318 men 'routed them' and brought back all the goods and captives that had been taken (14:1–16). Jacob in blessing his sons compares the tribes that will be descended

[50] Here used by Joseph of himself, but he is pretending to be an Egyptian.

[51] On the importance of courage in heroic society, MacIntyre, *After Virtue*, 115–17.

from them to a variety of animals, lions, strong asses, vipers, deer, wild asses and ravening wolves (Gen 49:9–27). All these images express the hope that the tribes will be so strong that they will not be pushed around. 'The wicked flee when no one pursues, but the righteous are bold as a lion' (Prov 28:1). But their strength should not be a licence for violence and savagery. While praising the other tribes for their strength, Jacob condemns Simeon and Levi for their violent impetuosity: 'in their anger they slay men, and in their wantonness they hamstring oxen' (49:6; cf. 9–27). In Chapter 3 we noted that one of the thrusts of Genesis appeared to be its commendation of peaceable relations that the patriarchs tried to pursue. But these images from Genesis 49 show the implied author valued peace that grew out of a benign exercise of strength, not a peace that was the result of an inability to resist. He would have concurred with Ps 127:5:

> Happy is the man who has his quiver full of them (sons)
> He shall not be put to shame when he speaks with his enemies in the gate.

The abhorrence of wanton violence by the strong is also evident in the thumbnail sketch of Lamech in 4:23–24 who boasts of slaying a man for wounding him, a young man for striking him. It is to curb the multiple revenge of men like Lamech, that Genesis 9:5–6 introduces the principle of talion, that is an eye for an eye or in his case a life for a life.

If Genesis thus endorses strength and courage without glorifying violence, on the other hand it disapproves of timidity. Hardly ever is fear justified and very often it leads to wrong. It is fear for his life that leads Abraham in both Egypt and Gerar to hide the fact that Sarah is his wife. Years later Isaac's fear prompts him to act similarly (12:10–20; 20:1–17; 26:7–11). It was fear for his life that prompted Lot to offer his daughters to the mob of Sodom (19:4–8), and later to live in a cave rather than in Zoar (19:30). Jacob's fear about the possibility of harm befalling Benjamin delayed his reconciliation with Joseph, while Judah's fears for Shelah led to the unusual behaviour of Tamar (42:4; 43:10; 38:11). In only two circumstances does Genesis approve of fear. One is the fear of God's presence as Jacob exclaimed at Bethel (28:17): 'How awesome is this place.' The other is the fear that is caused by sin as Adam experienced in the garden (3:10), Abimelech and his men after discovering Sarah's status (20:8), and Joseph's brothers when various things happened to them which made them think their guilt was catching up on them (42:35; 43:18). Otherwise fear always seems to be misplaced, so that often the opening words of a vision are 'Fear not' (15:1; 21:17; 26:24; 46:3). Similarly the book of Judges seems to regard fear in battle as inappropriate. The LORD tells Gideon to proclaim to his army 'Whoever is fearful and trembling, let him return home' (Judg 7:3). Yet Gideon himself is often afraid. Despite the command to destroy the altar of Baal, he delays till nightfall 'because he was too afraid of his family and the men of the town' (6:27). After the double sign of the fleece he is still fearful about leading the people into battle until he is reassured by hearing the Midianite dream (7:10–15). Barak too shows unnecessary hesitancy before leading Israel into battle (4:8–9).

Genesis does not just admire physical strength and courage, but economic strength. While this could hardly be described as a virtue, the book does take a positive attitude to wealth, frequently drawing attention to the patriarchs' prosperity and the way it keeps on increasing (12:16; 13:2; 15:1; 24:35; 26:12–14; 27:28). Jacob, who runs away from Canaan with nothing, returns with huge flocks and herds (30:43 – 32:5). Joseph, who is sold into Egypt as a slave, becomes the most powerful man in the land after Pharaoh and presumably one of the richest (41:41–49). Several of the tribal blessings celebrate the future prosperity of the tribes (49:11–12, 20, 26).

However, the wealthy patriarchs are also portrayed as generous. Their riches are acquired by honest hard work (26:12; 30:29–43) and by unexpected gifts (12:16; 20:16), but usually they are not portrayed as grasping or anxious to hang on to it at all costs. Abraham allows Lot to choose which part of the land to settle in, so Lot picks the well-watered Jordan valley (13:9–10). Having recovered all the booty taken by the kings of the north, Abraham refuses to take any for himself, declaring to the king of Sodom 'I would not take a thread or a sandal-thong or anything that is yours, lest you should say, "I have made Abram rich"' (14:23). Abraham's generosity is evident in the feast he prepares for his three visitors (18:6–8). Abraham also sends extravagant presents to Rebekah's family, as Jacob does later to Esau and the authorities in Egypt: in these cases gifts were the conventional way of ingratiating oneself with strangers, so we should not be too surprised by them (24:22, 53; 33:10–11; 43:11). Joseph's famine-relief measures are within the Old Testament a paradigmatic example of the rich helping the poor. Though buying their cattle, land, and labour strikes the Western reader as harsh, it was an accepted way of dealing with poverty and ensuring the poor would be guaranteed a job and food for the rest of their lives. That is why they gratefully declare 'You have saved our lives' (47:25).[52] This model of the wealthy righteous who are generous to the poor is reaffirmed many times in the Psalms and wisdom books: Job in this respect is just like the patriarchs of Genesis (cf. Ps 112; Job 31; Prov 22:9).

[52] The arrangements Joseph made for the Egyptians parallel the provisions of Lev 25 for impoverished Israelites. Slavery under a benevolent lord in biblical times was analogous to employment today, whereas freedom was closer to modern self-employment with all the risks that entails. For fuller discussion see Wenham, *Genesis 16–50,* 448–52; and Gregory C. Chirichigno, *Debt Slavery in Israel and the Ancient Near East* (JSOTSup 141, Sheffield: JSOT Press, 1993), 302–43.

Whereas Genesis approves of wealth properly acquired and generously distributed, grasping at wealth or meanness towards God and man is implicitly criticised. Abel gave of the firstlings of his flock, whereas Cain only offered *some* of the fruit of the ground, and this was not acceptable as a sacrifice (4:2–5).[53] Lot picked what seemed the best of the land, but that was before God destroyed the cities of the plain (13:10). The king of Sodom is portrayed as ungrateful, suspicious and stingy in his confrontation with Abraham (14:21–24). The methods of Jacob and Rebekah to acquire the blessing from Isaac with all the prosperity that it conveyed were certainly underhand, and though they were successful in the short term, they entailed misery for all of them in the longer term. So none of Genesis' examples of acquisitive behaviour can be taken as a recommendation of it.

The scenic mode of writing preferred by Old Testament storytellers contains much conversation between the actors and a few longer speeches. Given the great interest of the wisdom literature in the use and abuse of speech it seems likely that there is an implicit didactic intent behind some of the speeches recorded in Genesis, though once again we must be wary of reading in ideas that are foreign to the author's way of thinking.

Several of the episodes that are described more fully in Genesis contain powerful speeches, which have long attracted the admiration of commentators and literary critics. It therefore seems likely that eloquence and persuasiveness in speech are here being celebrated: 'With patience a ruler may be persuaded, and a soft tongue will break a bone' (Prov 25:15). Sternberg has offered a brilliant analysis of Abraham's servant's speech to Laban, which shows how the servant describes Isaac's situation and his own experience at the well in such a way as to compel Laban and Bethuel to assent to a marriage between Isaac and Rebekah.[54] Universally admired is the speech of Judah in Genesis 44:18–34, the longest in Genesis, in which Judah paints so evocatively the pathetic situation of Jacob, if his favourite son Benjamin is not allowed to return home. Again it shows great skill in leaving out any points that may offend Joseph and harping on those aspects that are most likely to appeal to his charity. Joseph himself is portrayed as not simply a good interpreter of dreams but as an eloquent advisor whose proposals are immediately accepted by Pharaoh (41:25–37). Abraham is not the master of the long speech, but he is portrayed as an effective and persistent negotiator. His plea for Sodom begins by appealing to God's justice,

[53] Cf. Wenham, *Genesis 1–15*, *ad loc*.

[54] Sternberg, *Poetics*, 145–52. Some of Sternberg's comments on the servant's speech suggest he is misleading his hearers. This is unfair: rather he is highlighting those aspects of the situation that he thinks most likely to persuade his hearers, just as Hamor and Shechem do in 34:21–23 (*Poetics*, 464–6).

'Shall not the Judge of all the earth do right?' (18:25) and continues with an appeal to divine compassion, so that by the end God agrees: 'for the sake of ten I will not destroy it' (18:32). His negotiating skills are much in evidence in buying a plot of land in which to bury Sarah. Offers and counter-offers are made until Abraham obtains what he really wants, the freehold possession of the cave of Machpelah and the land that surrounds it.[55]

If persuasive eloquence is a virtue that is commended in Genesis, has it anything to say about the misuse of speech? This is very difficult to determine, partly because there are so many potential abuses, and so much depends on the conventions of the culture and the intonation of the speech which we cannot recover. For example, Esau's 'Let me eat of some of that red pottage' (25:30) could be taken as abruptly uncouth, but his use of *na'* usually translated 'please' and a high-flown term for 'eat' could suggest that he is not quite at death's door, and that he therefore had no excuse for selling his birthright. On the other hand the king of Sodom's demand 'give me the persons' (14:21) sounds both blunt and rude. But does that necessarily indicate the author's disapproval? It is hard to be sure, so we shall focus on those rare occasions where a comment within the narrative indicates a moral judgement. In 27:35 Isaac says to Esau, 'Your brother came with guile,' and 34:13 notes that 'the sons of Jacob answered Shechem and his father deceitfully'. Though translated differently in the RSV the phrase, *bemirmah* means 'with deceit' and denotes a deliberate deception. Later Jacob himself is deliberately deceived by his father-in-law Laban, in what the author of Genesis views as divine retribution for Jacob's deception of his own father. In 34:13 'with deceit' is clearly the narrator's comment on Jacob's sons' negotiating line. This probably indicates the book's rejection of deceitful speech.[56] There is no comment from the narrator on the deliberate deception of the Pharaoh in Genesis 12:10–20, or Abimelech in 20:1–16 and 26:6–11, but as we have already observed it seems likely that he concurred with the rebuke delivered to the patriarch by the king. Genesis records a number of heated arguments, between the herdsmen of Lot and Abraham, between Sarah and Hagar, Isaac and the herdsmen of Gerar, Rachel and Leah, Jacob and his sons, Joseph and his brothers. Given the book's antipathy to conflict, and especially between relatives (cf. 13:8), it seems likely that it would share the attitude of Proverbs 'It is an honour for a man to keep aloof from strife, but every fool will be quarrelling' (Prov 20:3). But in view of the complexity of many disputes, it is difficult to be sure

[55] For a discussion of the dynamics of the negotiations cf. Licht, *Storytelling*, 20–3.

[56] By itself in this passage alone, *bemirmah* need not indicate authorial disapproval, but in the light of its earlier usage in 27:35 it seems highly likely that this is a negative comment too.

how Genesis expects its readers to react to the quarrels it relates: rarely can all the blame be attached to one side. Indeed the book often shows how both parties see the situation, so that the reader does not come down too firmly on one side or the other. Nevertheless it does implicitly advocate a pacific approach to problems.

Many of these disputes occur within families and tend to tear them apart. Within the traditional world-view that the Old Testament reflects, family solidarity is very important. In the decalogue, 'Honour your father and mother' is the first commandment dealing with social as opposed to religious obligations, indicating that filial duty is a very high priority. Thus Genesis repeatedly observes that brothers, even if long estranged, come together to bury their fathers (25:9 (Isaac and Ishmael); 35:29 (Jacob and Esau); 50:4–14 (Joseph and his brothers)). Filial loyalty demanded that sons should cover up their parents' mistakes.[57] But Ham did the very opposite: he broadcast his father's folly, and it was left to Shem and Japhet to cover their drunken father's nakedness. It is therefore not surprising that Noah cursed Ham, but blessed his other sons (9:20–27). There are several striking parallels between the flood story and the overthrow of Sodom: one is that both stories are followed by the surviving righteous father being disgraced by his children. In the case of Lot his daughters make him drunk and make him involuntarily commit incest with them (19:30–38). The narrator does not regard it as necessary to comment: the parallel with Noah and Ham is obvious, so that if Ham was cursed for his indiscretion, how much more blameworthy is the behaviour of Lot's daughters. In a similar way the narrator makes no comment about Reuben's incestuous relationship with Bilhah (Gen 35:22). Only in Jacob's deathbed blessing is the action denounced (49:4). Perhaps from the author's perspective the cruellest aspect of the sale of Joseph into Egypt was not his fate so much as the way his father suffered as a result of being led to believe Joseph was dead. 'All his sons and all his daughters rose up to comfort him; but he refused to be comforted, and said, "No, I shall go down to Sheol to my son mourning"' (37:35; cf. 42:38; 43:14).

The converse of filial duty is parental love for their children. This is expressed every time a child is born through the name that is given them. Eve speaks for every mother in Genesis as she greets her first child with the words, 'I have gotten a man with the help of the LORD' (4:1). The names of Abraham's two sons, Ishmael (God hears) and Isaac (he laughs) convey the sense of gratitude to God and the joy associated with children. Parental concern for their children's welfare was supposed to continue through life. Abraham is said to have been

[57] According to the Ugaritic Aqht epic (fourteenth century B.C.) a son should take his father by the hand when he's drunk, and carry him when he's sated with wine (*ANET*, 150).

very distressed when told to send Ishmael away, and he does his best to provide for him (21:11–14). Similarly Jacob's affection for Joseph and Benjamin is one of the leitmotifs of chapters 37–50.

But obviously it is Jacob's preference for Joseph and Benjamin, the sons of Rachel, that leads the other sons to hate Joseph (37:3–4). Similarly it was Isaac's fondness for Esau (25:28) that led him to summon him and leave Jacob out of the farewell paternal blessing. This flew in the face of convention[58] which demanded that all the sons should be blessed by a father before he died (cf. Gen 49), and triggered Rebekah's scheme to acquire the blessing by deceit. Favouritism breaches family solidarity which the Old Testament values so highly. Laban emerges from the pages of Genesis as a devious grasping figure, the antithesis of many of the virtues the patriarchs exemplify. But at least he shows concern for his daughters' welfare, when they and Jacob run off (31:43–50). One may even wonder if his insistence that Jacob marry Leah as well as Rachel might not be a perverse application of the solidarity principle. It certainly did not lead to solidarity within Jacob's family. Chapter 30 of Genesis records the bitter rivalry between Leah and Rachel, the one desperate for her husband's affection and the other for children. This resulted not merely in Jacob's uninterest in Leah's sons but also in her daughter Dinah. His apparent indifference to her rape led to the most vicious incident in the book.

Brothers were duty-bound to care for each other. If someone fell into debt, it was his brother's duty to buy him out if he could (Lev 25:25, 48–49). In the case of murder, it was the victim's brother who was expected to catch and execute the murderer if he could (Num 35:12). In the case of Dinah, as she was unmarried she was still the responsibility of Jacob her father. But his inaction led to her brothers assuming the role of avenger on her behalf with the consequences later described.

Family solidarity seems sometimes more apparent by its absence than its presence in Genesis. But I argued in Chapter 3 that one of the chief thrusts of the book is on the necessity for reconciliation between family members and indeed between the Israelites and their neighbours. Though in the period of the united monarchy this could be read as an essentially political message, its rationale is the principle of family solidarity. These neighbouring peoples were essentially 'brothers' and therefore there should be no strife between them (13:8). It is the sense that blood relationships are vitally important that makes Cain's murder of Abel so shocking, and the plans of Esau and Joseph's brothers to kill their hated brother so alarming. What should be the strongest bond of loyalty between human beings is perverted into the worst expression of hatred.

[58] K. H. Keukens, 'Der irreguläre Sterbesegen Isaaks: Bemerkungen zur Interpretation von Gen 27:1–45', *BN* 19 (1982), 43–56.

But as we have seen earlier, Genesis shows this hatred being overcome in dramatic fashion. Esau runs to greet his long-lost brother, and for his part Jacob declares, 'Seeing your face is like seeing the face of God, with such favour have you received me' (33:10). Similarly Joseph weeps for joy when he tells his brothers who he is and urges them 'do not be distressed, or angry with yourselves, because you sold me here; for God sent me before you to preserve life' (45:5). Joseph goes to great lengths to settle them in the best of the land, and to find them employment as Pharaoh's stockmen. Yet seventeen years later Joseph's brothers find it so difficult to believe that he has really forgiven them, that they invent a deathbed message from father Jacob to avert any revenge. 'Your father gave this command before he died, "Say to Joseph, Forgive, I pray you, the transgression of your brothers and their sin, because they did evil to you"' (50:17). This again reduces Joseph to tears, so shocked is he by the assumption that he would not forgive. For it is not simply that Genesis presupposes the duty of forgiveness, but that it values sincerity and integrity. The deviousness of Jacob and his sons is commented on unfavourably (27:35; 34:13), whereas Abimelech pleads for forgiveness from God because he acted 'in the integrity of my heart and the innocence of my hands' (20:5–6). Though such sincerity is not sufficient by itself to justify a course of action, Genesis implies that it is an important virtue that is a consequence or at least an aspect of the fear of God (20:11). Joseph is portrayed as one who fears God (42:18), so that his brothers' fear that his generosity towards them was merely out of deference to his father is hurtful. The fear of God and straightforwardness and keeping of promises are closely allied virtues in biblical thinking. As Psalm 15 puts it: he who would dwell on God's holy hill must speak the truth from his heart . . . and honour those who fear the LORD (2, 4). Joseph exemplifies both virtues in his career.

Finally in reviewing the virtues implicitly commended by Genesis, we should look at attitudes to the pleasures of life. Some philosophies, e.g. Stoicism, have valued emotional detachment and others commend asceticism. Neither is at all characteristic of Genesis. From Adam's shout of joy as he is introduced to Eve, 'This at last is bone of my bones . . .' to Joseph's tears at his brothers' fears, the leading characters all seem very ready to express their feelings (2:23; 50:17). The birth of children is the occasion of joy and laughter, most often encapsulated in the name given at birth (4:1; 21:7; 29:32 – 30:24; 41:51–52). At the end of life mourning is equally vigorous. Abraham's mourning and weeping for Sarah is mentioned in 23:2; Jacob refuses to be comforted when he hears of the supposed death of Joseph, while Judah predicts he will die of grief, should Benjamin not return home (37:35; 44:31). When Jacob does die, his sons mourn so long and loud for him, that the Canaanites comment: 'This is a grievous mourning to the Egyptians' and rename the place Abel-Mizraim, i.e. mourning of Egypt (50:11). Family reunions are marked by kissing, hugging and weeping (29:11, Rachel and Jacob; 29:13, Laban and Jacob; 33:4, Jacob and Esau; 45:14–15, Joseph and his brothers; 46:29, Joseph and Jacob) as are family partings (31:55, Laban and his daughters; 48:10, Jacob and his grandsons; 50:1, Joseph and Jacob). Joseph seems particularly emotional: apart from the occasions just listed, he turns aside to weep privately more than once (42:24; 43:30–31). Though Anglo-Saxon readers may tend to view Joseph's tearfulness as unmanly, this does not seem to be the perception of Genesis given the frequent references to men weeping in the book. Rather it is another mark of his exemplary character.

Anger is more rarely mentioned explicitly. Cain's anger presages his murder of Abel (4:5). Jacob is angry with Rachel for demanding a child (30:2) and with Laban for false accusations (31:36). Dinah's brothers are furious to hear of her rape, and Potiphar for Joseph's alleged assault on his wife (34:7; 39:19). Pharaoh was enraged by his cup-bearer and baker (40:2). On a number of occasions anger is expressed by various people without it being called anger (e.g. Pharaoh, 12:18–19; Sarah, 16:5; the angels, 19:16; Abimelech, 20:10; Abraham, 21:11; Abimelech, 26:10; Isaac, 26:27; Esau, 27:36; Jacob, 29:25; Leah, 30:15; Laban, 31:26; Jacob, 34:30; 37:10; Judah, 38:24; Jacob, 43:6; Joseph, 48:17–18.) In many of these cases the anger would appear to be justified, so it would not appear that Genesis is advocating passivity. But in none of these cases does the expressed anger lead to overreaction by the aggrieved party. They may act firmly – the Pharaoh expels Abraham from Egypt and Jacob demands his promised Rachel. But unlike Cain they do not commit murder. It could be that Genesis sees justified anger as a mark of a strong character, as long as it does not spill over into long-term resentment or exaggerated revenge. This would parallel its attitude to physical strength and courage, which are admired as long as not exercised to excess. On the other hand the failure to mention any emotional reaction by Jacob on two occasions when he should have been furious is eerie: it suggests something very amiss (34:5; 35:22).

Genesis also endorses the enjoyment of life's pleasures, such as food, wine and sex. There is no encouragement of ascetic abstinence, though it does point out the dangers of over-indulgence of the bodily appetites. Genesis 1 mentions that God provided mankind with food, and Genesis 2 that he planted a garden for Adam full of trees that were pleasant to look at and good for food.[59] Celebratory occasions involving plenty of eating and drinking continue to feature regularly in Genesis. Abraham

[59] Though this passage is primarily concerned with the act of disobedience involved in eating the one forbidden fruit, it does also draw attention to God's generous provision of many other enjoyable foods.

and Lot entertain the angels royally (18:2–8; 19:1–3). Isaac's weaning is marked by a great feast, so is the betrothal of Rebekah, the covenant with Abimelech, and Jacob's wedding (21:8; 24:54; 26:30; 29:22). Particularly splendid was the banquet thrown by Joseph to celebrate his brothers' arrival in Egypt (43:26–34). Food is meant to be enjoyed, indicates Genesis: it does not regard abstinence as virtuous.

But in the cases of Isaac and Esau the author seems to suggest that they had an obsession with food, which compromised their moral judgement. 'Isaac loved Esau, because he ate of his game' (25:28). This led to long-term favouritism which culminated in Jacob's exclusion from his father's farewell blessing (27:4). Once again the writer underlines Isaac's devotion to Esau because of the food he prepared: 'prepare for me savoury food, such as I love, and bring it to me that I may eat; that I may bless you before I die' (27:4). The whole deception episode revolves round preparing Isaac's favourite dish. Esau himself is portrayed as putting pleasure before principle in selling his birthright to Jacob. As we have already noted, it is not at all obvious that Esau was at death's door, rather hunger made him exaggerate. Yet he says, 'Of what use is a birthright to me?' So for some lentil stew Esau gave away his birthright, a move clearly disapproved of by the author who simply observes: 'Thus Esau despised his birthright' (25:32–34). These two stories suggest that though food is to be enjoyed, appetite must not overrule principle.

Similarly, Genesis appreciates wine yet is wary of overindulgence. It was Noah, 'a righteous man, blameless in his generation' who was the first wine maker: one could hardly give it a more venerable pedigree. The word translated 'feast' (*mišteh*) literally means 'drinking', so it may be assumed that wine was usually served at the feasts mentioned in Genesis (e.g. 19:3; 21:8; 29:22). Indeed plenty must have been served at Joseph's reunion party, for 'they drank and were merry with him' (43:34). In blessing Judah, Jacob predicts that his territory will be awash with wine: 'He washes his garments in wine and his vesture in the blood of grapes' (49:11).

While celebrating wine as a good gift from the creator (cf. Ps 104:15), Genesis also includes two stories illustrating its potential dangers. Noah, the inventor of wine, is the first to suffer from drinking too much (9:20–27), in an episode that echoes the fall in chapter 3.[60] Lot's daughters are chiefly to blame for the intoxication of their father, but as in the case of Noah it leaves a cloud over the last days of the one righteous man worthy to be rescued from Sodom (19:30–38).

Finally, sexual intercourse is viewed not just as a pleasure but as a duty within marriage. 'Be fruitful and multiply' is the first command

[60] Antony J. Tomasino, 'History Repeats Itself: The "Fall" and Noah's Drunkenness', *VT* 42 (1992), 128–30.

given to the human race in Genesis 1 and the promise of numberless descendants is central to the promise to Abraham. The genealogies record the success of many generations in fulfilling their duty. Attempts to evade this duty by Onan and Judah lead to the former dying and the latter being made a laughing-stock by Tamar, his daughter-in-law (Gen 38). Despite the potential for the abuse of the sexual appetite Genesis contains few examples of this apart from the rape of Dinah. There is of course plenty of tension within marriage caused by bigamy and childlessness, but apart from the threat caused by potentially adulterous rulers and a rich man's wife, marriage is portrayed as a secure and valued institution in Genesis.

Thus out of the stories of Genesis we can build up a catalogue of the virtues as they are perceived by the author, an identikit picture of the righteous. He or she is pious, that is prayerful and dependent on God. Strong and courageous, but not aggressive or mean. He or she is generous, truthful and loyal, particularly to other family members. The righteous person is not afraid to express emotions of joy, grief or anger, but the last should not spill over into excessive revenge, rather he should be ready to forgive. Finally righteousness does not require asceticism: the pleasures of life are to be enjoyed without becoming a slave to them.

These virtues may sound commonplace, but just because they are widely shared in great literature and in many societies does not mean they are trite. Rather it points to their universality. Booth points out that great works of literature such as Shakespeare's have universal appeal because their norms are widely shared.

> It is true that these beliefs are for the most part self-evident, even commonplace – but that is precisely because they are acceptable to most of us. Shakespeare requires us to believe that it is right to honor our fathers, and that it is wrong to kill off old men like Lear or grind out the eyes of old men like Gloucester. He insists that it is always wrong to use other people as instruments to one's own ends, whether by murder or slander, that it is good to love, but wrong to love selfishly, that helpless old age is pitiable, and that blind egotism deserves punishment.[61]

While many of the individual virtues endorsed by the Old Testament would be admired in many cultures, the precise constellation of accepted virtues varies from society to society, from philosopher to philosopher. MacIntyre observes that the concept of a virtue 'always requires for its application the acceptance of some prior account of certain features of social and moral life in terms of which it has to be defined and explained'.[62] Thus Homer's society operated on the heroic model for

[61] Wayne C. Booth, *The Rhetoric of Fiction* (Chicago and London: University of Chicago Press, 1961), 141.

[62] MacIntyre, *After Virtue*, 174.

whom the paradigm of excellence is the warrior. Everyone had their allotted role in this family-based structure, so to be virtuous was to fulfil that role excellently. Thus strength, courage, cunning and fidelity, which help the individual achieve his or her role, are key virtues. For Aristotle the virtues enabled a person to achieve *eudaimonia*, happiness, prosperity and the contemplation of the divine. As an Athenian gentleman the prerequisites for achieving these goals were wealth, freedom and intelligence. Thus barbarians and slaves could not achieve *eudaimonia* or be truly virtuous. In more modern times Benjamin Franklin set out his vision of the virtues, which was controlled by the principle of utility. Thus he valued cleanliness, silence, industry and acquisitiveness, for these help one to achieve success.

It is therefore worth enquiring whether there is a unifying principle that holds together the various Old Testament virtues that we have identified. Is there a goal to which their practice leads beyond the immediate horizon of the narrative? Is there a *telos* to human behaviour that the Old Testament believes that virtue leads to?

The great collections of law in Leviticus and Deuteronomy both make plain the rewards of obeying the law: they both conclude with a section of blessings which spell out the consequences of obeying the law and a longer section of curses describing the costs of disobedience. According to Leviticus 26 there will be abundant harvests (vv. 3–5), peace including freedom from attack by wild animals and victory over their enemies (vv. 6–8), many children (v. 9), and God's presence with them (vv. 11–13). Deuteronomy 28:1–14 contains a similar set of blessings for obedience. Peace, prosperity, children, and the presence of God seem to be the goals endorsed by the psalms and wisdom books too (e.g. Ps 15; 24; 42; 122; 127–8; Job 31; Prov 31). All these goods are summed up in the term 'blessing'.

Our concern, though, is with the narrative books. Do they share these goals of human existence too? The storyline of Judges cataloguing one disaster after another makes it difficult to be sure what the implied author's goals were. However, the deuteronomistic phraseology and formulae used by the author surely suggest that he would endorse Deuteronomy's goals of peace, good harvests, children and the divine presence. Many of the episodes are the more poignant, when they are seen as a commentary on the failure to achieve these goals. Israel's repeated subjugation by their enemies, the lack of peace, the loss of crops to invaders (6:3–4), and the sacrifice of Jephthah's daughter (11:34–40), are all reminders of how far short of the ideals Israel has fallen.

In the case of Genesis similar goals are apparent from a study of the opening chapters and the promises made to the patriarchs, which reaffirm God's primal intentions for man.[63] If the creation of human

[63] Cf. Clines, *Theme*, 29.

beings is the climax of creation in Genesis 1:1 – 2:3, the divine rest on the sabbath is the goal of creation. The garden of Eden was once a place of harmony, where God walked in the cool of the day conversing with Adam. The first command given to Adam and reaffirmed to Noah is 'Be fruitful and multiply'. Land, descendants and security arising from God's protective presence are at the heart of the patriarchal promises, which suggests that Genesis' idea of blessing is not very different from that expressed in Leviticus and Deuteronomy. But while Deuteronomy looks for peace as a result of Israel's enemies being defeated, Genesis looks rather for the blessing of the nations through Abraham's offspring.

The virtues we have identified in Genesis relate quite clearly to these goals. Piety for example presupposes the possibility of drawing near to God. Courage is encouraged by the conviction that God is with the patriarchs. Loyalty to other family members by spouse, parent or child reflects the importance of continuing the line of promise. Aristotle understood the practice of virtue not simply to be a means to achieving the good life for man, but 'the exercise of the virtues is a necessary and central part of such a life, not a mere preparatory exercise to secure such a life'.[64] It would seem that the Old Testament would agree. It is in living the God-approved lifestyle that his people draw near to him and experience his presence in their daily life, so making that life more like that pictured in Eden and promised to the patriarchs.

The role of the community in biblical ethics

A focus on the virtues implied by the Old Testament writers may unwittingly lead to an individualistic interpretation of its ethics, that is quite off-key. We have observed that family solidarity and filial loyalty are most important virtues in the traditional perspective of the Old Testament. But recently Hauerwas and Birch are among those who have rightly drawn attention to the communal setting of biblical ethics: that is the biblical text with its didactic message is at once the product of a community and also designed to create and perpetuate a community. Our rhetorical analyses of Genesis and Judges have emphasised the historical settings of these works and the way that their message reflects the ethos of the implied authors. According to Birch we should envisage groups behind these texts, not an individual writer.[65] Now while the individual writer may reflect the values of the group in society to which he belongs, this is questionable: prophets for example were rather

[64] MacIntyre, *After Virtue*, 140.

[65] B. C. Birch, 'Moral Agency, Community, and the Character of God in the Hebrew Bible', *Semeia* 66 (1994), 25–6.

solitary figures, and it is by no means clear that the author of a challenging text like Genesis or Judges necessarily enjoyed wide support in Israel.

However Birch is much more justified in claiming that 'the biblical text is directed to the formation of community'. We argued above that the books of Genesis and Judges were putting forward programmes that affected the whole community. Genesis is both justifying the Davidic monarchy and pleading for reconciliation between groups within Israel such as the tribes, and between Israel and its neighbours such as the Philistines and Aramaeans. Judges is arguing the merits of a certain type of royal leadership and criticising fiercely the tribe of Benjamin and the leadership it offered. In both cases the authors are attempting to influence the shape of the whole nation.

Hauerwas has argued that the Christian community has been, indeed was intended to be, shaped by the story of Jesus set out in the gospels.[66] Birch applies this notion to the Old Testament. He sees the story of the Exodus and the law-giving at Sinai as defining Israel's relationship to God. The way that this story was retold in the annual passover celebrations determined the shape of Israel as a community. It is into this story of redemption from Egypt that the law-giving is set, and this informs Israel's understanding of its ethical responsibility. Many of the slave laws reflect Israel's memory of its own period in bondage in Egypt. When a slave is released, he must be treated generously for this reason. 'You shall remember that you were a slave in the land of Egypt, and the LORD your God redeemed you' (Deut 15:15).

Birch thus understands the narrative as directed at forming the character of Israel as a nation: it defines the national identity. But the laws themselves are directed at individuals and extended families and tribes within the nation. So too the stories of Genesis and Judges deal with groups and families who were parts of the much broader people, and they too have an educational function showing how the parts should relate to the whole. 'You shall be to me a kingdom of priests and a holy nation' (Exod 19:6) sums up the individual and corporate vision of Exodus. A collection of holy individuals makes a holy nation, which can serve as mediator between God and all the nations of the world. Or, as the promise to Abraham put it, 'In you shall all the families of the earth find blessing' (Gen 12:3). Thus the cultivation of individual virtues is only a means to creating holy people who in turn make up the holy nation. The stories of Genesis show how this process may start to

[66] At many points Hauerwas has drawn attention to the importance of the biblical narratives for the formation of a Christian ethical community. 'The moral use of scripture, therefore, lies precisely in its power to help us remember the stories of God for the continual guidance of our community and individual lives.' Stanley Hauerwas, *A Community of Character: Toward a Constructive Christian Social Ethic* (Notre Dame: University of Notre Dame Press, 1981), 66.

happen, while the book of Judges shows how the neglect of virtue leads first individuals and then the whole nation into a moral nose-dive.

The imitation of God as integrating ethical principle

In this chapter we have tried to make two main points. First that the ethical expectations of the Old Testament are higher than the legal rules. Laws define a floor of tolerable behaviour. Break them and punishment follows. But that does not mean that simply keeping the laws is sufficient. It is not enough to avoid worshipping other gods: the LORD wants Israel to love him with their whole heart, mind and strength. It is not good enough not to commit adultery, the Old Testament expects husbands and wives to love, care for and protect each other. Ethical duty involves much more than keeping the law.

The second point that has emerged is that by portraying the heroes of Genesis repeatedly acting in certain ways the book is implicitly defining certain virtues and vices, encouraging its readers to imitate the former and avoid the latter. We suggested that courage, honesty, family loyalty, generosity, eloquence, toughness in the face of wrong, but a readiness to forgive were some of the virtues Genesis implicitly commends. These virtues again cannot be defined by law: rather the stories offer paradigms of behaviour that apply in various situations.[67] They certainly imply that usually the patriarchs acted much better than merely abiding by the letter of the law. Is there any principle that brings together both these aspects of a duty to do better than the minimum of just keeping the law and the ideals of virtue often exemplified in the behaviour of various actors?

It has been observed that many laws and ethical demands often have a motive clause attached which justifies the course of behaviour required.[68] Some of these clauses appeal to God's behaviour to justify human action. The decalogue says: 'Remember the sabbath day . . . for in six days the LORD made the heaven and earth . . . and rested the seventh day' (Exod 20:8, 11). The book of the covenant urges compassion for debtors, 'for I am compassionate' (Exod 22:27). Leviticus urges, 'Be holy, for I am holy' (Lev 11:45). Deuteronomy forbids the taking of bribes, because God 'is not partial and takes no bribe' (Deut 10:17; 16:19). The motivation to act in certain ways because that is

[67] In this respect our attempt to define narrative ethics in terms of virtues resembles W. Janzen's paradigmatic approach in *Old Testament Ethics: A Paradigmatic Approach* (Westminster/John Knox Press: Louisville, 1994). Where I part company with his methodology is in deciding what is paradigmatic. He seems to rely on instinct to determine what is paradigmatic and what is not. In this chapter I have used the criteria of repetition, positive context and congruity with wisdom ethos to determine whether a trait is to be judged vice or virtue.

[68] Rifat Sonsino, *Motive Clauses in Hebrew Law* (Chico: Scholars Press, 1980).

how God acts is thus found in a wide variety of legal collections within the Pentateuch, and it therefore seems likely that it is assumed within the narratives as well.

The importance of the imitation of God as a focus of Old Testament ethical thinking has been recognised by various scholars. 'A person seeking a new way of life is called upon to take God as a model: "Good and straightforward is God, therefore he instructs sinners in the way. He guides the humble in justice and teaches the humble His way" (Ps 25:8–9).'[69] 'For the Old Testament as we have it ethics is a matter of imitating the pattern of God's own actions, in salvation and in creation, because these spring from a pattern which always exists in his own mind and by which he governs the world with justice and with mercy.'[70] 'The Life of God models the moral life. God as experienced by Israel and mediated to subsequent generations through the canon is to be imitated as moral agent, in both character and conduct.'[71]

The rationale for this demand is found in the opening chapter of Genesis: 'God created man in his own image' (1:27). The exact meaning of the image has been discussed at length, and the debate cannot be reviewed here.[72] It is now accepted on the basis of extra- and intrabiblical parallels that mankind is viewed as God's representative on earth. He is God's vice-gerent appointed to rule the earth in a godlike way. He is given dominion over other creatures (Gen 1:28; Ps 8:4–8). Human actions are expected to echo divine, whether in fruitfulness or in observing the sabbath (Gen 1:28; 2:1–3; Exod 20:11). It is not explicitly said that Noah observed the sabbath, but the flood story does make it clear that he operated on a weekly cycle like God's (8:10, 12).

Kings and commoners must exhibit divine virtues in their behaviour, pursuing justice and caring for the poor (Deut 10:17–19; 14:28–29; Job 29:12–17; Ps 72). Fidelity, love, generosity, and forgiveness are displayed in God's dealings with mankind, and men should treat their fellow human beings in similar fashion.

God as the almighty creator is portrayed in Genesis 1 and 2 as boundless in power, yet very concerned for and generous to his creatures, especially man. Later on, in his promises to the patriarchs, his generosity is once more emphasised, as he promises them land and numerous descendants. We have noted that the wealth of the patriarchs is viewed positively by Genesis: it shows them enjoying God's blessing, 'entering into the life of God'.[73] Abraham's generosity towards Lot giving him (13:9) choice of the land, and to the king of Sodom restoring all his

[69] Falk, *Religious Law*, 25.

[70] J. Barton, 'Approaches to Ethics in the Old Testament', in *Beginning Old Testament Study* (ed. J. W. Rogerson, London: SPCK, 1982), 130.

[71] Birch, 'Moral Agency', 31.

[72] But see Westermann, *Genesis 1–11* , 147–61; G. J. Wenham, *Genesis 1–15*, 27–40.

[73] Birch, 'Moral Agency', 30.

property mirrors the generosity of God. God, who preserved life in the ark, later sent Joseph to Egypt to preserve life there (6:19–20; 45:5). Divine generosity is one of the great themes of Deuteronomy. Israel must respond to God's generosity by giving herself to God in loyalty and service.[74] Generosity must characterise human relationships too. Thus loans must be given, even if there is little hope of their repayment. Manumitted slaves must be given a golden handshake (Deut 15:7–18). 'The righteous is ever giving liberally and lending' (Ps 37:26).

An aspect of God's generosity is his compassion and mercy. He forgives sinners. His creatures must behave likewise. 'You shall not take vengeance or bear any grudge against the sons of your own people; but you shall love your neighbour as yourself' (Lev 19:18). That forgiveness is a divine attribute that man should imitate is illustrated in the Jacob and Esau story. When Jacob comes back from Paddan-Aram to meet Esau, he treats Esau like God. He sends him a *minḥah*, normally a kind of sacrifice, 'for he thought "I may make atonement before him"' (Gen 32:20). Then Esau runs to meet Jacob and greets him with open arms, and Jacob comments, 'to see your face is like seeing the face of God'. In other words Esau has behaved like God by so freely forgiving Jacob's offences. Joseph shows similar generosity in forgiving his brothers.

'The LORD' is 'a God merciful and gracious, slow to anger and abounding in steadfast love and faithfulness, keeping steadfast love for thousands, forgiving iniquity and transgression and sin, but who will by no means clear the guilty.' So Exodus 34:6–7 sums up God's character, which is illustrated throughout the biblical narrative and celebrated in nearly every psalm. Yet it is precisely these qualities that God looks for among his people: they are to reflect, even positively imitate his character. Israel is to be loving and faithful: 'Now Israel what does the LORD your God require of you, but to fear the LORD your God, to walk in all his ways, to love him, to serve the LORD your God with all your heart and with all your soul' (Deut 10:12). More often than not the patriarchs exemplify this devotion in their own lives.

It is not just in the vertical God–man relationship that these virtues should be practised, but in the horizontal intrahuman relationships. Loyalty within the family and to one's neighbours was so taken for granted that the law hardly bothers to mention it except in a situation where loyalty to God must take precedence (Deut 13:7–11). Genesis tends to take loyalty for granted, shocking its readers more by its breach than celebrating its expected practice, whether in the story of Cain and Abel, Jacob and Esau, or Joseph and his brothers. But the reconciliation of Jacob with Esau, and Joseph with his brothers shows what ought to

[74] J. G. McConville, *Law and Theology in Deuteronomy* (JSOTSup 33, Sheffield: JSOT Press, 1984), 10–20.

be the case. Commenting on Judah's speech offering to stay instead of Benjamin, Sternberg comments, 'it surely manifests nothing short of a transformation, from subnormal to abnormal solidarity'.[75]

But this loyal, generous and forgiving God has his limits: 'he will by no means clear the guilty.' This is repeatedly demonstrated in Genesis. The flood and the destruction of Sodom show divine judgement on a grand scale, the suffering of Jacob as a result of his deception of Isaac and the temporary infertility of the women of Gerar show it on an individual level (20:18). And though the law encourages human judges to be equally firm in punishing sin (Exod 23:7; Deut 13:9; 19:21; 25:12), Genesis gives few examples of people taking revenge into their own hands:[76] it seems more interested in encouraging peacemaking than justifying revenge.[77]

Genesis thus sets out a very lofty ideal of human behaviour. It does not show its heroes simply keeping the law in their individual actions or illustrating typical human virtues. Rather it sets out a vision of human beings made in the image of God, his representatives on earth, and therefore obligated to try and imitate God in their dealings with one another and with other creatures. Sometimes the stories of Genesis show the patriarchs acting in exemplary fashion: they not only keep the law, model virtue, but exhibit truly godly characteristics as those made in the image of God should. Sometimes though they fall very far short. Admittedly they rarely break the laws set out later in the Pentateuch, but some of their actions are a travesty of godliness. But most often their behaviour is mixed, neither outstandingly virtuous nor catastrophic, perhaps somewhat better than the typical ancient reader but not too much better: good enough to be an inspiration, but not such paragons as to discourage the implied reader from trying to emulate them. Nevertheless their mixed ethical achievement does not generate a sense of complacency in the reader, rather it serves as a reminder that God still keeps his promises and is loyal to his people despite their shortcomings.

[75] Sternberg, *Poetics*, 308. Cf. Alter, *Art of Biblical Narrative*, 174–5: 'His entire speech is motivated by the deepest empathy for his father, by a real understanding of what it means for the old man's very life to be bound up with that of the lad.'

[76] The most obvious example is Gen 34, where it is not immediately obvious where the writer's sympathy lies. See Chapter 6 for further discussion.

[77] Falk observes that man should not try to imitate every attribute of God. Humans are neither omniscient nor omnipotent and therefore some divine actions cannot be replicated. Falk, *Religious Law*, 25.

6

SOME PROBLEMATIC TALES

The preceding chapters have sought to establish general principles for the ethical interpretation of the Old Testament. We have stressed the importance of the implied author as a point of reference in interpretation. We are not looking at the attitudes of the actors within the story, but trying to discover the outlook of the implied author to the stories he tells and the message he is trying to convey through them. This led us to stress the importance of the rhetorical function of each book, of discovering what Genesis and Judges are trying to say in general terms to their implied audiences. The point being made by any part of the book must be congruent with the book's overall message.

In the last chapter we then turned to discuss how we could determine the author's ethical stance. It was argued that although the law gives some clues to the writers' outlook, it represents the floor of acceptable behaviour not its ceiling. Biblical narrators hoped that their characters would do more than observe the letter of the law. We argued that repeated patterns of behaviour, e.g. displays of courage, generosity, or eloquence, in positive contexts suggest that they are being displayed as models of virtue which should be imitated. Further it was proposed that the idea of the imitation of God held together the network of virtues and ethical ideals that the biblical writers were implicitly promoting through these texts.

By the use of these criteria it becomes possible to see more clearly the authorial stance on many of the problematic passages in Genesis. It does not admire the patriarchs declaring their wives to be their sisters. These episodes involve deceit, fear, lack of care for the wife, and unconcern that such deception could lead the Egyptians to sin. In the case of Jacob's trickery to obtain the blessing, the author does not place the whole blame on him: he draws attention to Isaac's favouritism and the way he allows his appetite to override principle. Nevertheless the brunt of the blame is laid on Jacob, and Rebekah to a lesser extent. His barefaced lie is not excused either in chapter 27 or later in the book. The rest of his career is lived under its shadow. Forced to run from home, he himself is deceived first by his father-in-law and later by his sons. By chapter 33 he has acknowledged the injustice of his action as he symbolically gives back the blessing to Esau, but he does not escape the aftermath of his action until Joseph summons him to join the reconciled brothers in Egypt (Gen

46). In this way the author makes it plain how he views Jacob's action.

But in chapter 34, the story of the rape of Dinah, readers have the utmost difficulty in deciding what the author thinks about the events described. Readers are rarely unclear what they think about the rape and the subsequent massacre, but on whose side is the writer? Some think he blames Jacob, others his sons. Some hold that he views Shechem as a scoundrel, others think he was not a bad bloke. To judge from the literature we are little closer to agreement now than two thousand years ago! I shall therefore quickly review some of the readings that have been proposed before attempting to show how rhetorical criticism and the general ethical stance of Genesis may clarify the issues.

The book of *Jubilees* (mid-second century B.C.)[1] sees the behaviour of Shechem as totally reprehensible and makes it appear even worse than it does in Genesis. 'Dinah was snatched away to the house of Shechem . . . He lay with her and defiled her, but she was little, only twelve years old' (*Jub* 30:2). *Jubilees* goes on to ascribe the massacre of the Shechemites to the judgement of God: 'the LORD handed them over into the hand of the sons of Jacob' (30:6). For this writer the Dinah story shows that intermarriage with Gentiles is completely out of the question, and that Simeon and Levi were quite justified in opposing it so vigorously. Indeed their names were recorded in heaven, and Levi was rewarded with the priesthood for his zeal (30:17–23). Even Jacob is portrayed as tacitly approving their actions: his protest in Genesis 34:30 is only alluded to in *Jubilees* 30:25, while his curse on their actions in Genesis 49:5–7 is omitted entirely.

Josephus (late first century A.D.) comes down firmly on Jacob's side against his sons. He rewrites the account of their assault on the city, saying it took place at night during a Shechemite festival, which does not sound quite so bad as in Genesis where the Shechemites' weakness is due to their submission to circumcision as demanded by the sons of Jacob. But even so Josephus is blunt. They 'perpetrated this deed without their father's sanction', and Jacob was 'aghast at the enormity of these acts and indignant at his sons' (Josephus, *Antiquities* 1. 340–1).

Later Jewish tradition as represented by *Genesis Rabbah* does not attach much blame to Jacob or his sons but to Dinah. 'Dinah went out' is seen as the cause of the whole problem. Her behaviour invited trouble: 'Simeon and Levi acted in Shechem with a reason, *And they said: Should one deal with our sister as with a harlot?* Said they: What mean they by treating us as public property? And what caused this? The fact that Dinah the daughter of Leah went out.'[2]

[1] For discussion of date see O. S. Wintermute in ed. J. H. Charlesworth, *The Old Testament Pseudepigrapha II* (Garden City: Doubleday, 1985), 43–5.

[2] *Midrash Rabbah* 80:2 (trans. by H. Freedman, 3rd edn., New York: Soncino Press, 1983), 736.

John Calvin in his commentary on Genesis allows that Dinah may be partially to blame, claiming that this is the attitude of the author. 'It is not to be doubted that Moses in part casts the blame of the offence upon Dinah herself, when he says, "she went out to see the daughters of the land;" whereas she ought to have remained under her mother's eyes in the tent.'[3] Although Shechem 'grievously sinned', in Calvin's eyes he partially made up for it by his subsequent affection for Dinah and his eagerness to marry her whatever the cost. Jacob's inactivity he ascribes to his devastation by the event. 'The sense then is, that he was so oppressed with insupportable grief that he held his peace.'[4] But no excuses are allowed for Levi and Simeon.

> Shechem . . . had acted wickedly and impiously; but it was far more atrocious and wicked that the sons of Jacob should murder a whole people, to avenge themselves of the private fault of one man. It was by no means fitting to seek a cruel compensation for the levity and rashness of one youth, by the slaughter of so many men.[5]

Practically no aspect of their revenge escapes Calvin's scathing censure: their abuse of circumcision, their deceit, the massacre, the taking of booty and finally their retort to Jacob's rebuke, 'Should he treat our sister like a harlot?' 'Their own answer not only breathes a barbarous ferocity, but shows they had no feeling . . . Thus we are taught, how intemperate anger deprives men of their senses.'[6]

More recent commentators have generally had little to say about the moral dimensions of Genesis 34; instead they focus their attention on historical and source-critical issues.[7] But this truce has been shattered by modern narrative critics, who are as divided about this chapter as *Jubilees* and Josephus and argue their case as bitterly as the actors in the story itself.

Meir Sternberg's classic study of Old Testament narrative technique, *The Poetics of Biblical Narrative* devotes a whole chapter to arguing that Genesis 34 is persuading the reader that Levi and Simeon's revenge on the city of Shechem was justifiable, whereas Jacob in not reacting failed in his duty.

Sternberg begins by noting the author's categorical condemnation of the rape. 'Shechem . . . saw her, and he took her and lay with her and

[3] J. Calvin, *A Commentary on Genesis II* (1554, ET, J. King 1847; reprinted London: Banner of Truth, 1965), 218.

[4] Calvin, *Genesis II*, 220.

[5] Calvin, *Genesis II*, 220.

[6] Calvin, *Genesis II*, 229.

[7] Two exceptions are G. von Rad, *Genesis*[2] (OTL, London: SCM Press, 1972), 334–5, who in various passing comments shows more sympathy with Dinah's brothers than with Jacob; and W. Brueggemann, *Genesis* (Atlanta: John Knox, 1982), 275–80, who comes down strongly for Jacob against his sons.

abused her' (34:2). The last two verbs, 'lay with' and 'abused' are loaded terms which express the author's repudiation of the act. 'Lay with'[8] by itself would condemn the action, but the final verb 'abuse', 'humiliate' underlines the censure. By Old Testament standards it is just plain wrong: 'such a thing ought not to be done' (34:7).

But verse 3 moderates the shock and explains why Shechem wanted to marry Dinah and was even prepared to accept circumcision to achieve this goal. 'His soul was drawn to Dinah . . . he loved the maiden and spoke tenderly to her.' Sternberg comments: 'The feeling moderates the impression of barbarity given by the act.'[9] And because the narrator tells us this we can be sure of Shechem's sincerity. Although his affection for Dinah by no means makes up for his previous treatment of her, it does put him in a better light than Amnon who, having raped his half-sister Tamar, then sent her away (2 Sam 13:18).

After its action-packed opening the story suddenly slows down, as we are told that though 'Jacob heard that he had defiled his daughter Dinah . . . he held his peace' (34:5). This, Sternberg argues, is not how a father should behave when he hears his daughter has been raped. At least David was very angry when he heard of the assault on Tamar (2 Sam 13:21), and Jacob was inconsolable when he concluded that Joseph was dead (Gen 37:34–35). But he does not feel anything, say anything, or do anything about his daughter's plight. Sternberg argues that this reflects the fact that Dinah was Leah's daughter, not Rachel's, and as Jacob never loved Leah, so he never loved her children. So he left all the discussion to his sons, whose anger at the wrong done to their sister was exacerbated by her father's apparent lack of concern. By contrast Hamor, Shechem's father, plays a vigorous part in the negotiations on behalf of his son (e.g. vv. 6, 8, 18, 20, 24), which highlights the inactivity of Jacob.

But the way Hamor and Shechem put their request for intermarriage with the Israelites without any acknowledgement of the wrong done to Dinah further prejudices the reader against them. Though their proposal of intermarriage and free trade sounds generous, and the offer of unlimited marriage payments flamboyant, Sternberg argues that they are negotiating from a position of strength because they have detained Dinah in their house.[10] This almost necessitates the brothers' resort to guile and violence.

'The sons of Jacob answered . . . deceitfully' is one of the rare moments where an Old Testament writer unequivocally reveals his moral perspective. But, as Sternberg notes, the writer then appears to

[8] 'Lie with' (*šakab 'et*) is always used of irregular sexual intercourse, Paul Noble, *Bib Int* 4 (1996), 178–9. It is not clear whether the irregularity is that the act is premarital, forced, or exogamous (Shechem was a Canaanite) or all three.

[9] Sternberg, *Poetics*, 447.

[10] Sternberg, *Poetics*, 456.

try to mitigate the deceit by the comment, 'because he (who) had defiled their sister Dinah'. This clause is redundant and it seems to be added deliberately to moderate the reader's condemnation of their deceit. According to Sternberg, mentioning the brothers' deceitfulness before their speech which embodies it reduces its negative impact on the reader. On the other hand Hamor and Shechem's own speech to their fellow citizens contains a certain amount of deceit as well, harping on the economic dominance over the Israelites they will enjoy, climaxing with the prospect: 'Will not their cattle, their property and all their beasts be ours?' (34:23).

Thus by underlining the wrongfulness of Dinah's rape, highlighting the failure of Jacob to defend her honour, drawing attention to the power of the Shechemites and the deceitfulness of their leaders, the author of Genesis 34 has endeavoured to put the sons of Jacob in the best possible light. They were right to be very angry, but they could not do much for their sister without resort to underhand means. Nevertheless, Sternberg admits, 'the reprisal is out of all proportion to the crime'.[11]

But the writer does not give up trying to minimise the blame to be attached to Simeon and Levi for their assault on the city. They are most concerned with rescuing Dinah, that is why they had to kill all the men of the city including Hamor and Shechem, for she was detained in Shechem's house. They were Dinah's full brothers, as v. 25 again reminds the reader. It was the other sons of Jacob, who after the massacre of the male inhabitants of the city entered it 'hyena-like' and plundered the flocks and herds, 'their wealth, all their little ones and their wives' (vv. 28–29). Thus 'the debunking of the majority brings out the consistency of . . . Simeon and Levi'.[12] 'These two gradually move from off stage to on stage to central position: their idealistic and uncompromising stance makes them the most intricate, colourful, and attractive characters in the story.'[13]

They are of course given the last word in the story. Their ringing riposte to their father's protest about their action – 'Should he treat our sister like a harlot?' (v. 31) – 'vibrates with the sense of injury that drove them to seek redress in the sword'.[14] By contrast, Jacob's wimpishness reveals 'himself as the tale's least sympathetic character'.[15] Sternberg holds that if Jacob had rebuked his sons for the massacre, the abuse of circumcision or even breach of contract, we might have sympathised with his remarks. But all he is apparently worried about is the danger of a Canaanite backlash (v. 30) which could endanger

[11] Sternberg, *Poetics*, 467.
[12] Sternberg, *Poetics*, 472.
[13] Sternberg, *Poetics*, 473.
[14] Sternberg, *Poetics*, 474.
[15] Sternberg, *Poetics*, 473.

his own skin. He was not concerned to prevent exogamous marriage, something no patriarch should acquiesce in.

Having argued passionately that Genesis most clearly endorses Simeon and Levi, Sternberg admits right at the end that things are not quite so clear-cut.

> The dilemma raised by the story is so complex and each choice so problematic that he (i.e. the narrator) cannot fully identify with any of the positions taken. After all, whatever Jacob's callousness and selfishness, he does right to think of the safety of his house. Whereas the brothers do right to champion Dinah; but they pay the price in deceit and bloodshed, they increasingly act from personal motives rather than horror of exogamy and in disregard for consequences rather than out of trust in God's providence, which validates their proceeding (35:5) after the event. From the narrator's vantage point, therefore, none of the dramatised views rises above the level of stuff for plot and polyphony. Yet his rhetorical maneuvers throughout, the final set of oppositions, and, above all, his giving the last word – and what a last word! – to Simeon and Levi, leave no doubt where his sympathy lies.[16]

A completely different reading of the story has been offered by Fewell and Gunn.[17] Whereas Sternberg maximises the blame on Jacob, Hamor and Shechem and seeks to exonerate Simeon and Levi, Fewell and Gunn seek to show that Jacob, Hamor and Shechem were attempting to act in the best interests of Dinah and that Simeon and Levi's actions are quite inexcusable.

Fewell and Gunn begin by arguing that Shechem's treatment of Dinah was not as reprehensible as generally supposed. They translate verse 2b: 'Shechem took her and lay with her and raped her.' The terms used here, they claim, are descriptive not evaluative. Though they suppose most readers will condemn rape, they do not think the author is being especially condemnatory. In fact the kindly attitude of Shechem expressed in verse 3, 'he loved the young woman, and he spoke to the young woman's heart' puts him in a quite positive light. Indeed they claim that his advances were well received, for 'speaking to her heart' means 'touching her heart'. So Dinah was reassured, and far from being detained in Shechem's house probably remained there voluntarily. 'However one views the rape, one must acknowledge that the narrator tips the balance in Shechem's favour: Shechem moves from raping an object to loving a woman and seeking to make restitution for the wrong he has done her.'[18] He is prepared to pay any bride price to marry Dinah properly.

[16] Sternberg, *Poetics*, 475.

[17] Danna N. Fewell and David M. Gunn, 'Tipping the Balance: Sternberg's Reader and the Rape of Dinah', *JBL* 110 (1991), 193–211.

[18] Fewell and Gunn, 'Tipping the Balance', 197.

Fewell and Gunn view Jacob's silence as benign and prudent. He wants to consult with his sons before reacting. When they returned and took over the negotiations with Hamor and Shechem, Jacob was happy with the terms they were proposing, not realising his sons' insincerity. He did not object to intermarriage on principle. 'Jacob's silence derives from caution rather than apathy.'[19] 'His apparent acceptance of the settlement with Hamor might suggest that he saw the advantage for his daughter.'[20]

Whereas Sternberg sees the brothers as essentially motivated by concern for their sister's welfare and honour, Fewell and Gunn see them as self-interested. 'Their anger stems from the reckless act against Israel.'[21] What matters to them is that the family has been put to shame, not that Dinah has suffered injury. Hence the massacre of the citizens of Shechem was not a rescue operation to extricate Dinah (she may have been quite happy where she was), but straightforward revenge by the sons of Jacob for the offence against the family. Furthermore Simeon and Levi should not be seen as high-minded idealists, and the other brothers as greedy looters. 'In the end, however, whether Simeon and Levi are implicated in the pillaging or not matters little. Their grossly disproportionate response remains just that.'[22]

Their final outburst 'Should he treat our sister as a harlot?', which for Sternberg demonstrates their idealism, proves nothing of the kind. 'What they really mean is that their honor cannot be bought – which means that no restitution to Dinah herself is satisfactory. The injury is an injury to them and they seek revenge.'[23] And whereas Jacob's complaint that their action has endangered him is dismissed by Sternberg as expressing cowardly self-interest, Fewell and Gunn view it as the exasperation of a wise peace-loving man whose hopes have been dashed by his sons' folly.

> Jacob's initial silence is wisdom in the face of a potentially explosive situation for his family as a whole. In fact, by avoiding confrontation, he allows the Hivites to offer a potential solution of restitution. Jacob has also been deceived by his sons' conditions. His anger is understandable. His sons have usurped his authority, deceived him in the process, and acted without responsibility. They leave him to face the consequences, him and the rest of the family.[24]

That two such diametrically opposed interpretations of a passage should be commended by well-known scholars is remarkable: those

[19] Fewell and Gunn, 'Tipping the Balance', 198.
[20] Fewell and Gunn, 'Tipping the Balance', 210–11.
[21] Fewell and Gunn, 'Tipping the Balance', 199.
[22] Fewell and Gunn, 'Tipping the Balance', 205.
[23] Fewell and Gunn, 'Tipping the Balance', 207.
[24] Fewell and Gunn, 'Tipping the Balance', 208.

actors in the story that Sternberg commends are those most criticised by Fewell and Gunn, while those preferred by Fewell and Gunn are damned by Sternberg. The ordinary reader of the Old Testament marvels at the scholarly legerdemain and asks what is the trick: is the text really open to such diverse readings?

Fewell and Gunn's article provoked a fiery response from Sternberg[25] and an attempt to adjudicate between them by Noble.[26] It is not necessary to summarise the arguments here, but to concur with Noble that in many particulars Sternberg stands on firmer exegetical ground than his opponents. It is not true that the Hebrew verbs translated 'lay with her and humbled her' are merely descriptive and do not carry a strong condemnation of the deed as Fewell and Gunn assert. They are also wrong to argue that Shechem's speaking to Dinah's heart means that he touched her heart and did win her over. Though that clearly was his intention, there is nothing in the text to demonstrate he achieved it. So Fewell and Gunn's claim that she stayed in Shechem's house willingly is without foundation. On the other hand neither does the text say she was detained there: that is Sternberg's presumption.

Fewell and Gunn try to minimise Shechem's offence and maximise Dinah's acquiescence in her situation partly to justify Jacob's apparent indifference. If his daughter was happy, Jacob did not have to worry about the situation too much. After all Deuteronomy 22:28–29 prescribes marriage in cases of premarital intercourse. And since Judah married a Canaanite, Jacob would not have been worried about Dinah marrying Shechem.[27] Sternberg has no difficulty in showing this is a most unlikely reading of Genesis 34. Deuteronomy, in allowing marriage after premarital intercourse, is only envisaging what should be done if both parties are Israelite, for it strictly forbids intermarriage with the people of Canaan. Both Abraham and Isaac had strong views about avoiding intermarriage with Canaanites, while Judah's experience with Shua had disastrous consequences (38:1–11).[28] So here too Sternberg's interpretation is more plausible than Fewell and Gunn's: Jacob ought to have been worried by the prospect of his daughter marrying a Canaanite.

But to resolve these points of difference in Sternberg's favour is not to concede that his whole position is correct. There are too many gaps in the story to be sure how they ought to be filled: the presuppositions of the interpreter are liable to have a large effect on how these uncertainties are tackled. Fewell and Gunn appeal to a feminist worldview to substantiate their position, while Sternberg is adamant that a

[25] 'Biblical Poetics and Sexual Politics: From Reading to Counterreading', *JBL* 111 (1992), 463–88.

[26] Paul Noble, 'A "Balanced" Reading of the Rape of Dinah: Some Exegetical and Methodological Observations', *Bib Int* 4 (1996), 173–203.

[27] Fewell and Gunn, 'Tipping the Balance', 206, 210.

[28] Sternberg, 'Biblical Poetics and Sexual Politics', *JBL* 111 (1992), 484–5.

competent reader must not only understand the nuances of biblical Hebrew, but also understand the theology and ethics that inform the writers of the Old Testament.

> Each language reflects (some would say, conditions) a world view, and each representation carries an evaluation of the represented life. This interdependence holds truer than ever for the Bible, where none of the components (the language, the world, the ideology) leads an independent existence outside the text – as usual in modern writing – but all need to be recovered from the text, so that they stand or fall together.[29]

Failure to recognise or acknowledge the basic tenets of the biblical writers will produce incompetent readers. 'You must follow the implicit ground rules or exclude yourself. If anything, a reader unable or unwilling to postulate the articles of faith (from God downwards) will forfeit competence as a hopeless counterreader.'[30] It is Sternberg's appeal to the sense of Hebrew words in other contexts and his reliance on legal texts from Deuteronomy and Genesis against exogamy that give his interpretation the edge over Fewell and Gunn.

However, we argued in the previous chapters that we cannot appeal just to the law to establish the ethical expectations of the biblical writers. We need to consider the rhetorical purpose of each book and to recognise that the writers do not just evaluate their characters against the basic level of behaviour enshrined in the law, but against the ideal of the imitation of God and the characteristic virtues that the godly should embody.

Set against this wider background Genesis 34 is particularly problematic, so that it is not surprising that commentators have come to quite diverse conclusions. On the one hand Genesis does emphasise the sacred duty of Abraham's descendants to marry within the family and not to marry Canaanites. The longest tale in Genesis, often called the wooing of Rebekah, is a commentary on this point (Gen 24). Similarly Isaac and Rebekah despatched Jacob to Paddan-Aram to find a wife, because they said they could not stand the prospect of him marrying a local Hittite girl (27:46 – 28:2). It therefore seems certain that Dinah should not have had sexual relations with Shechem in any circumstances, simply because he was a Canaanite.

Additionally it seems highly likely that their offence was viewed as very serious because it was premarital. The law to which Fewell and Gunn appeal to show that ancient Israel handled such situations calmly does little to help their case. Not only does it not deal with mixed-race unions, but it imposes such penalties on premarital sex that it would have been the height of folly to indulge in it. Exodus 22:16–17 allows

[29] Sternberg, 'Biblical Poetics and Sexual Politics', 469.
[30] Sternberg, 'Biblical Poetics and Sexual Politics', 469.

the couple to marry if the man gives the marriage present to the girl's father. This marriage present, often equivalent to several years' wages (cf. Gen 29:18–20), was negotiated with the bride's father before betrothal. In such an irregular situation as Shechem and Dinah's the least punishment the man could hope to escape with was having to give an inflated marriage present. Shechem appears to recognise this when he says: 'Ask of me ever so much as marriage present and gift, and I will give according as you say to me; only give me the maiden to be my wife' (34:12).

However, the law in Exodus also allows the girl's father to refuse marriage and yet require the payment of the marriage present! In effect to demand enormous damages for the man's misbehaviour. Perhaps Shechem's final plea – 'only give me the maiden to be my wife' – reflects a fear that he could face such a sanction. Finally it is likely that where rape could be proved, the punishment of the man would be even more severe: this appears to be the situation in Deuteronomy 22:28–29, but this is not certain.[31] Nor is it certain that Dinah was raped rather than seduced.[32] But whatever the precise definition of Shechem's crime, there is no doubt that by the implied author's standards it was doubly serious, being both exogamous and premarital. It was not something that could or should have been ignored. Jacob's apparent unconcern was not the right response.

If the author did not believe Jacob should have turned a blind eye to Shechem's fault, does that mean he endorses the sons' revenge? In Chapter 3 we argued that one of the primary thrusts of Genesis is to advocate reconciliation between former enemies and peaceful relations between warring parties. In particular Joseph's reconciliation with his brothers and Jacob's with Esau suggested that the Israelite tribes should live together peaceably with each other and with the Edomites. Abraham is also portrayed as seeking peace with his nephew Lot, with Abimelech, king of Gerar and with the Hittites of Kiriath-arba. Likewise Isaac seeks a peaceable accommodation with Abimelech. Jacob before the Dinah affair had bought land from the sons of Hamor, which again implies that he was on good terms with them (33:19). It was Shechem who

[31] The relationship of the law in Deut 22:28–29 to that in Exod 22 is problematic. Deuteronomy would appear to be dealing with rape 'and seizes her', whereas in Exodus the woman consents 'if a man seduces' (so J. L. Saalschütz, *Das mosaische Recht*[2] (Berlin: Carl Heymann, 1853; reprinted 1974), 581; for the view that both cases assume the woman's consent see Hugenberger, *Marriage as Covenant*, 251–61. Deuteronomy requires witnesses, 'and they are found', but no witnesses are mentioned in Exodus. Could this be that in a consensual situation both parties agree to what happened, but in a violent one it is the woman's word against the man's? In any case Deuteronomy certainly penalises premarital intercourse very heavily by demanding fifty shekels (eight years' wages of a shepherd) and removing the right of divorce.

[32] L. M. Bechtel, 'What if Dinah is not Raped? (Genesis 34)', *JSOT* 62 (1994), 19–36.

upset the apple cart. But the brothers' overreaction made a bad situation worse, as Jacob puts it, 'you have made me odious to the inhabitants of the land' (34:30). But by denying the last word to Jacob and ending with the defiant protest, 'Should he treat our sister as a harlot', the author prevents moral closure and leaves the reader to ponder what should be done in a situation of competing moral imperatives: is the pursuit of peace or the vindication of a sister more important?[33] We are left to reflect for fifteen long chapters, until Jacob gives his final word in 49:5–7.

Our short-term conclusion must surely be that no one comes out of this episode very creditably on the Israelite side, let alone the Shechemite side. But despite making themselves odious to the Canaanites and failing to live by the law, let alone the higher ethic that the book of Genesis suggests the people of God should live by, Jacob and his sons escape scot-free. Instead of being wiped out by a counterattack as Jacob feared, 'a terror from God fell upon the cities that were round about them, so that they did not pursue the sons of Jacob' (Gen 35:5). Here as in many other Old Testament stories God treats his people much more kindly than they deserve in order to demonstrate his faithfulness to his promises.

The story of Gideon

In Chapter 4 we reviewed the rhetorical function of the book of Judges and accepted the common view that it portrays the religious and moral degeneration of the nation that could only be stopped by the establishment of the monarchy. We noticed that the first judge seemed to be nearly perfect morally and as a leader, whereas the last judge, Samson, was a caricature of all that was expected of a judge. The last few chapters of the book where there is no judge or leader of any sort show the nation dissolving into moral and political anarchy. But in between we have Gideon – according to some interpretations an outstanding deliverer of the nation, but according to others fatally flawed – reflecting the failings of Israel as a whole. How should his story be read? Is Gideon implicitly held up as an example to follow, or is his career a warning? By looking at another ambiguous tale we hope to derive principles that can be helpful in reading other problematic passages.

Within the Bible, comments on Gideon are very brief, just emphasising that God worked through him to deliver Israel from their oppressors. For Isaiah (9:4) the 'day of Midian' was one of the great

[33] It is evident that neither side are paragons of Old Testament virtue. Honest forthright speech is what the righteous should utter, cf. Chapter 5 above, but 'the sons of Jacob answered . . . deceitfully' (34:13). On the other hand fear of others is not justified either, because God was with Jacob and promised to keep him wherever he went (28:15), yet in this episode Jacob seems to be paralysed by fear from beginning to end.

triumphs of the past, which will be re-enacted when the new son of David comes (cf. Ps 83:9–12). Hebrews lists Gideon among the great heroes of the past, who 'through faith conquered kingdoms, enforced justice, received promises' (Heb 11:32–33). But usually the stress is on the persistent waywardness of the nation, despite which God rescued them from their oppressors (1 Sam 12:11; Neh 9:27–28; Pss 78:56-66; 106:34–46).

But outside Scripture Gideon has widely been perceived as an immaculate hero whose conduct is in every respect exemplary. Josephus as usual paints his career in glowing colours, 'a man of moderation and a model of every virtue'.[34] He leaves out those features that might not appeal to a Gentile reader, e.g. destroying the Baal altar, killing the Midianite kings, and making an ephod, while underlining his possession of the key virtues of wisdom, courage, temperance, justice and piety.

> . . . wisdom, as seen by his ability to use calculated reflection in making decisions; courage, as seen particularly by his ability to overcome the Midianites with a meager force of three hundred cowards; temperance, as seen by the modesty which he displays when he is approached to undertake his mission against the Midianites; justice as seen by the fact that all his pronouncements of judgement had binding weight; and piety, as seen by his being described as 'beloved of G–d'.[35]

This essentially uncritical praise of Gideon has dominated Christian approaches to Judges as well: commentators praise him for his faith and modesty, only his misuse of the ephod attracting censure, something already criticised in the text itself (Judg 8:27).

The holistic reading of Webb introduced a more nuanced perspective on the Gideon story. Webb divides the narrative of Gideon into two parts. In the first, chapters 6–7 Gideon is presented essentially positively, whereas chapter 8 draws attention to some of his negative traits. Webb notes the parallels to the call of Moses in Judges 6. Both are called when hiding from their enemies. Both are told 'I have sent you' (Judg 6:15; Exod 3:12). Like Moses Gideon protests that he is inadequate for the task (Judg 6:15; Exod 3:11). Both are reassured that God will be with them, receive a sign, and experience a fire theophany. Gideon's military tactics may echo Joshua's which he used against Jericho. He shows tact and diplomacy in handling the dispute with the Ephraimites. Even Gideon's fearfulness, which Webb points out is constantly drawn to the reader's attention, is seen by him as a positive feature in Gideon's character.[36]

[34] *Antiquities* 5. 230.

[35] Louis H. Feldman, 'Josephus' Portrait of Gideon', *Revue des études juives* 152 (1993), 27.

[36] B. G. Webb, *The Book of the Judges: An Integrated Reading* (JSOTSup 46, Sheffield: JSOT Press, 1987), 146–51.

> In this first major movement then, Gideon is a reluctant conscript, who distrusts his own competence and relies wholly upon Yahweh. In short, he is a model of Mosaic piety. He is commissioned by Yahweh and invested with Yahweh's spirit (6:34). The war in which he engages is holy war in which the victory is not his personal achievement but the gift of Yahweh.[37]

A different picture of Gideon emerges in chapter 8. He pursues the kings Zebah and Zalmunna in a ruthless vendetta. There is now no reference to Yahweh's guidance or empowerment, rather his success is achieved through his own strength of character and tactical skill. He is credited with saving Israel (8:22), whereas that honour is reserved to God alone (7:2). Similarly although he himself says that 'I will not rule over you . . . the LORD will rule over you', he looks like a king and acts like a king with his imperious manner, great wealth, many wives, and a son Abimelech, who succeeds him as ruler. However Webb is inclined to excuse the making of the ephod as 'an act of piety that goes wrong'.[38] Gideon had simply intended it to be a means of Israel consulting God so that theocratic rule would have been a reality. Unfortunately it became an object of worship. This is the final irony of the story: Gideon whose career began by overthrowing the worship of Baal at Ophrah ended his days presiding over the national apostasy.[39]

Amit is much more generous to Gideon. She regards him as the last of the delivering judges; she terms the next two major judges, Jephthah and Samson, the disappointing judges. But Gideon exemplifies the ideal saviour judge. Through the remarkable signs associated with his call and his spectacular victories achieved with minimal forces, God's involvement in Israel's salvation was made very clear.[40] And according to Amit Gideon was being quite honest when he declared he did not want to rule Israel, because the LORD was their true king. 'Gideon, on the other hand, replies that expectations of military deliverance must be placed upon God alone and not upon any human factor.'[41] The ephod was a means of securing continued direct divine guidance of Israel's affairs.

The only criticism of the ephod is found in 8:27b, 'All Israel played the harlot after it there, and it became a snare to Gideon and his family.'

[37] Webb, *Judges*, 151.

[38] Webb, *Judges*, 153.

[39] Webb, *Judges*, 153.

[40] 'The abundance of signs is not by chance. Its function is to lead the readers, together with the heroes of the narrated world, to the conclusion that Israel was saved by God's will and power, and that Gideon the deliverer is none other than a messenger who was set up by God, and who relies entirely upon God's encouraging signs.' Amit, *Judges*, 235; cf. 245.

[41] Amit, *Judges*, 97.

This comment is quite out of character with the rest of the Gideon cycle and 'is inconsistent with the positive atmosphere that accompanies the making of the ephod as a reaction of Gideon to the proposal of kingship'.[42] This leads Amit to argue that 8:27b is a later editorial insertion to explain why the nation had to be punished by the tyrannical rule of Abimelech which follows in the next chapter. By this interpolation 'some editor or copier attempted to justify God's behavior in relation to Gideon'.[43] Elsewhere in the Gideon story Amit finds no criticism of him. She praises his treatment of Succoth and Penuel as decisive and determined. 'Gideon chose to mete out to them a severe punishment, "that they may hear and fear".'[44] Amit observes that the author often draws attention to Gideon's fearfulness, which is even more pronounced than Barak's. She finds his lack of confidence in the fleece scene particularly surprising: after 'his possession by the Spirit of God and the mustering of the army . . . there should not be any reason for expressions of hesitation on his part'.[45] But she does not regard it as a defect in his character or lack of faith. Thus for Amit the characterisation of Gideon in Judges is almost entirely positive.

In contrast O'Connell sees Gideon as a flawed hero. He argues that Gideon's failings are reflected in the nation as a whole and particularly in those of his son Abimelech. The minor weaknesses of Gideon become major faults in Abimelech, so that by reading the two stories alongside each other the reader should become sensitive to the author's value judgements.

The first task given to Gideon after his call is the destruction of the altar to Baal and the Asherah near it. But already there are hints of future developments in his execution of this task: he does it by night and lies low when the sacrilege is discovered. In Gideon's reluctance to oppose Baal publicly O'Connell sees the seeds of three future errors. First, it foreshadows his cultic syncretism which climaxed in the worship of the ephod. Second, overfriendliness with the Canaanites led to him taking a Canaanite concubine and the birth of his fratricidal son Abimelech. Third, it hints at the ruthless reprisals Gideon will exact later upon those who fail to support him. Gideon's diffidence is also reprehensible and 'reflects an underlying lack of confidence in YHWH. He is afraid either to confront openly the foreign cult in his home city or to oppose the foreign threat in his tribal region'.[46]

O'Connell, like Amit, sees a parallel between Gideon manufacturing an ephod from the gold earrings that the Israelites took from the Midianites and Aaron making a golden calf from the earrings that Israel

[42] Amit, *Judges*, 230; cf. Hebrew original, 215.
[43] Amit, *Judges*, 232.
[44] Amit, *Judges*, 229, 236.
[45] Amit, *Judges*, 227.
[46] O'Connell, *Rhetoric*, 155.

had acquired from the Egyptians. O'Connell argues that this narrative analogy is deliberate and designed to portray Gideon as an instigator of cultic corruption.[47]

Furthermore Gideon's fearfulness and instability parallels the nation's (6:8–10; cf. 11, 13).

> Thus Gideon, like Barak, is a microcosm of Israel's reluctance to follow YHWH wholeheartedly. Gideon's reluctance to follow YHWH stems both from his fearfulness . . . and from his unwillingness to shun foreign cultic practices (8:27a). Israel's reluctance to follow YHWH could likewise be construed as stemming from their fearfulness to engage the enemy, exhibited in their retreat to the caves (6:2), and from their unwillingness to shun foreign cultic practices (6:10b). The irony of this characterization is that YHWH raises up a deliverer for Israel who is none other than Israel in miniature.[48]

But in the story of Gideon God's patience towards him despite all his faults and hesitations repeatedly emerges. 'YHWH is shown to be exceedingly gracious and patient towards both parties . . . namely Israel and Gideon.'[49] Earlier judges had their faults, but Gideon's were more serious: yet God still delivered his people through him showing how unmerited was his continuing kindness towards them.[50]

We could characterise the interpretations of Webb and O'Connell as the flawed-hero approach. It has been developed even further by Block,[51] who lists no less than sixteen points where Gideon's words or actions seem inappropriate in a divinely appointed deliverer of Israel. He notes Gideon's cynicism (6:13),[52] his demand for a sign (6:17), the Baal shrine at his family home (6:25), his fanatical pro-Baal neighbours (6:30), his reluctance to fight Midian despite being clothed with the Spirit (6:34–40), his continued fear (7:9–10), his appeal to the tribes to attack Midian when victory had been promised to the three hundred (7:7, 23), the non-mention of Yahweh's involvement in chapter 8 except in flippant asides (8:7, 19, 23), his ruthlessness towards Succoth and Penuel (8:16–17), his vendetta against Zebah and Zalmunna (8:19), and his demand that his young son slay them (8:20–21).

Block develops three points at greater length. In 6:32 Gideon's father apparently renames him Jerubbaal, 'Let Baal contend against him'. Block suggests that this is an *ad hoc* reinterpretation of Gideon's real

[47] O'Connell, *Rhetoric*, 162.

[48] O'Connell, *Rhetoric*, 163.

[49] O'Connell, *Rhetoric*, 168.

[50] O'Connell, *Rhetoric*, 171.

[51] Daniel I. Block, 'Will the Real Gideon Please Stand Up? Narrative Style and Intention in Judges 6–9', *JETS* 40 (1997), 353–66.

[52] George F. Moore, *A Critical and Exegetical Commentary on Judges* (ICC, Edinburgh: T&T Clark, 1895), 185, found scepticism in Gideon's words.

name Jerubbaal, which would naturally be interpreted 'Let Baal contend' or 'Let Baal prove himself to be great'. This would be the sort of name a worshipper of Baal would give to his child to honour the deity. The true legacy of Gideon is revealed in chapter 9, where his son Abimelech succeeds him and replicates his father's faults on a greater scale including the official worship of Baal-berith. Interestingly this chapter consistently refers to Gideon as Jerubbaal, implying that 'the god after whom he was named has taken up the challenge proposed by Joash (6:31–32) and, sad to say, has apparently successfully contended for himself and won'.[53]

Second, Block sees Gideon's apparent rejection of kingship as hypocritical, for despite his pious 'I will not rule over you . . . the LORD will rule over you', he certainly takes all the trappings of kingship: 1,700 shekels of gold, the royal pendants and the purple garments of the Midianite kings. Like other oriental kings he organises the cult, by setting up the ephod. He resides in 'his own house', which must have been a palace to accommodate his many wives and seventy sons: this apparent allusion to Deuteronomy 17:17 (the king must 'not multiply wives to himself') indicates not only that he was a king but that he flouted the law. Taking a Canaanite concubine was another breach of the law.

Third, the name given to his concubine's son – Abimelech – is suspicious. It could mean 'The king (=God) is my father', 'The king (=Gideon) is my father', or 'Melek (=Canaanite god) is my father'. Only the first interpretation absolves Gideon of syncretism or the claim to being a king. In that all the other Abimelechs in the Old Testament are non-Israelites Block thinks an innocent interpretation is unlikely. In the light of all this evidence Block finds it impossible to regard Gideon as a man of strong and pious devotion.

Once again the diversity of interpretation of these stories is striking. Is it possible to adjudicate between the very positive evaluation of Gideon by the tradition and modern interpreters such as Amit, and the negative assessments of writers such as Webb and Block? It is very difficult for so much depends on the assumptions of the reader. Sixteen reasons for supposing Gideon is not the paragon judge sounds impressive, but many of Block's points could be given a more innocent interpretation, as Block himself is aware. He hears 6:13, 'if the LORD is with us, why then has all this befallen us?', as a cynical response by Gideon to the angelic greeting. But he then observes '6:13 is certainly correct theologically, but the tone in his voice is quite wrong'.[54] Of course in a written text it is impossible to recapture the tone of voice. Detecting irony is another uncertain business and this makes Klein's

[53] Block, 'Will the Real Gideon', 365.
[54] Block, 'Will the Real Gideon', 359.

book, *The Triumph of Irony in the Book of Judges*[55] less than persuasive at times: what may strike one reader as ironic may seem the plain truth to others.

The Achilles heel in the very positive reading of Gideon is 8:27b 'all Israel played the harlot after it (the ephod) and it became a snare to Gideon and to his family'. As we noted above, Amit regards this as a later editorial addition to the text representing a negative judgement on Gideon, which links the fate of Abimelech to the sin of his father Gideon, whereas the earlier text simply related Abimelech's death to his own sin.[56] This hangs together with her view of the diachronic development of the book of Judges. But as we have argued earlier, we are not interested in the interpretation of events in the sources of Genesis or Judges, but in the way that the events are understood by the implied author which is expressed in the final form of the text. To argue that an earlier version of the Gideon story saw him as a perfect hero is no more relevant for our discussion here than it was for Gunkel to argue that the original teller of the story now found in Genesis 12:10–20 admired Abram's ability as a liar. It is enough to admit that the latest redactor of Judges 6–8 recognised Gideon's failing in this respect to dent the myth of him as the ideal judge. Nevertheless it raises the question as to whether allowing the ephod to be worshipped was Gideon's only mistake in the eyes of the implied author or whether this is just the tip of an iceberg of criticism.

There are three reasons for supposing that the Webb/Block interpretation of Gideon as the flawed hero is nearer the implied author's understanding than the alternative idealisation of him.[57] The first is that stories of Gideon and his son Abimelech form a distinct unit within the book, the tale of the house of Gideon. It appears that parallels between the careers of Abimelech and Gideon are deliberately drawn to shed light on each other. This means that some of the major faults of Abimelech are prefigured in the life of Gideon, so that where it is clear that the author condemns the former it is likely that he is also criticising the latter. The mistakes of Gideon are writ large in the career of Abimelech.

Gideon's public career began by him destroying the altar of Baal; the first thing that happened after his death was that the people of Israel made Baal-berith, the god of Shechem, their god (6:27–28; 8:33). Gideon was invited to rule over the men of Israel in the wake of his victory over the Midianites: Abimelech seized power over Shechem

[55] JSOTSup 68, Sheffield: JSOT Press, 1988.

[56] Amit, *Judges*, 230–2.

[57] For another example of a narrative that is superficially positive in its description of its hero, but in fact profoundly critical, see Jerome T. Walsh, 'The Characterization of Solomon in 1 Kgs 1–5', *CBQ* 57 (1995), 471–93.

(8:22; 9:1–6). Gideon took revenge on seventy-seven elders of Succoth, whereas Abimelech killed seventy of his brothers (8:14; 9:5). Gideon broke down the tower of Penuel and slew its men, but Abimelech burnt down the stronghold of Shechem, 'so that all the people died, about a thousand men and women' (8:17; 9:49). Gideon's last campaign ended with him inviting his son 'a youth' to kill Zebah and Zalmunna and his son refusing; Abimelech's last campaign ended with him asking 'a youth' his armour-bearer to kill him so that he could not have been said to die at a woman's hands, and so he died. It seems likely that the dark deeds of Abimelech cast a shadow over the parallel actions of his father.

The second reason for holding that Judges does not regard Gideon as beyond criticism arises from the express criticism of the apostate worship of the ephod, which he apparently sponsored. One way of reading 8:27 is that Gideon made the ephod in all innocence, and quite unexpectedly and contrary to his intentions 'all Israel played the harlot after it'. But this surely presupposes a rather naive Gideon with very little control over the people, who have just invited him to rule over them. Furthermore the description of the manufacture of the ephod does sound uncannily like that of the golden calf. Both were made from earrings taken from foreigners, and both became very quickly a focus of illicit worship.[58] So it is doubtful whether the author regarded the making of the ephod as beyond cavil: there is a suspicion of compromise about it at least. And looking back earlier in his career there are other points where Gideon seems less than whole-hearted in his obedience to the LORD. When first told to destroy the altar of Baal, he delayed till night-time, 'because he was too afraid of his family and the men of the town to do it by day' (6:27). Furthermore although he is the only judge to have been called by the angel of the LORD, he demands and is given quite a few signs to reassure him, which are not really necessary. Then in the great battle against the Midianites he seems to disobey God's directions at certain points. He summoned support from Asher, Zebulon and Naphtali, but then the LORD sent all save 300 home again 'lest Israel vaunt themselves against me, saying "My own hand has delivered me"' (7:2). So Gideon duly sends them home, but immediately after the spectacular rout of the Midianites, he again summons even more tribes than before, Naphtali, Asher, all Manasseh and Ephraim (7:23–24). Indeed one may ask why Gideon told the 300 chosen men to shout 'For the LORD and for Gideon!'; the addition of 'for Gideon' would seem to be out of kilter with God's express wish that only he should be glorified in this victory (7:2). These deviations between commands and their fulfilment may appear slight, but when set against the exact obedience of Noah, Moses and Joshua, they may

[58] Cf. O'Connell, *Rhetoric*, 162.

be significant and may have led eventually to Gideon accepting the rule over Israel that he admitted belonged to the LORD alone (8:23).

Finally if one assumes that the author of Judges presupposed a similar pattern of virtuous behaviour as Genesis and the wisdom books, there are two areas where Gideon clearly falls short of the ideal. All readers are struck by his fearfulness. Despite a theophanic call Gideon repeatedly has to be reassured that God is with him and he will succeed. He is afraid to destroy the Baal altar by day (6:27). After being clothed with the Spirit he needs to be reassured by the wet and dry fleece sign (6:34–40). Then just before the battle, too afraid to go alone, he takes his servant Purah to spy on the Midianites (7:9–14). Set against the commands of the law and fearlessness of Joshua, Gideon's timidity stands out: he does not really believe God will do what he has promised (cf. Deut 20:1–9; Josh 1:1–9). Indeed his own challenge to the troops that anyone fearful should return home (Judg 7:3) would have ruled himself out had he acted on it!

The other area where Gideon seems to fall somewhat short is in the ferocity with which he takes revenge. War is inevitably brutal and bloody, but that does not mean that anything goes: Amos' oracles against the nations particularly focus on war crimes, presupposing that every ancient nation knew that there were certain rules that ought to govern the conduct of war (Amos 1–2). Deuteronomy, despite its advocacy of holy war against the Canaanites, does encourage magnanimity in the conduct of war against other nations if they are prepared to surrender (Deut 20:10–20), a policy clearly followed by Joshua (Josh 9). Genesis too encourages peaceable relations with Israel's neighbours and reconciliation with former enemies. But Gideon is portrayed in Judges 8 as pursuing a personal vendetta against the Midianites and taking harsh revenge on Israelite cities that had not supported him wholeheartedly. And as we have already noted, his son was even more belligerent. So although 'the land had rest for forty years in the days of Gideon', the writer leaves the impression that it was a rather uneasy peace. Though Gideon was a better ruler than his son, he fell short of the standards of his predecessors, especially Joshua, or the ideals expressed in such passages as Psalm 72.

In short there are many aspects of Gideon's character and actions that raise questions: like the other judges he is not meant to be imitated in every detail. But he is a great example of how God can act through less than perfect people. The story of Gideon, like the rest of Judges, demonstrates God's power over Israel's enemies and their gods. It demonstrates the LORD's faithfulness to his covenant despite Israel's infidelity and his patience towards those whom he calls to lead his people despite their own wavering faith and obedience.

7

NEW TESTAMENT PERSPECTIVES

> We will read the Bible seriously only when we use it to guide our thought towards a *comprehensive* moral viewpoint, and not merely to articulate disconnected moral claims. We must look within it not only for moral bricks, but for indications of the order in which the bricks belong together.[1]

O'Donovan's comment applies not just to naive appeals to proof texts to establish 'biblical' principles of ethics, but to many serious studies of biblical ethics. We have noted the blind spot of many Old Testament scholars towards the ethics of the narratives with all their attention being focused on the legal, prophetic and wisdom texts. The same oversight tends to characterise New Testament scholarship in its approach to Old Testament ethical teaching: much attention is given to the law and the prophets whose importance for the understanding of New Testament texts is inescapable, but the great storyline, in which the law and the prophets are just episodes, rarely receives the attention it deserves.

Yet the First Gospel begins with a genealogy of Jesus that traces his origin back to Abraham, while St Luke takes his genealogy back to Adam (Luke 3:23–38). Jesus himself refers to a variety of characters from the Old Testament to make points for his contemporary hearers: Noah, Abraham, Lot's wife, Moses, David, Solomon, the Queen of Sheba, Elijah, Elisha and Jonah, which suggests that he saw the whole Hebrew Bible as normative and relevant. Most interesting is the remark in Matthew 23:35 (cf. Luke 11:51) 'from the blood of innocent Abel to the blood of Zechariah the son of Barachiah', the first and last murder victims in the Hebrew canon:[2] this suggests reading the whole Old Testament for its moral implications. Similarly Paul frequently mentions Adam and Abraham as archetypes of sin and faith. He views Israel in the wilderness as a type of the Church, so that the latter should learn from the former's mistakes (1 Cor 10:1–11). The epistles of James, Peter, John and Jude, and particularly the epistle to the Hebrews, make

[1] Oliver O'Donovan, *Resurrection and Moral Order: An Outline for Evangelical Ethics* (Leicester: InterVarsity Press, 1986), 200.

[2] Gen 4:10; 2 Chr 24:22. 'Abel's martyrdom is the first, and comes near the beginning of the first book of the canon; Zechariah's martyrdom is the last, and comes near the end of the last book. All the martyrdoms from Abel to Zechariah are therefore equivalent to all the martyrdoms from one end of the Jewish Bible to the other.' Roger T. Beckwith, *The Old Testament Canon of the New Testament Church* (London: SPCK, 1985), 215.

frequent reference to Old Testament stories not simply to show the theological continuity between the testaments, but to draw out the ethical implications of the Old Testament for the New Testament Church. Though most often these appeals to Scripture seem to be designed to encourage global virtues such as faith or warn against general vices such as disobedience, quite specific sins, e.g. sexual immorality, greed, idolatry, or positive virtues such as hospitality, modesty, perseverance, and prayerfulness are illustrated by reference to Old Testament narratives. Encapsulating the general view of the New Testament writers towards the reading of the Old is 2 Timothy 3:16: 'All scripture is inspired by God and profitable for teaching, for reproof, for correction, and for training in righteousness, that the man of God may be complete, equipped for every good work.' Here the value of the whole Old Testament Scripture for ethical instruction is clearly highlighted. But as is well known, the ethics of the two testaments are often held to be at odds with each other. Marcion, though frequently execrated, is often covertly followed.[3] In this chapter, then, we wish to review the New Testament's use of Old Testament narratives for ethics, and ask how far its fresh perspectives involve radically new moral stances.

Ben Witherington in *Paul's Narrative Thought World* has drawn attention to the importance of the Old Testament story for Paul's theology. In his vision of human history there are four major stories: (1) the story of a world gone wrong, i.e. the fall of Adam and the consequences described in Genesis 1–11; (2) the story of Israel in that world; (3) the story of Christ; 'and (4) the story of Christians, including Paul himself, which arises out of all three of these previous stories and is the first full instalment of the story of a world set right again.'[4] Paul's theology is set within the framework of this grand narrative which begins with creation and ends with Christ's second advent and the resurrection of the dead. For Jews and Paul the story of salvation began with the call of Abraham. With him began the process of the retrieval of fallen mankind and the restoration of Eden. 'When Paul thinks of the human beginnings of paradise regained, he thinks of that first great example of faith. Paul does not believe that there are several stories of God's redeeming work; there is essentially only one that leads from Abraham to Christ and beyond.'[5]

In defining a right relationship with God Paul does not think of law courts, but of 'God's gracious choice of Abraham and Abraham's grateful trusting response'.[6] It is the unity and continuity of God's saving

[3] Cf. O'Donovan's unease with the storyline of Joshua, *Resurrection*, 158.

[4] Ben Witherington III, *Paul's Narrative Thought World: The Tapestry of Tragedy and Triumph* (Louisville: Westminster/John Knox Press, 1994), 5.

[5] Witherington, *Paul's Narrative*, 38.

[6] Witherington, *Paul's Narrative*, 38.

purpose that explains Paul's use of Scripture. The whole Old Testament looks forward to Christ and thus is especially relevant to the followers of Christ, who constitute the final community of God. 'For Paul there is one Holy Writ for all God's people and one continuous people of God from Abraham through Moses to Christ and beyond.'[7] It is this unity of God's purpose and the continuity of his people that allows Paul to draw all sorts of analogies between the experiences of Israel in the Old Testament and the Church in the New. In Romans 4 Paul sees Abraham as the paradigm for all true believers.[8] Romans 5–6 make heavy use of the story of Adam,[9] while chapters 9–11 are a long reflection on the history of Israel.[10] Witherington observes that, unlike much Jewish thinking on the Old Testament which emphasises the roles of Moses and David in their history, Paul's thought is dominated by Adam and Abraham. He suggests that this was because Paul was 'trying to ground his own telling of the drama of salvation in the more universal stories . . . that would be more congenial for Gentiles to appropriate, identify with, and in some respects model themselves on'.[11] But whatever Paul's reason for focusing on these stories more than others in the Old Testament, Witherington is in no doubt that the principle controlling Paul's thought is the oneness of God, of his people and his plan of salvation. This enables Paul to draw all sorts of analogies between the Old Testament and the New without any allegorical contrivance.[12]

Witherington is primarily interested in the structure of Paul's theology and how it is embedded in his view of saving history that culminates in Christ. Apart from such major issues as faith and obedience, ethical concerns are secondary to Paul's thought, at least as he is conventionally expounded.[13] But given his understanding of the unity of God, the divine purpose and the people of God, one would expect him to find a unity of ethic before and after Christ. The one God who revealed himself to his people before Christ was the same God who revealed himself in Christ.

[7] Witherington, *Paul's Narrative*, 38.

[8] Witherington, *Paul's Narrative*, 43.

[9] Witherington, *Paul's Narrative*, 251.

[10] Witherington, *Paul's Narrative*, 62.

[11] Witherington, *Paul's Narrative*, 129–30.

[12] Witherington, *Paul's Narrative*, 52.

[13] Rosner points to the scholarly neglect of Paul's dependence on the Old Testament as a source of his ethics. He shows in a detailed study of 1 Cor 5–7 that Paul is constantly relying on the ethical norms of the Old Testament, especially Deuteronomy and the prophets. Brian S. Rosner, *Paul, Scripture and Ethics* (Arbeiten zur Geschichte des antiken Judentums und des Urchristentums 22, Leiden: Brill, 1994), 12. Tomson notes how Paul's interest in ethics pervades his epistles. He likens 1 Corinthians to *responsa*, letters written in answer to halakhic questions by medieval rabbis, and notes that according to early Jewish tradition Gamaliel (Paul's teacher) and Shimon, Gamaliel's son, wrote such letters. Peter J. Tomson, *Paul and the Jewish Law: Halakha in the Letters of the Apostle to the Gentiles* (Assen: Van Gorcum, 1990), 86.

Thus it is likely that Paul expected the same principles to govern the behaviour of the people of God before and after Christ. This is clearly his argument when it comes to faith and works: as Abraham was justified by faith without works, so is the Christian believer.

The same is true when it comes to the details of behaviour. In 1 Corinthians 10 Paul draws out four lessons from the stories in Exodus and Numbers: 'Do not be idolaters as some of them were' (1 Cor 10:7; cf. Exod 32); 'We must not indulge in immorality as some of them did' (1 Cor 10:8; cf. Num 25); 'We must not put the Lord to the test, as some of them did'(1 Cor 10:9; cf. Num 21:4–9); 'Nor grumble as some of them did' (1 Cor 10:10; cf. Num 16). This chapter is remarkable for the way it identifies the experiences of the exodus generation of the Israelites with those of the Corinthian church. Passing through the Red Sea is equated with Christian baptism and the manna from heaven with the bread of the eucharist. More striking still is the identification of the rock which brought forth water in the wilderness with the accompanying presence of Christ.[14]

But just as remarkable is the familiarity it presupposes with the details of the wilderness wanderings. Paul does not mention the making or worship of the golden calf when condemning idolatry: he simply refers to the eating and dancing that followed its creation. One rather marginal quote was enough to identify the episode in question. The references to the incidents with Baal Peor, the fiery serpents and the rebellions of Korah, Dathan and Abiram are equally allusive. Anyone who did not know the stories of Numbers very well would hardly see the point of these allusions, let alone find them persuasive arguments in favour of Paul's ethic. This passage shows that the Corinthian church was well versed in the Old Testament, knew its stories intimately and recognised their authoritative relevance.

We have already noted that Paul's preferred appeal was to the stories of Adam and Abraham, probably because they appeared more easily applicable to Gentiles. But in these cases too he seems to presuppose a close acquaintance with the details of each story. His discussion of the proper demeanour of men and women in worship is based on a close reading of Genesis 1–2 (1 Cor 11:2–15; cf. 2 Cor 11:3). He argues that since Abraham was pronounced righteous (Gen 15:6) before he was circumcised (Gen 17:24–27), this shows the primacy of faith (Rom 4). Later in the same chapter he draws out the nature of faith by discussing a detail in the story. 'He did not weaken in faith when he considered his own body, which was as good as dead because he was about a hundred years old' (Rom 4:19). Later when he discusses the mystery of the Jewish rejection of Christ, he spends much time on the

[14] For the pervasiveness of this type of approach in the New Testament, see Anthony T. Hanson, *Jesus Christ in the Old Testament* (London: SPCK, 1965).

family feuds and intrigues that characterised the behaviour of Abraham's descendants (Rom 9:6–13).

Other New Testament writers also seem to expect their readers to be intimately aware of Old Testament narratives and be alert to their ethical implications. The epistle of James concentrates on issues of behaviour to such an extent that it feels like an Old Testament wisdom book. He of course stresses Abraham's good works as well as his faith, citing his readiness to sacrifice Isaac as an illustration. He mentions Rahab's welcome of the spies as another example of good works (Jas 2:21–25). The prophets and Job are cited as exemplars of steadfastness under suffering (Jas 5:10–11), and Elijah of persistence in prayer (Jas 5:17). Once again very little extra information is given: James expects his readers to be totally familiar with these stories and to recognise their relevance.

In a similar way the epistles of Peter, John and Jude and the book of Revelation allude to Old Testament stories to underline their points. For example: 'if he rescued righteous Lot, greatly distressed by the licentiousness of the wicked . . . then the Lord knows how to rescue the godly from trial' (2 Pet 2:7–9); 'Balaam loved gain from wrong-doing, but was rebuked for his own transgression; a dumb ass spoke with human voice and restrained the prophet's madness' (2 Pet 2:15–16); 'Cain . . . murdered his brother . . . Because his own deeds were evil and his brother's righteous' (1 John 3:12); 'Woe to them! For they walk in the way of Cain, and abandon themselves for the sake of gain to Balaam's error, and perish in Korah's rebellion' (Jude 11). Once again the terse allusiveness of most of the references to the Old Testament shows that the authors presuppose their readers will be most familiar with them and be able to identify their situation with that of their predecessors.

As Witherington pointed out in the case of Paul this identification of the contemporary New Testament scene with the Old Testament situation arises out of a conviction of the oneness of God's saving purpose and the unity of the people of God before and after Christ. This same conviction is expressed most vividly in the epistle to the Hebrews which abounds with allusions to Old Testament heroes and the encouragement their example offers to the New Testament believer. Whereas other books of the New Testament tend to draw attention to the mistakes of the past as warnings to the present, Hebrews is balanced towards the positive. It does of course contain dire warnings against apostasy, 'Take care, brethren, lest there be in you an evil unbelieving heart' as there was among the followers of Moses (Heb 3:12–19; cf. 12:25–29). But the positive notes are much more dominant.

Jesus 'was faithful . . . just as Moses also was faithful in God's house' (Heb 3:2); Aaron 'was called by God' (5:4); 'Abraham having patiently endured, obtained the promise' (6:15). Chapter 11 is totally given over to a review of those who by faith persevered and overcame great odds – Abel, Noah, Abraham, Sarah, Jacob, Joseph, Moses, Rahab – and then concludes with this peroration:

> And what more shall I say? For time would fail me to tell of Gideon, Barak, Samson, Jephthah, of David and Samuel and the prophets – who through faith conquered kingdoms, enforced justice, received promises, stopped the mouths of lions, quenched raging fire, escaped the edge of the sword, won strength out of weakness, became mighty in war, put foreign armies to flight . . .
>
> Therefore since we are surrounded by so great a cloud of witnesses . . . let us run with perseverance the race that is set before us. (Heb 11:32–34; 12:1)

Once again it is noticeable that the author presupposes not just a familiarity with the stories of the Old Testament but that there is a continuity between those people and his readers. They are part of the one people of God sharing in one story of salvation. That is why the achievements of the Israelites of the past should inspire the Christians of the first century.

But can this theological continuity be maintained in the realm of ethics? Does not the New Testament advocate a quite different stance in such areas as the food laws, marriage and divorce, and violence? We shall conclude our study by looking afresh at these issues, and how far they require us to modify the ethical continuity apparently assumed by New Testament writers.

The food laws exemplify concepts such as purity and uncleanness which to the modern mind have little obvious connection with morality. But to understand the different approaches of the Old and New Testaments we do need to define what constituted purity and cleanness and how sin and uncleanness were related.

The rules about purity and cleanness are clearly set out in the Old Testament, but penetrating the rationale behind them has proved more difficult. However, the introduction of anthropological methods of enquiry has shed much light on the biblical notions, for similar ideas of purity and uncleanness are found in many traditional societies and serve to define hierarchies, acceptable and unacceptable modes of behaviour and even the boundaries of society itself.[15]

[15] Mary Douglas, *Purity and Danger* (London: Routledge & Kegan Paul, 1966), was a seminal work to which all modern discussions of biblical notions of impurity are deeply indebted. These include E. Feldman, *Biblical and Post-Biblical Defilement and Mourning: Law as Theology* (New York: Ktav, 1977); Walter Houston, *Purity and Monotheism: Clean and Unclean Animals in Biblical Law* (JSOTSup 140, Sheffield: JSOT Press, 1993); Philip P. Jenson, *Graded Holiness: A Key to the Priestly Conception of the World* (JSOTSup 106, Sheffield: JSOT Press, 1992); G. J. Wenham, *The Book of Leviticus* (Grand Rapids: Eerdmans, 1979); D. P. Wright, 'Unclean and Clean (OT)', *Anchor Bible Dictionary* VI, 729–41.

The Old Testament traces the knowledge of the distinction between clean and unclean back to primeval times,[16] for Noah was told to take into the ark seven pairs of every type of clean animal and one pair of each unclean animal (Gen 7:2–3). But the detailed regulations about purity are nearly all contained in the book of Leviticus 11–15, 21–22.[17]

The key principle is that God is the supremely holy being, and anyone who wishes to come into his presence must be holy too. But uncleanness is a bar to holiness: indeed if any unholy person comes into contact with the holy, he will die, as Uzzah did when he touched the ark of the covenant (e.g. 2 Sam 6:6–7). Numbers 4 is concerned that if the Levites just see the ark, they may die. It is therefore of vital importance to know what constitutes uncleanness, which has a variety of causes and different degrees of severity. The basic idea is that the clean may enter God's presence in worship, but the unclean must not. Domesticated clean animals may be sacrificed, but others may not. Only 'clean' people, i.e. those unpolluted by discharges or other problems should enter the sanctuary to offer sacrifice. Leviticus 11–22 gives a full treatment of these issues.

Leviticus 11 classifies living creatures into clean and unclean. Clean may be eaten, and some of the clean creatures may be sacrificed, but unclean may not. Cud-chewing animals with split hooves (e.g. cattle, sheep), are clean and may be eaten, but others (e.g. pigs, camels, rock badgers) are unclean. Other rules define which birds and aquatic creatures are unclean.

This sort of uncleanness is quite benign. It just means these creatures may not be eaten. Unclean creatures do not pollute unless they are dead. You do not become unclean by touching a live camel, for example. But all animals, whether clean or unclean when alive, when dead will make those who touch them unclean (Lev 11:28, 31, 39). Even more polluting are human corpses. So holy people like priests and Nazirites are forbidden to mourn for the dead, lest they make themselves unclean (Lev 21:1–12; Num 6:1–12). Laity who become unclean by touching a corpse remain so for a week and must undergo a special decontamination rite as prescribed in Numbers 19: failure to do so may lead to being 'cut off', that is premature death.

[16] The idea certainly antedates the Old Testament, for concepts of cleanness and impurity are well attested among Israel's neighbours such as the Egyptians, Mesopotamians and the Hittites.

[17] The date of these laws is problematic. The text traces them back to the covenant at Sinai (thirteenth century B.C.), but standard critical theory places their redaction in the fifth century. But like many other aspects of pentateuchal criticism this is now a matter of intense debate; cf. G. J. Wenham, 'Pondering the Pentateuch', *The Face of OT Studies: A Survey of Contemporary Approaches* (ed. David W. Baker and Bill T. Arnold, Grand Rapids/Leicester: Baker/Apollos, 1999), 116–44.

Some bodily discharges also make people unclean. Mothers are polluted by the puerperal discharge for forty days after giving birth to a son, and for eighty days after bearing a daughter (Lev 12). Sexual intercourse pollutes both parties for a day and menstruation makes a woman unclean for a week (Lev 15:18–19). Long-term discharges from the sexual organs make people unclean for as long as the discharge continues.

Skin diseases, often mistranslated as leprosy, may also make a person unclean. Psoriasis or eczema could produce some of the symptoms described in Leviticus 13. It is the symptoms that determine whether a skin complaint is clean or not: active, sore, peeling conditions make a person unclean, whereas stable conditions, e.g. baldness or leukoderma, are classed as clean. Similar principles are applied to determine whether moulds or fungi (again called in Hebrew 'skin disease') affecting garments or houses are serious. Anyone suffering from a polluting skin condition remains unclean until it clears up. In general short-term human uncleanness may be cleared by waiting a day and washing in water. When a condition causing long-term uncleanness clears up, e.g. skin disease, the sufferer has also to offer a sacrifice to be ritually clean again (Lev 14).

Whereas the above naturally occurring conditions pollute the person involved and anyone he or she comes in contact with, some sins may cause a much more serious pollution; they pollute not just the sinner but the land and even the sanctuary itself.[18] For example Leviticus 18 gives a long list of forbidden sexual relationships including incest, adultery, homosexuality and bestiality, which are said to pollute those involved and the land (Lev 18:24–25). It was these practices that Leviticus says led to the previous inhabitants of Canaan being 'vomited out'. So it warns Israel that if they do the same, they may be exiled from the land or the offender will be cut off, i.e. die by supernatural causes (Lev 18:25, 28–29). Idols and idolatry are also polluting. Worship of other gods, consulting the dead or possession of idols makes the perpetrators, the land, and the sanctuary unclean (Lev 18:21; 20:2–5; Ezek 20:7, 18). Homicide is another sin that pollutes the land (Num 35:33–34). The uncleanness caused by these sins is so serious that only the death of the sinner suffices to cleanse it.

These different types of uncleanness may be classified according to the severity of their effects. At the one extreme is the uncleanness that occurs naturally, which needs no cleansing, such as that associated with certain animals. Then come the uncleannesses that can be dealt with simply by washing. More serious, but still natural, are the types of uncleanness associated with bodily discharges, which require the

[18] On moral impurity see Jonathan Klawans, 'The Impurity of Immorality in Ancient Judaism', *JJS* 48 (1997), 1–16.

offering of sacrifice. Finally at the other extreme is the uncleanness generated by idolatry, homicide, or illicit sex, which can be countered only by the death of the offender and the day of atonement ceremonies. Often the milder forms of uncleanness are classified as ritual, and the more serious as moral. However it is preferable to see them as forming a continuum.

Tolerated		*Prohibited*	
Nonsacrificial	Sacrificial	Unintentional	Intentional
e.g. menstruation	e.g. skin disease	e.g. forgotten cleansing	e.g. homicide, idolatry

Holiness

Opposite uncleanness in the ritual system stands holiness; a look at this concept may clarify the Old Testament understanding of uncleanness.

Holiness is intrinsic to God's character and everything that belongs to him. Israel is frequently urged to 'Be holy, for I am holy'. God's name, which expresses his character is holy, so to swear falsely or resort to idolatry profanes his name. Anyone or anything given to God becomes holy. Thus the priests' portions of the sacrifices are holy, as are the tabernacle and its equipment. Priests, Levites and Nazirites (the Old Testament equivalent of monks and nuns) are regarded as holy. In a more general sense the whole nation of Israel is set apart from other nations to serve God and is therefore described as holy.

But does holiness mean anything more than set apart for God? What is it about God that makes him holy in himself? This is more difficult to answer. Mary Douglas suggested that holiness involves wholeness and completeness. This means that holy men like priests have to be free of deformity and physical handicap. Animals offered to God must be free of blemish. Holy behaviour involves moral integrity: thus theft, dishonesty, double-dealing and hypocrisy are all incompatible with holiness.[19]

Though wholeness partially captures what the Old Testament means by holiness, it is more precisely encapsulated in the notion of full and perfect life. God is the source of life and so holiness virtually equates to the life-giving power of God. The Garden of Eden is not only pictured as the place where God dwelt, but its verdant vegetation, four rivers and the tree of life all strengthen the association between God, holiness and life. Similar ideas are reflected in the laws about sacrifice and priests, forbidding the offering of blemished animals or the participation of handicapped priests in worship: it is not the abnormality of blemishes

[19] Douglas, *Purity*, 53.

and handicaps that prevents such people or animals joining in worship, but their lack of perfect life. Those who come into the presence of God must demonstrate they have perfect life.

Since God is the perfectly holy, the unclean are those opposed to God, or who fall short of his perfection. Hence idolatry, which involves worshipping another god, is one of the most severe forms of uncleanness; it pollutes the idolater, the land, and the sanctuary. But divine holiness does not merely demand total religious and moral commitment, it means life. God himself is full and perfect life, so that death is the very antithesis of holiness. Thus it is not surprising that homicide generates an intense form of uncleanness. Thus uncleanness is very often associated with death. The Old Testament thus operates with the following polarities:

God	sin
life	death
holiness	uncleanness

The world and its contents are viewed as revolving around two poles, the holy God of life, and sin/death, the unclean. Israel, the people of God, is called to be holy, 'because I the LORD am holy' (Lev 20:26). This means shunning those sins that are the antithesis of holiness, such as idolatry, murder, and sexual immorality. Sexual congress is the most powerful and godlike of all human powers, in that it enables man to be like God creating other beings in his own image, but its misuse is viewed by the Old Testament as gravely as idolatry or homicide.

If the quintessence of uncleanness is death, it becomes clear why corpses are regarded as so polluting. These apparently harsh regulations declare very loudly one aspect of God's character: he is life, perfect life, both morally and physically. He is opposed to death: those who willingly or even involuntarily embrace actions that lead to death separate themselves from God.

The food laws

Of the three key principles in the Jewish dietary laws, no consumption of blood, no mixing of meat and milk in the same meal, and the avoidance of certain foods altogether, only the last is spelled out in detail in the Old Testament. The ban on blood is mentioned immediately after the flood in Genesis 9:4, where the consumption of meat is first permitted with the proviso, 'Only you shall not eat flesh with its life, that is, its blood.' The later law in Leviticus 17 threatens anyone who does eat blood with 'cutting off', i.e. premature death. For Deuteronomy to eat meat from which the blood has not been drained is incompatible with Israel's vocation to be a holy nation.

Once again the tie-up between holiness and life on the one hand and uncleanness and death on the other is apparent in the blood ban. Because blood represents the life of the animal it is sacred, it belongs to God, therefore man should not consume it even in 'profane' slaughter (Deut 12:20–25). Animals that die naturally have their life blood still in them, so they are banned from consumption by the holy people of Israel. But foreigners who are not in this close relationship with God may eat the flesh of such carcasses (Deut 14:21).

Three times the law insists, 'You shall not boil a kid in its mother's milk' (Exod 23:19; 34:26; Deut 14:21), and this is the basis of the Jewish ban on eating meat and milk products at the same meal. The original circumstances of the ban are obscure. It could be that like the blood ban it is inculcating respect for life. A kid should be living on its mother's milk not being cooked in it. Such a dish subverts the natural order, and confuses the realms of life and death in an unacceptable way.

However the other food laws (Lev 11; Deut 14) do not immediately seem to fit this understanding of uncleanness. It is not apparent, for example, why pigs and camels and crabs are unclean whereas sheep, goats, or salmon are classified as clean. The criterion that clean land animals must have cloven hooves and chew the cud is only another way of defining the classes clean and unclean: it does not explain why there should be different classes in the first place. The same may be said about the distinction between fish with scales and fins, which are clean, and other water creatures that are not. When it comes to the birds, Leviticus and Deuteronomy simply give a list of twenty hard-to-identify birds which are unclean and therefore may not be eaten, and declare the others clean.

Over the centuries various theories have been put forward to explain these food laws. But anthropological explanations that see these food rules as both symbolic and social have most to commend them. These rules are symbolic in expressing a society's self-understanding and social in that they tend to support the boundaries and hierarchies of that society. M. Douglas has put forward several possible explanations of this type. In *Purity and Danger* (1966) she argued that wholeness, holiness and cleanness were closely related ideas in biblical thinking. As already noted above this is an important insight.

She later noted in *Implicit Meanings* that the cleanness rules structure the bird, animal, and human realms in a similar way.[20] Both the realms of birds and beasts contain a mixture of clean and unclean species. The clean may be eaten, the unclean may not. Within the clean group there is a sub-group of animals or birds that may also be sacrificed, e.g.

[20] Mary Douglas, *Implicit Meanings: Essays in Anthropology* (London: Routledge & Kegan Paul, 1975).

sheep, pigeons. This threefold division of the bird and animal kingdoms corresponds to the divisions among human beings. Mankind falls into two main groups, Israel and the Gentiles. Within Israel only one group may approach the altar to offer sacrifice, the priests. This in turn matches the law's understanding of sacred space. Outside the camp is the abode of Gentiles and unclean Israelites. Ordinary Israelites dwell in the camp, but only priests may approach the altar or enter the tabernacle tent.

These distinctions made in the food laws between clean and unclean foods thus match the divisions among mankind, between Israel the elect nation and the non-elect Gentiles. They served to remind Israel of her special status as God's chosen people. Just as God had selected just one people to be near him, so Israel had to be selective in her diet. Through this system of symbolic laws the Israelites were reminded at every meal of their redemption to be God's people. Their diet was limited to certain meats in imitation of their God, who had restricted his choice among the nations to Israel. It served also to bring to mind Israel's responsibilities to be a holy nation. As they distinguished between clean and unclean foods, they were reminded that holiness was more than a matter of meat and drink but a way of life characterised by purity and integrity.

These food laws not only reminded Israel of her distinctiveness, they served to enforce it. Jews faithful to these laws would tend to avoid Gentile company, lest they were offered unclean food to eat. This may partially explain the reluctance of Daniel and his friends when exiled in Babylon to eat the food provided by the royal court: they feared they might be defiled, so they insisted on eating only vegetables (cf. Dan 1:8–16).

These food laws also fit into the broader framework of the uncleanness laws. If God is identified with life and holiness and uncleanness is associated with death and opposition to God, the food laws symbolise that Israel is God's people called to enjoy his life, while Gentile idolaters are by and large opposed to him and his people and face death. The food laws also underline respect for life directly as well as symbolically. Eating meat is described as a concession in Genesis 9:1–4. And it may only be eaten if the blood is drained out first, 'for the life is . . . the blood' (Lev 17:11). Consumption of the life liquid, blood, is thus banned. Furthermore wanton slaughter of living creatures is also discouraged by the limited number of animals classified as clean. In both ways then these food laws tended to promote respect for life.

In the prophetic literature the terms 'clean' and 'unclean' are much less common. That is not to say the prophets were not familiar with the ideas but they focus on the worst types of prohibited uncleanness attributable to human sin, not on tolerated types of uncleanness caused by bodily functions. Thus Hosea 5:3 accuses Israel of contracting uncleanness through unfaithfulness to the LORD, which he calls spiritual harlotry. Hosea 6:7–10 associates uncleanness with murder and infidelity to the covenant. Isaiah 30:22 and Jeremiah 2:7; 7:30 declare that idolatry defiles the land and the sanctuary.

But it is the priest/prophet Ezekiel, brought up strictly to avoid uncleanness (Ezek 4:14), who makes most use of the concept in his condemnation of Israel. Though he knows the laws on naturally occurring uncleanness (Ezek 44:25; cf. 22:26 alluding to Lev 10:10–11), he repeatedly focuses on the uncleanness caused by Israel's moral and spiritual apostasy, particularly bloodshed and idolatry, which he terms harlotry (e.g. Ezek 22:3–4, 11, 27; 33:25–26; 36:17–18).

Jewish beliefs in the first century

Among first-century Jews purity laws were both important and controversial: different groups had quite different interpretations and applications of the biblical laws. The concern to be ritually clean is shown both by archaeology and the texts relating to this period. Many Jewish ritual baths, *miqveh*s, dating from the first century have been discovered. More than a sixth of the Mishnah (completed *c.* A.D. 200) is concerned with purity regulations and the New Testament often refers to Jewish beliefs about uncleanness as well as using the terminology of purity and uncleanness in its own way.

This overview of the Old Testament and early Jewish thinking about purity and uncleanness allows us to assess the New Testament approach more clearly. When it comes to sins which cause uncleanness the continuity between the testaments is clear. Like the prophets the New Testament writers affirm that idolatry, sexual immorality, and murder cause grave uncleanness. According to Jesus, 'What comes out of a man makes him unclean . . . evil thoughts, sexual immorality, theft, murder, adultery, greed . . .' (Mark 7:15, 20–23).[21] Frequently the demons cast out by Jesus are termed 'unclean spirits' (e.g. Mark 1:23, 26–27). This fits the Old Testament conception that the essence of uncleanness is opposition to God. In the epistles uncleanness is sometimes sandwiched between sexual immorality and greed, which is idolatry (e.g. Eph 5:3; Col 3:5) again reflecting Old Testament thought patterns. However as in the prophets and Mark 7:21 and Matt 15:19 uncleanness is most often associated with sexual sin (e.g. Rom 1:24; Gal 5:19; 1 Thess 4:7), so that impurity is virtually identified with misuse of sex.

In these respects the New Testament teaching fully underlines the Old Testament view of uncleanness, but in other respects it transforms it. Transformation rather than abrogation would seem to describe the

[21] On the probability that this reflects the teaching of Jesus, cf. N. T. Wright, *Jesus and the Victory of God* (London: SPCK, 1996), 396–8.

New Testament's handling of the uncleanness caused by disease or discharge and the food laws. Instead of keeping his distance from those afflicted with uncleanness Jesus touches them, thereby making himself unclean. Thus he touches lepers, a woman suffering from a flow of blood, and even corpses, healing the former and bringing the dead back to life (e.g. Mark 1:40–41; 5:21–43). The Old Testament uncleanness laws declared God was the source of perfect life and therefore only the healthy could approach him in worship. But the Old Testament rarely offered healing to the unclean (e.g. 2 Kgs 5:14). People could pray for it, but then had to wait patiently. But Jesus inaugurated the new creation and the eschatological reign of God, when God drew near to the sufferers and healed them personally. His miracles had the effect of including 'within the people of YHWH . . . those who had formerly been outside'.[22]

The healing miracles 'might also be seen as the breaking in of the new order planned by the creator god'. In them 'we glimpse something beyond the simple reconstitution of Israel' . . . 'When Israel was restored, the whole creation would be restored.'[23] In other words Jesus' apparent disregard for the uncleanness regulations signalled no disrespect for them, rather it was a declaration that their most fundamental values were being fulfilled. The uncleanness laws witnessed to a picture of God who was the source of perfect life and wholeness: only those who enjoyed full and perfect health were judged fit to enter the temple and experience God's presence. Now with the new creation inaugurated by Jesus those he healed were freed from uncleanness and were able to draw near to God.

This new creation according to biblical and first-century Jewish thought was to embrace not just Jews but all nations. It is this conviction that drives the transformation of the laws on unclean foods. The Jerusalem council reaffirmed the ban on the consumption of blood (Acts 15:20): this is perfectly congruent with both testaments' respect for life and its Giver.[24] But when it comes to laws forbidding the eating of certain types of creature a different stance is adopted.

These food laws reminded the Jews of their special status as the one people chosen by God. The clean (edible) creatures symbolised Israel,

[22] Wright, *Jesus*, 192.

[23] Wright, *Jesus*, 193.

[24] For a discussion of the Jerusalem decrees see Tomson, *Paul and the Jewish Law*, 178–84. He points out that the Western text bans idol food, blood, and unchastity, which could be understood to be prohibiting idolatry, homicide, and illicit sex, the three cardinal sins of Judaism (cf. discussion above of the most serious forms of uncleanness), whereas the Eastern text and Textus Receptus include a ban on 'strangled meat', that is non-kosher meat from which the blood has not been drained. He points out that both the Eastern and Western church, as late as the fifth century, widely followed this prohibition of eating meat containing blood.

whereas the unclean (prohibited) foods symbolised the Gentile nations. But in the new creation the people of God is open to people of all nations, not just Jews, hence it is inappropriate for the food laws which symbolise segregation to be maintained. In Matthew and Mark, Jesus' critique of the food laws (Matt 15:16–17; Mark 7:18–19) is immediately followed by the story of the Syro-Phoenician woman (describing herself as a dog, i.e. unclean), whose daughter, possessed by an unclean spirit, was healed by Jesus (Matt 15:21–28; Mark 7:24–30).

Jesus' ministry and teaching thus laid the foundation for outreach to the Gentiles and the abolition of the food laws, but in Acts 10 the decisive step is taken.[25] Peter has a vision in which a heavenly voice commands him to kill and eat unclean animals. He responds: 'Surely not, Lord! I have never eaten anything impure or unclean.' While Peter is still perplexed by the vision, men sent by Cornelius, a Roman centurion, come asking for Peter to visit him. When he arrives at the house of Cornelius, Peter explains why he came: 'It is against our law for a Jew to associate with a Gentile or visit him. But God has shown me that I should not call any man impure or unclean' (Acts 10:14, 28). The significance of this Cornelius episode is underlined by Luke recounting it three times in Acts 10, 11 and 15. The Jerusalem council confirmed that it was right to include Gentiles within the Church and simultaneously to abrogate the main food laws. The only uncleanness regulations they imposed concerned idolatry, sexual immorality, and blood, which were the worst types of uncleanness in the Old Testament (Acts 15:20). Paul takes it for granted that the other food laws no longer apply to Christians (e.g. 1 Cor 8:8; 1 Tim 4:3–5). Thus the reappraisal of the laws on unclean food like that on unclean persons is not seen by New Testament writers as contradicting the Old Testament so much as reaffirming the realisation of its hopes with the coming of Christ and the inauguration of a new creation, in which there is neither Jew nor Gentile, and everyone, including the unclean, may be restored to fulfil God's purposes.

New creation is also the key to the New Testament's apparent rejection of the Old Testament stance on marriage and divorce. As is well known, the Old Testament allows polygamy: patriarchs and kings often have several wives. From the laws it is apparent that divorce was also permitted in Old Testament times (e.g. Deut 24:1–4). What is less obvious is that, as elsewhere in the ancient world, a double standard operated with regard to adultery. A married woman who was unfaithful to her husband was guilty of adultery against her husband, but a married man who was unfaithful to his wife was not regarded as committing

[25] Cf. L. William Countryman, *Dirt, Greed and Sex* (London: SCM Press, 1989), 67–9.

adultery against her.[26] In other words there was an asymmetry in the marriage relationship: a wife was bound exclusively to her husband, but he was not bound exclusively to her.

This inequality in the marriage bond was challenged by Jesus when he said: 'Every one who divorces his wife and marries another commits adultery, and he who marries a woman divorced from her husband commits adultery' (Luke 16:18; cf. Mark 10:11). On the face of it this saying is just condemning remarriage after divorce. Divorce followed by remarriage counts as adultery. Nevertheless it is an extraordinary statement, for it is the act of divorce that allows a man under modern law or ancient Jewish law[27] to marry another woman without being regarded as adulterous. The essential clause in a Jewish bill of divorce is: 'Thou art free to marry any man.'[28] But the implication of Jesus' statement is that divorce procedures do not give those involved freedom to remarry: they are still bound to each other so that a second relationship counts as adulterous.

But striking as this is, it is not the most revolutionary aspect of Jesus' teaching on marriage. It should be noted that the charge of adultery here applies to the husband, who under conventional thinking would not have been regarded as committing adultery by initiating a second relationship. As already mentioned a wife committed adultery by being unfaithful but a husband did not. Yet here he is said to commit adultery, as Mark 10:11 makes clear, against his wife. In other words both husband and wife, not the wife alone, are bound to exclusive loyalty to each other. By this saying Jesus introduced full equality into marriage. The double standard is overthrown.

It is overthrown in another respect too. Divorce makes a second union lawful. It therefore follows that if Jesus is condemning second unions after divorce, he must also be rejecting second unions before divorce. In other words he is outlawing polygamy as well, which would also be contrary to true equality between spouses. Thus this saying is very original, indeed revolutionary, when set against its Jewish background. By declaring remarriage after divorce adulterous, it rules out real divorce, polygamy and male infidelity. The contrast between the teaching of Jesus and the practice and law of the Old Testament could hardly be sharper.

Given the obvious contradiction between his teaching and Old Testament practice, it is not surprising that the Pharisees came to test him, i.e. to trap him in debate. In the first century Shammaite and

[26] A man who had intercourse with a married woman other than his wife was guilty of adultery against her husband.

[27] For full discussion see David W. Amram, *The Jewish Law of Divorce according to the Bible and Talmud* (New York: Hermon Press, 1975).

[28] Gittin 9:3.

Hillelite Pharisees were debating what grounds legitimated divorce, so Jesus was asked whose views he favoured: 'Is it lawful to divorce one's wife for any cause?' (Matt 19:3). In replying to the Pharisees Jesus clarifies the theology behind his novel views. He goes back to creation arguing on the basis of Genesis 1 and 2 that monogamous life-long union is God's intention for marriage. Divorce was a later concession to human frailty, not the creator's will.

> He answered, 'Have you not read that he who made them from the beginning made them male and female, and said, "For this reason a man shall leave his father and mother and be joined to his wife, and the two shall become one"? So they are no longer two but one. What therefore God has joined together, let no man put asunder.' They said to him, 'Why then did Moses command one to give a certificate of divorce, and to put her away?' He said to them, 'For your hardness of heart Moses allowed you to divorce your wives, but from the beginning it was not so.' (Matt 19:4–8)

For our present discussion it does not matter how the exception clause in 19:9 should be understood.[29] What is striking is Jesus' appeal to the story of creation over against the legal texts. The kingdom of God inaugurates a new era in which God's intentions for his creation will be realised.

> By quoting Genesis 1:27 and 2:24 to undermine Deuteronomy 24:1–3, Jesus was in fact making it clear that the story to which he was obedient was that in which Israel was called by YHWH to restore humankind and the world to his original intention . . . the last days must fulfil the creator's intention . . . (Jesus) believed himself to be inaugurating the great time of renewal spoken of in the prophets, when the law would be written on the hearts of YHWH's people.[30]

In this respect Jesus' transformation of marriage is like his treatment of the uncleanness rules. On the face of it there is confrontation and abrogation of the old rules, but at a deeper level there is a reaffirmation of God's original creative purposes for the human race. Man was made in the divine image, but this is marred by physical disabilities on the one hand and sin on the other. Jesus proclaims a new age when the divisions between races and between married partners have no more place, so that the rules which attempted to control the effects of sin and uncleanness have no more relevance.

[29] Matt 19:9 is often supposed to represent a softening of Jesus' teaching against divorce introduced by Matthew or the Church. Cf. Raymond F. Collins, *Divorce in the New Testament* (Collegeville: Michael Glazier, 1992), 207–31. But this is contextually unlikely: G. J. Wenham, 'Matthew and Divorce: an Old Crux Revisited', *JSNT* 22 (1984), 95–107, and William A. Heth and G. J. Wenham, *Jesus and Divorce*[2] (Carlisle: Paternoster Press, 1997).

[30] Wright, *Jesus*, 285–6.

The same pattern of thought explains Jesus' attitude to violence: in the new creation there will be no more conflict and no more retaliation. The prophets looked forward to an age when

> they shall beat their swords into ploughshares
> and their spears into pruning hooks;
> nation shall not lift up sword against nation,
> neither shall they learn war any more. (Isa 2:4)

They awaited a time when Jerusalem would be a city undisturbed by war or other conflict: 'Thus says the LORD of hosts: Old men and old women shall again sit in the streets of Jerusalem each with staff in hand for very age. And the streets of the city shall be full of boys and girls playing in its streets' (Zech 8:4–5).

Contradicting many of his contemporaries who believed this new age would be brought about by violent revolution against foreign oppression, Jesus insisted that it was not only characterised by non-violence but initiated by the non-violent. The antitheses of the Sermon on the Mount reach their climax with two final contrasts outlawing revenge:

> You have heard that it was said, 'An eye for an eye and a tooth for a tooth.' But I say to you, Do not resist one who is evil. But if any one strikes you on the right cheek, turn to him the other also.
>
> You have heard that it was said, 'You shall love your neighbour and hate your enemy.' But I say to you, Love your enemies and pray for those who persecute you, so that you may be sons of your Father who is in heaven. (Matt 5:38–39, 43–45)

Jesus acted like this at his trial and crucifixion. Peter appeals to Christians to follow their Lord's example. 'Christ also suffered for you, leaving you an example, that you should follow in his steps . . . When he was reviled, he did not revile in return' (1 Pet 2:21, 23). Likewise when Paul thinks about Christ's earthly career his thought is dominated by Jesus' obedience unto death and the hope that he too will share in Christ's suffering and resurrection. Furthermore he appeals to believers to act similarly.[31] 'Bless those who persecute you; bless and do not curse them . . . Repay no one evil for evil' (Rom 12:14, 17). Indeed Paul may not just be appealing to Jesus' example here, but alluding to his teaching in the Sermon on the Mount.[32]

[31] 'Paul does not think it is ridiculous idealism to appeal to the example of Christ as a moral pattern for believers: rather, he believes by God's Spirit and grace Christians can be obedient even unto death.' Witherington, *Paul's Narrative*, 104.

[32] James D. G. Dunn, *Romans II* (WBC, Dallas: Word, 1988), 745; David Wenham, *Paul: Follower of Jesus or Founder of Christianity?* (Grand Rapids: Eerdmans, 1995), 250–2; Richard B. Hays, *The Moral Vision of the New Testament* (Edinburgh: T&T Clark, 1997), 330.

But as Hays points out the New Testament's witness against violence only makes sense in an eschatological perspective. The Church is meant to embody non-violence in the present as a pledge of the future new creation. 'As a mundane proverb, "Turn the other cheek" is simply bad advice. Such action makes sense only if the God and Father of Jesus Christ actually is the ultimate judge of the world *and* if his will for his people is definitively revealed in Jesus.'[33] After incisively criticising various Christian approaches which relativise the New Testament's witness against violence, Hays raises the conflict with the Old, especially its laws and prophetic calls in God's name to wage war. How can the two testaments' approach to violence be reconciled? In his view they cannot, and Christians must follow the teaching of the New in preference to that of the Old.

> If irreconcilable tensions exist between the moral vision of the New Testament and that of particular Old Testament texts, the New Testament vision trumps the Old Testament. Just as the New Testament texts render judgements superseding the Old Testament requirements of circumcision and dietary laws, just as the New Testament's forbidding of divorce supersedes the Old Testament's permission of it, so also Jesus' explicit teaching and example of non-violence reshapes our understanding of God and of the covenant community in such a way that killing enemies is no longer a justifiable option.[34]

Though many would endorse this view, it is in effect writing off much of the Old Testament as irrelevant, for most of its narratives concern conflict within families, between tribes and between nations. Yet as we saw the New Testament writers presuppose an intimate knowledge of the Old Testament by their readers and a recognition that whatever was written in former times was written for our instruction.

I have argued that where the New Testament is apparently abrogating Old Testament laws on impurity and marriage, it is more accurately read as reaffirming the creator's ideals for his creation. What was tolerated by the law (e.g. bigamy), did not reflect God's creative ideal (e.g. monogamy). Can the same be said about violence?

Genesis opens with an account of God creating the world in six days and resting on the seventh. The completed creation is described as 'very good' (1:31) but the goal of creation is the sabbath day of rest. Eden is pictured as a garden of peace, with harmony between God and his creation, man and the animals, man and wife. This tranquillity is shattered by Adam's disobedience and mutual recriminations ensue. The next stage in the downward spiral is Cain's murder of Abel, and soon afterwards comes the twice-repeated comment that

[33] Hays, *Moral Vision*, 338.

[34] Hays, *Moral Vision*, 336.

'the earth was filled with violence' (6:11–13) and the decision to destroy the world in a flood is announced. It is after the flood that the first legally formulated divine decree is pronounced: 'Whoever sheds the blood of man, by man shall his blood be shed' (9:6). Were not God the speaker one might be tempted to dub this a counsel of despair: the human race is, despite the flood experience, incorrigibly perverse and will not give up its violence: only the threat of the death penalty will prevent it degenerating again into total violence. Yet God's desperation is embedded in a threefold reaffirmation of his first command to man, 'Be fruitful and multiply' (9:1, 7; cf. 1:28). God wants the earth to be filled with human beings created in his image, and by implication living in love and harmony and not destroying each other.

Sadly this vision of peace is rarely realised in Genesis, but the patriarchs are portrayed as endeavouring to live peaceably with their relatives and foreign neighbours (e.g. Gen 13:8; 14:22–24; 21:22–34; 31:44–54; 34:30). Both the Jacob and Joseph cycles climax with great scenes of reconciliation between brothers who had previously plotted to kill each other (Gen 33:4–11; 45:1–20). The book reaches its peak with Jacob's blessing, a vision of the twelve tribes each enjoying prosperity and security in their allotted territories. It is thus clear that Genesis views the conflicts with which its pages are filled as a declension from the harmony of the first creation and that it looks forward to a restoration of true peace in the land promised to the forefathers.

Similarly Deuteronomy, the most militant book of the law, looks forward to a time when the LORD 'gives you rest from all your enemies, round about, so that you live in safety' (Deut 12:10). It closes like Genesis with a blessing from its central character portraying this golden age.

> So Israel dwelt in safety,
> the fountain of Jacob alone,
> in a land of grain and wine;
> yea his heavens drop down dew.
> Happy are you, O Israel! Who is like you,
> a people saved by the LORD,
> the shield of your help,
> and the sword of your triumph!
> Your enemies shall come fawning to you;
> and you shall tread upon their high places. (Deut 33:28–29)

Thus the stories of conflict and the laws which try to regulate it are in the Pentateuch prefaced and closed with a vision of peace. God's primal intentions for mankind will, declares the Pentateuch, be realised at last. This vision was reaffirmed by the prophets, psalmists, and even those historians who chronicled the nation's sad history of war and defeat.[35]

The laws touching on divorce and bigamy reflected a toleration of these practices rather than approval. The same is true of the laws on war. Even in a God-directed campaign against Midian, killing the enemy pollutes the soldiers involved. 'Encamp outside the camp seven days; whoever of you has killed any person, and whoever has touched any slain, purify yourselves and your captives on the third day and on the seventh day' (Num 31:19). Deuteronomy groups together most of its laws on warfare in chapters 20–21. In the middle of them there is a law prescribing what is to be done if someone is found dead in the countryside. The elders of the nearest village must perform a rite to exonerate themselves and cleanse the land of blood guilt (21:1–9). If one person's death is taken so seriously, the death of many in war cannot have been a matter of indifference to the legislators.

Now it cannot be denied that many people in Old Testament times tended to glorify war as they have in many cultures before and since, but that certainly is not the stance of the implied authors of Genesis and Judges. Despite the fact that many of the military campaigns they relate were sanctioned by God, they would surely say, 'From the beginning it was not so'. Indeed if Israel had not sinned, says Judges, they would not have been overrun by their enemies. The book of Judges presupposes that God wants Israel to enjoy peace at home and abroad, but it shows that the nation's methods of trying to achieve peace led to ever greater external oppression and internal, intertribal strife.

So unlike Hays I do not think the testaments are deeply opposed when it comes to violence. Both testaments see human violence and conflict as contrary to God's will. Both encourage the people of God to make peace and promote reconciliation. Both look for a future era in which God will be acknowledged as king by all and peace will reign. Where they differ is in affirming that the new creation has been inaugurated and the reign of God has begun with the coming of Jesus. But this is not to contradict the Old Testament, rather it is to affirm its fulfilment.

[35] Susan Niditch, *War in the Hebrew Bible* (New York: Oxford University Press, 1993), 139–49, draws attention to the fact that Chronicles, the last book in the Hebrew canon, depicts God's unhappiness with warfare forbidding David to build the temple because he was a warrior and had shed blood (1 Chr 28:3).

CONCLUSIONS

In our opening chapters we explored the notions of the implied author and the implied reader, and sought to distinguish them from the more familiar ideas of author and reader. In modern literature it is usually possible to distinguish the real author from the implied author. Much is known about the life and views of C. S. Lewis apart from his writings, and sometimes it is possible to distinguish his real beliefs and practices from those he implicitly or explicitly endorsed in his books. In other words the views of the implied author C. S. Lewis may not always concur with those of the real author. In the case of biblical writings though, we can only deal with implied authors for we know them only through their works; we do not have independent access to their lives and thoughts apart from the books ascribed to them.

In reading texts it is often difficult to pick up the stance of the implied author. The reader must ask constantly whether the deeds described and the words spoken really represent the standpoint of the author. Who are the reliable characters in the narrative who reflect the implied author's view? Who does he consider admirable and who does he despise? In modern literature an additional problem may be caused by the narrator's unreliability. Though the reader automatically assumes the narrator's voice represents the author's, this may not be the case. However in the biblical texts we have focused on, we found no reason to distinguish the narrator's standpoint from the implied author's.

But we argued that it is most important to distinguish the implied author's ethical stance from that of the characters within the story. In recounting the nation's past its storytellers have a didactic purpose, but that certainly does not mean that they approved of all they described. We argued with several recent studies that nearly every episode in Judges is shadowed by the implied author's critique, a critique that becomes harsh and strident as the nation spirals into moral and political anarchy. The book of Genesis on the other hand is more positive. A sunny start in chapters 1 and 2 is followed by the avalanche of sin in chapters 3–11. Then come the patriarchs, whose erratic progress demands careful reading, but we argued that they were often viewed as paradigmatic for their successors, exhibiting patterns of behaviour that should be emulated. Nevertheless the author does not gloss over their mistakes, and he shows that God's promises are gradually fulfilled, thus demonstrating that divine grace, not judgement will prevail.

Within these narratives it is often difficult to establish the authors' standpoints, for they rarely make their judgements explicit. Though some have argued that the authors evaluated their characters against the standards expressed in the law, I have proposed that the laws in the Pentateuch represent the floor of acceptable behaviour, not the ideal. The creation of man and woman in the divine image implied that human beings are expected to imitate the divine virtues, whether that involves observing the sabbath (Gen 2:1–3) or exercising forgiveness towards those that have wronged them (Gen 33:10; 50:19–21).

Further we argued that Genesis 1–2 gives a picture of the author's vision of God's purposes for mankind and in particular of relationships between the sexes. It is noticeable that divine bounty provided Adam with just one wife, and that he for his part was totally satisfied with this provision. Indeed the narrator declares that this is a pattern for every marriage: 'for this reason a man leaves his father and mother and cleaves to his wife' (Gen 2:24). The author reinforces the point that monogamy was the divine intention by portraying negatively every case of polygamy: either the husband is vicious, e.g. Lamech, or the relationship is an unhappy one, e.g. Esau, Jacob (Gen 4:23–24; 26:34–35; 29:30 – 30:23). The same stance is taken in the laws regulating marriage: the one law dealing with bigamy is concerned to limit the animosity generated by a bigamous relationship (Deut 21:15–17). While clearly the law tolerates bigamy, such a regulation shows it does not recommend it.

Genesis contains no example of divorce[1] so we cannot be sure how the author viewed it. Nevertheless his comments on the paradigm marriage are striking. The man is to cleave (*dabaq*), i.e. stick firmly, to his wife. She becomes one flesh and bone with her husband, i.e. as closely related to him as his natural blood relatives (Gen 2:23–24).[2] None of this suggests a relationship that could or should be easily broken. Again the rare mentions of divorce in the law suggest a practice tolerated by lawgivers rather than approved (e.g. Lev 21:14; Deut 24:1-4).[3] It would therefore appear that the implied author of Genesis would not have disagreed with Jesus' evaluation of the situation. 'For your hardness of heart Moses allowed you to divorce your wives, but from the beginning it was not so' (Matt 19:8). The creator's intention was for life-long monogamy as Adam and Eve enjoyed, not the turbulent polygamy of Lamech and Jacob.

[1] Hagar's expulsion was not divorce because she was only Sarah's maid. For a discussion of surrogate marriage in Bible times cf. Thomas L. Thompson, *The Historicity of the Patriarchal Narratives* (BZAW 133, Berlin: W. de Gruyter, 1974), 252–69.

[2] Wenham, *Genesis 1–15*, 70–1.

[3] For discussion see R. Westbrook, 'The Prohibition on Restoration of Marriage in Deuteronomy 24:1–4', in *Studies in the Bible 1986* (ed. S. Japhet, Scripta Hierosolymitana 31, Jerusalem: Magnes Press, 1986), 387–405.

A similar logic, I have argued, explains the New Testament's approach to the uncleanness laws and to violence. At the heart of the uncleanness regulations is an affirmation that God is the source of life in its completeness. Therefore acts such as homicide, which are contrary to life, are defiling, and people who in their physical condition do not show fullness of life are unclean and so must be excluded from God's presence in worship. But Jesus proclaims the inauguration of the new creation in which God's original creative purposes will be fulfilled. Therefore those who under the Old Testament dispensation were unclean because of sin or their bodily condition may now enter the kingdom of God, because the creator himself will restore them to newness of life.

Violence is intrinsically anti-life. Unchecked it will lead to death. So the Old Testament, like the New, regards it as inherently inimical to God's purpose. The goal of God's creation in Genesis 1:1 – 2:3 was God's rest on the sabbath day. The garden of Eden was characterised by harmony between the sexes, between humans and animals, between God and man, until conflict was introduced into all these spheres by sin. Thereafter violence spiralled out of control with Cain murdering his brother, Lamech boasting of seventy-sevenfold vengeance, till eventually the world was filled with violence, prompting God to send the flood.

After the flood a central divine priority was to control human violence, so the first law enacted forbade the consumption of blood and instituted capital punishment for murder (Gen 9:4–6). Here, as in many laws and narratives dealing with violence, the implied authors would surely agree that 'in the beginning it was not so, but for the hardness of human hearts' God allowed punishment, which is a violent response, of individual offenders, and even war against sinful nations, including Israel. In other words, God tolerated violence although his long-term goal was peace.

Jesus declared that with his coming the reign of God was beginning and the world was being recreated, an age in which all violence is out of place. This is why his followers must eschew revenge. But if violence of any sort is out of place in the new creation, does this mean that the Church may quietly jettison all the Old Testament narratives which are so full of conflict?[4] Had the kingdom fully come or the new creation been completed with his first coming, we could doubtless do so. But he taught his disciples to pray 'Thy kingdom come, thy will be done on earth as it is in heaven', implying that the new creation was far from

[4] This is what Hays seems to be discreetly recommending. Christians 'will read the Old Testament in such a way that its portrayals of God's mercy and eschatological restoration of the world will take precedence over its stories of justified violence'. Hays, *Moral Vision*, 337.

complete. The coming of the kingdom may be more apparent in the Christian era than it was before Christ, but it is still partial. The Church today, like Israel of old, still hopes and prays for the consummation. It still has to live in a world distorted by hardness of heart and not as it was in the beginning. It still lives in a world where sin and violence are endemic. Individual Christians and the Church are afflicted by both. They need the laws and narratives of the Old Testament to remind them of the creator's ideals and how to handle situations which fall short of these ideals. In this way the experience of the saints of the Old Testament has much to teach those of the New.[5] But to work this out in detail is beyond the scope of this book. I shall simply end with two points that are less obscure.

First, the Old Testament witnesses to God's tolerance. The LORD urges Israel: 'You shall love the LORD your God with all your heart, and with all your soul and with all your might', 'you shall love your neighbour as yourself'; indeed to imitate God himself: 'be holy, for I am holy' (Deut 6:5; Lev 19:18; 11:45). But there is a great gap between these lofty ideals and the law. People were not punished for not loving God with their whole heart, only for brazen disloyalty expressed by active idolatry. Similarly lack of love towards one's neighbours did not attract judicial sanction, only actions that seriously harmed them, such as theft, murder or adultery. On such deeds the law came down very hard, but though God wanted his people to love him wholeheartedly and their neighbours as themselves, he put up with much less. As the psalmist put it:

> The LORD is merciful and gracious,
> slow to anger and abounding in steadfast love.
> He does not deal with us according to our sins,
> nor requite us according to our iniquities.
> For he knows our frame;
> he remembers that we are dust. (Ps 103:8, 10, 14)

If the gap between divine ideals for human behaviour and the law's requirements witnesses to God's long-suffering and tolerance, the second clear point that the narratives demonstrate is his faithfulness to his promises despite the unfaithfulness of his people. There are many episodes in Genesis where it is apparent that the patriarchs do not obey or show the faith they should, yet despite their slips God remains faithful, indeed rescues them from the problems they create for themselves. This pattern is even more prominent in Judges. The nation's repeated

[5] It is striking that Oliver O'Donovan in *The Desire of the Nations: Rediscovering the Roots of Political Theology* (Cambridge: Cambridge University Press, 1996), appeals as much to the Old as to the New Testament to develop a modern Christian political theology.

lapses into apostasy do not prevent the LORD from answering their cries for deliverance. Even Samson, who gives away the secret of his God-given strength, has his prayer for vindication answered. God's faithfulness is not nullified by Israel's unfaithfulness (cf. Jer 31:35–37).

God's character as it emerges in the stories of the Old Testament is thus pre-eminently marked by tolerance and faithfulness. That is why St Paul could assure his readers that 'whatever was written in former days was written . . . that by the encouragement of the scriptures we might have hope' (Rom 15:4). Read sensitively they may still do the same today.

WORKS CITED

ALEXANDER, T. DESMOND, 'Genealogies, Seed and the Compositional Unity of Genesis', *TynBul* 44 (1993), 255–70.

ALEXANDER, T. DESMOND, 'Messianic Ideology in the Book of Genesis', in *The Lord's Anointed: Interpretation of Old Testament Messianic Texts* (ed. Philip E. Satterthwaite, Richard S. Hess and Gordon J. Wenham, Carlisle: Paternoster Press, 1995), 19–39.

ALTER, ROBERT, *The Art of Biblical Narrative* (New York: Basic Books, 1981).

AMIT, YAIRAH, *The Book of Judges: The Art of Editing* (Hebrew) (Jerusalem: Bialik, 1992; ET, J. Chipman, Biblical Interpretation Series 38, Leiden: Brill, 1999).

AMRAM, DAVID W., *The Jewish Law of Divorce according to the Bible and Talmud* (New York: Hermon Press, 1975).

AUGUSTINE, ST., *City of God* (trans. Marcus Dods, Edinburgh: T&T Clark, 1884).

BACH, ALICE, 'Rereading the Body Politic: Women and Violence in Judges 21', *Bib Int* 6 (1998), 1–19.

BAR-EFRAT, SHIMON, *Narrative Art in the Bible* (ET, D. Shefer-Vanson, JSOTSup 70, Sheffield: Almond Press, 1989).

BARR, JAMES, *Comparative Philology and the Text of the Old Testament* (Oxford: Clarendon Press, 1968).

BARTON, JOHN, 'Approaches to Ethics in the Old Testament', in *Beginning Old Testament Study* (ed. John W. Rogerson, London: SPCK, 1982), 113–30.

BARTON, JOHN, 'The Basis of Ethics in the Hebrew Bible', *Semeia* 66 (1994), 11–22.

BECHTEL, LYN M., 'What if Dinah is not Raped? (Genesis 34)', *JSOT* 62 (1994), 19–36.

BECKWITH, ROGER T., *The Old Testament Canon of the New Testament Church* (London: SPCK, 1985).

BENDOR, S., *The Social Structure of Ancient Israel: The Institution of the Family from the Settlement to the End of the Monarchy* (Jerusalem: Simor, 1996).

BERG, W., 'Der Sündenfall Abrahams und Saras nach Gen 16:1–6', *BN* 19 (1982), 7–14.

BERGE, K., *Die Zeit des Jahwisten* (BZAW 186, Berlin: W. de Gruyter, 1990).

BERLIN, ADELE, *Poetics and Interpretation of Biblical Narrative* (Sheffield: Almond Press, 1983).

BIRCH, BRUCE C., 'Divine Character and the Formation of Moral Community', in *The Bible in Ethics: The Second Sheffield Colloquium* (ed. John W. Rogerson, Margaret Davies, M. Daniel Carroll R., JSOTSup 207, Sheffield: JSOT Press, 1995), 119–35.

BIRCH, BRUCE C., 'Moral Agency, Community, and the Character of God in the Hebrew Bible', *Semeia* 66 (1994), 23–41.

BIRD, PHYLLIS A., 'The Harlot as Heroine: Narrative Art and Social Presupposition in Three OT Texts', *Semeia* 46 (1989), 119–39.

BLENKINSOPP, JOSEPH, *The Pentateuch* (London: SCM Press, 1992).

BLOCK, DANIEL I., 'Will the Real Gideon Please Stand Up? Narrative Style and Intention in Judges 6–9', *JETS* 40 (1997), 353–66.

BOLING, ROBERT G., *Judges* (AB, Garden City: Doubleday, 1975).

BOOTH, WAYNE C., *The Rhetoric of Fiction* (Chicago and London: University of Chicago Press, 1961).

BOOTH, WAYNE C., *The Company We Keep: An Ethics of Fiction* (Berkeley and Los Angeles: University of California Press, 1988).

BROWN, WILLIAM P., *Character in Crisis* (Grand Rapids: Eerdmans, 1996).

BRUEGGEMANN, WALTER, 'The Kerygma of the Priestly Writers', *ZAW* 84 (1972), 397–414.

BRUEGGEMANN, WALTER, *Genesis* (Atlanta: John Knox, 1982).

BURROWS, MILLAR, *The Basis of Israelite Marriage* (New Haven: American Oriental Society, 1938).

CALVIN, JEAN, *A Commentary on Genesis II* (1554; ET, J. King, 1847, London: Banner of Truth, 1965).

CARR, DAVID, '*Biblos geneseos* Revisited: A Synchronic Analysis of Patterns in Genesis as Part of the Torah', *ZAW* 110 (1998), 159–72, 327–47.

CASSUTO, UMBERTO, *A Commentary on the Book of Genesis, Vol. 1* (Jerusalem: Magnes Press, 1961).

CESSARIO, ROMANUS, *The Moral Virtues and Theological Ethics* (Notre Dame: University of Notre Dame Press, 1991).

CHIRICHIGNO, GREGORY C., *Debt Slavery in Israel and the Ancient Near East* (JSOTSup 141, Sheffield: JSOT Press, 1993).

CLINES, DAVID J. A., *The Theme of the Pentateuch* (JSOTSup 10, Sheffield: JSOT Press, 1978).

CLINES, DAVID J. A., *Job 1–20* (WBC, Dallas: Word, 1989).

CLINES, DAVID J. A., *What Does Eve Do to Help?* (JSOTSup 94, Sheffield: JSOT Press, 1990).

COLLINS, RAYMOND F., *Divorce in the New Testament* (Collegeville: Michael Glazier, 1992).

CORBETT, EDWARD P. J., *Classical Rhetoric for the Modern Student*[3] (Oxford: Oxford University Press, 1990).

COUNTRYMAN, L. WILLIAM, *Dirt, Greed and Sex* (London: SCM Press, 1989).

DALLEY, STEPHANIE, *The Myths of Mesopotamia* (Oxford: Oxford University Press, 1990).

DAUBE, DAVID, 'Concessions to Sinfulness in Jewish Law', *JJS* 10 (1959), 1–13.

DAVIES, G. H., 'Judges 8:22–23', *VT* 13 (1963), 151–7.

DEIST, F. E., '"Murder in the Toilet" (Judges 3:12–20)', *Scriptura* 58 (1996), 263–72.

DOUGLAS, MARY, *Purity and Danger* (London: Routledge & Kegan Paul, 1966).

DOUGLAS, MARY, *Implicit Meanings: Essays in Anthropology* (London: Routledge & Kegan Paul, 1975).

DRIVER, SAMUEL R., *The Book of Genesis*[3] (London: Methuen, 1904).

DUNN, JAMES D. G., *Romans II* (WBC, Dallas: Word, 1988).

EPSTEIN, LOUIS M., *Marriage Laws in the Bible and the Talmud* (Cambridge: Harvard University Press, 1942).

ESLINGER, LYLE M., *Kingship of God in Crisis: a Close Reading of 1 Samuel 1–12* (Sheffield: Almond Press, 1985).

EXUM, J. CHERYL, 'Feminist Criticism: Whose Interests are Being Served?', in *Judges and Method* (ed. Gale A. Yee, Minneapolis: Fortress Press, 1995), 65–90.

FALK, ZEEV W., *Religious Law and Ethics: Studies in Biblical and Rabbinical Theonomy* (Jerusalem: Mesharim, 1991).

FALK, ZEEV W., 'Law and Ethics in the Hebrew Bible', in *Justice and Righteousness* (ed. Henning G. Reventlow and Yair Hoffmann; JSOTSup 137, Sheffield: JSOT Press, 1992), 82–90.

FELDMAN, LOUIS H., 'Josephus' Portrait of Gideon', *Revue des études juives* 152 (1993), 5–28.

FELDMAN, E., *Biblical and Post-Biblical Defilement and Mourning: Law as Theology* (New York: Ktav, 1977).
FEWELL, DANNA N. and GUNN, DAVID M., 'Tipping the Balance: Sternberg's Reader and the Rape of Dinah', *JBL* 110 (1991), 193–211.
FOH, SUSAN T., 'What is the Woman's Desire?', *WTJ* 37 (1974/75), 376–83.
FOKKELMAN, J. P., *Narrative Art in Genesis* (Assen: Van Gorcum, 1975).
FRETHEIM, TERENCE E., *The Pentateuch* (Nashville: Abingdon Press, 1996).

GABRIEL, J., 'Die Kainitengenealogie: Gen 4:17–24', *Bib* 40 (1959), 409–27.
GOOD, E. M., *Irony in the Old Testament*[2] (Sheffield: Almond Press, 1981).
GORDON, ROBERT P., 'A House Divided: Wisdom in OT Narrative Traditions', in *Wisdom in Ancient Israel* (ed. John Day, Robert P. Gordon and Hugh G. M. Williamson, Cambridge: Cambridge University Press, 1995), 94–105.
GUNKEL, HERMANN, *Genesis*[9] (Göttingen: Vandenhoeck & Ruprecht, 1977).
GUNN, DAVID M., *The Story of King David: Genre and Interpretation* (JSOTSup 6, Sheffield: JSOT Press, 1978).
GUNN, DAVID M., *The Fate of King Saul: An Interpretation of a Biblical Story* (JSOTSup 14, Sheffield: JSOT Press, 1980).
GUNN, DAVID M., 'Reading Right', in *The Bible in Three Dimensions* (ed. David J. A. Clines, Stephen E. Fowl, Stanley E. Porter, JSOTSup 87, Sheffield: JSOT Press, 1990), 53–64.

HAAS, P., '"Die he shall surely die": The Structure of Homicide in Biblical Law', *Semeia* 45 (1989), 67–87.
HABEL, NORMAN C., *The Book of Job* (OTL, London: SCM Press, 1985).
HANSON, ANTHONY T., *Jesus Christ in the Old Testament* (London: SPCK, 1965).
HASEL, GERHARD F., 'The Polemic Nature of the Genesis Cosmology', *EvQ* 46 (1974), 81–102.
HAUERWAS, STANLEY, *A Community of Character: Toward a Constructive Christian Social Ethic* (Notre Dame: University of Notre Dame Press, 1981).
HAUERWAS, STANLEY and PINCHES, CHARLES R., *Christians among the Virtues* (Notre Dame: University of Notre Dame Press, 1997).
HAYS, RICHARD B., *The Moral Vision of the New Testament* (Edinburgh: T&T Clark, 1997).

HETH, WILLIAM A. and WENHAM, GORDON J., *Jesus and Divorce*[2] (Carlisle: Paternoster Press, 1997).

HETTEMA, THEO L., *Reading for Good: Narrative Theology and Ethics in the Joseph Story from the Perspective of Ricoeur's Hermeneutics* (Kampen: Kok Pharos, 1996).

HOUSTON, WALTER, *Purity and Monotheism: Clean and Unclean Animals in Biblical Law* (JSOTSup 140, Sheffield: JSOT Press, 1993).

HUGENBERGER, GORDON P., *Marriage as Covenant* (VTSup 52, Leiden: Brill, 1994).

JACKSON, BERNARD S., *Essays in Jewish and Comparative Legal History* (Leiden: Brill, 1975).

JANZEN, WALDEMAR, *Old Testament Ethics: A Paradigmatic Approach* (Louisville: Westminster/John Knox, 1994).

JENSON, PHILIP P., *Graded Holiness: A Key to the Priestly Conception of the World* (JSOTSup 106, Sheffield: JSOT Press, 1992).

JÓNSSON, GUNNLAUGUR A., *The Image of God: Gen 1:26–28 in a Century of OT Research* (ConBOT 26, Lund: Almqvist & Wiksell International, 1988).

KEUKENS, K. H., 'Der irreguläre Sterbesegen Isaaks: Bemerkungen zur Interpretation von Gen 27:1–45', *BN* 19 (1982), 43–56.

KLAWANS, JONATHAN, 'The Impurity of Immorality in Ancient Judaism', *JJS* 48 (1997), 1–16.

KLEIN, LILLIAN R., *The Triumph of Irony in the Book of Judges* (JSOTSup 68, Sheffield: JSOT Press, 1988).

KRUSCHWITZ, ROBERT B. and ROBERTS, ROBERT C., *The Virtues: Contemporary Essays on Moral Character* (Belmont: Wadsworth, 1987).

LASINE, STUART, 'Guest and Host in Judges 19: Lot's Hospitality in an Inverted World', *JSOT* 29 (1984), 37–59.

LICHT, JACOB, *Storytelling in the Bible* (Jerusalem: Magnes Press, 1978).

LIMBURG, JAMES, *Jonah: a Commentary* (London: SCM Press, 1993).

LONGACRE, R. E., *Joseph: a Story of Divine Providence* (Winona Lake: Eisenbrauns, 1989).

MACINTYRE, ALASDAIR, *After Virtue: A Study in Moral Theory* (London: Duckworth, 1981).

MCCONVILLE, J. G., *Law and Theology in Deuteronomy* (JSOTSup 33, Sheffield: JSOT Press, 1984).

MEYERS, CAROL L., *Discovering Eve* (New York: Oxford University Press, 1988).

MILGROM, JACOB, *The JPS Torah Commentary: Numbers* (Philadelphia: JPS, 1990).

MOBERLY, R. WALTER L., *At the Mountain of God* (JSOTSup 22, Sheffield: JSOT Press, 1983).

MOBERLY, R. WALTER L., *The Old Testament of the Old Testament* (Minneapolis: Fortress Press, 1992).

MOORE, GEORGE F., *A Critical and Exegetical Commentary on Judges* (ICC, Edinburgh: T&T Clark, 1895).

MORAN, WILLIAM L., 'The Ancient Near Eastern Background of the Love of God in Deuteronomy', *CBQ* 25 (1963), 77–87.

NIDITCH, SUSAN, *War in the Hebrew Bible* (New York: Oxford University Press, 1993).

NOBLE, PAUL, 'A "Balanced" Reading of the Rape of Dinah: Some Exegetical and Methodological Observations', *Bib Int* 4 (1996), 173–203.

NOTH, MARTIN, *Überlieferungsgeschichtliche Studien* (1943), partial ET = *The Deuteronomistic History* (JSOTSup 15, Sheffield: JSOT Press, 1981).

NUSSBAUM, MARTHA C., *Love's Knowledge: Essays on Philosophy and Literature* (Oxford/New York: Oxford University Press, 1990).

O'CONNELL, ROBERT H., *The Rhetoric of the Book of Judges* (VTSup 63, Leiden: Brill, 1996).

O'DONOVAN, OLIVER, *Resurrection and Moral Order: An Outline for Evangelical Ethics* (Leicester: InterVarsity Press, 1986).

O'DONOVAN, OLIVER, *The Desire of the Nations: Rediscovering the Roots of Political Theology* (Cambridge: Cambridge University Press, 1996).

OTTO, ECKART, *Theologische Ethik des Alten Testaments* (Stuttgart: Kohlhammer, 1994).

OTTO, ECKART, 'Aspects of Legal Reforms and Reformulations in Ancient Cuneiform and Israelite Law', in *Theory and Method in Biblical and Cuneiform Law* (ed. Bernard M. Levinson; JSOTSup 181, Sheffield: JSOT Press, 1994), 160–96.

PATRICK, DALE and SCULT, ALLEN, *Rhetoric and Biblical Interpretation* (JSOTSup 82, Sheffield: Almond Press, 1990).

PENNANT, DAVID F., 'Alliteration in Some Texts of Genesis', *Bib* 68 (1987), 390–2.

PROUSER, O. HORN, 'The Truth about Women and Lying', *JSOT* 61 (1994), 15–28.

RAD, GERHARD VON, *OT Theology I* (ET, D. M. G. Stalker, Edinburgh: Oliver & Boyd, 1962).

RAD, GERHARD VON, *Genesis*[2] (OTL, London: SCM Press, 1972).

RIMMON-KENAN, SHLOMITH, *Narrative Fiction: Contemporary Poetics* (London: Routledge, 1983).

ROSNER, BRIAN S., *Paul, Scripture and Ethics* (Arbeiten zur Geschichte des antiken Judentums und des Urchristentums 22, Leiden: Brill, 1994).

SAALSCHÜTZ, J. L., *Das mosaische Recht*[2] (Berlin: Carl Heymann, 1853; reprinted 1974).

SELDEN, RAMAN, WIDDOWSON, PETER and BROOKER, PETER, *A Reader's Guide to Contemporary Literary Theory*[4] (Hemel Hempstead: Prentice-Hall, 1997).

SKINNER, JOHN, *A Critical and Exegetical Commentary on Genesis*[2] (ICC, Edinburgh: T&T Clark, 1930).

SODEN, WOLFRAM VON, 'Etemenanki von Asarhaddon nach der Erzählung vom Turmbau zu Babel und dem Erra-Mythos', *UF* 3 (1971), 253–63.

SONSINO, RIFAT, *Motive Clauses in Hebrew Law* (Chico: Scholars Press, 1980).

STERNBERG, MEIR, *The Poetics of Biblical Narrative* (Bloomington: Indiana University Press, 1985).

STERNBERG, MEIR, 'Biblical Poetics and Sexual Politics: From Reading to Counterreading', *JBL* 111 (1992), 463–88.

STONE, KENNETH A., *Sex, Honor and Power in the Deuteronomistic History* (JSOTSup 234, Sheffield: JSOT Press, 1996).

STORDALEN, T., 'Genesis 2, 4: Restudying a *locus classicus*', *ZAW* 104 (1992), 163–77.

STRUS, A., *Nomen-Omen* (AnBib 80, Rome: Biblical Institute Press, 1978).

SWEENEY, MARVIN A., 'Davidic Polemics in the Book of Judges', *VT* 47 (1997), 517–29.

THOMPSON, THOMAS L., *The Historicity of the Patriarchal Narratives* (BZAW 133, Berlin: W. de Gruyter, 1974).

TOMASINO, ANTONY J., 'History Repeats Itself: The "Fall" and Noah's Drunkenness', *VT* 42 (1992), 128–30.

TOMSON, PETER J., *Paul and the Jewish Law: Halakha in the Letters of the Apostle to the Gentiles* (Assen: Van Gorcum, 1990).
TOSATO, A., 'The Law of Lev 18:18: A Reexamination', *CBQ* 46 (1984), 199–214.
TSEVAT, M., 'Bethulah', *TDOT* 2.338–43.

VAUX, ROLAND DE, *Ancient Israel* (ET, J. McHugh, London: Darton, Longman & Todd, 1961).
VAWTER, BRUCE, *On Genesis: A New Reading* (New York: Doubleday, 1977).

WALSH, JEROME T., 'Genesis 2:4b – 3:24: A Synchronic Reading', *JBL* 96 (1977), 161–77.
WALSH, JEROME T., 'The Characterization of Solomon in 1 Kgs 1–5', *CBQ* 57 (1995), 471–93.
WEBB, BARRY G., *The Book of the Judges: An Integrated Reading* (JSOTSup 46, Sheffield: JSOT Press, 1987).
WEINFELD, MOSHE, *Deuteronomy and the Deuteronomic School* (Oxford: Clarendon Press, 1972).
WENHAM, DAVID, *Paul: Follower of Jesus or Founder of Christianity?* (Grand Rapids: Eerdmans, 1995).
WENHAM, GORDON J., 'The Deuteronomic Theology of the Book of Joshua', *JBL* 90 (1971), 140–8.
WENHAM, GORDON J., 'Betulah, "A Girl of Marriageable Age"', *VT* 22 (1972), 326–48.
WENHAM, GORDON J., *The Book of Leviticus* (Grand Rapids: Eerdmans, 1979).
WENHAM, GORDON J., 'The Restoration of Marriage Reconsidered', *JJS* 30 (1979), 36–40.
WENHAM, GORDON J., 'Matthew and Divorce: an Old Crux Revisited', *JSNT* 22 (1984), 95–107.
WENHAM, GORDON J., *Genesis 1–15* (WBC, Waco: Word Books, 1987).
WENHAM, GORDON J., 'Method in Pentateuchal Source Criticism', *VT* 41 (1991), 84–109.
WENHAM, GORDON J., 'Attitudes to Homosexuality in the OT', *ExpTim* 102 (1991), 359–63.
WENHAM, GORDON J., *Genesis 16–50* (WBC, Dallas: Word Books, 1994).
WENHAM, GORDON J., 'The Akedah: A Paradigm of Sacrifice', in *Pomegranates and Golden Bells: Studies in Honor of Jacob Milgrom* (ed. David P. Wright, David N. Freedman and Avi Hurvitz, Winona Lake: Eisenbrauns, 1995), 93–102.

WENHAM, GORDON J., 'The Priority of P', *VT* 49 (1999), 240–58.
WENHAM, GORDON J., 'Pondering the Pentateuch', in *The Face of OT Studies: A Survey of Contemporary Approaches* (ed. David W. Baker and Bill T. Arnold, Grand Rapids/Leicester: Baker/Apollos, 1999), 116–44.
WESTBROOK, RAYMOND, 'The Prohibition on Restoration of Marriage in Deuteronomy 24:1–4', in *Studies in the Bible 1986* (ed. Sara Japhet, Scripta Hierosolymitana 31, Jerusalem: Magnes Press, 1986), 387–405.
WESTBROOK, RAYMOND, *Studies in Biblical and Cuneiform Law* (Paris: Gabalda, 1988).
WESTERMANN, CLAUS, *Genesis 1–11: A Commentary* (ET, J. J. Scullion, London: SPCK, 1984).
WESTERMANN, CLAUS, *Genesis 12–36: A Commentary* (ET, J. J. Scullion, London: SPCK, 1986).
WESTERMANN, CLAUS, *Die Geschichtsbücher des Alten Testaments* (Gütersloh: C. Kaiser/Gütersloher Verlag, 1994).
WHITE, HUGH C., *Narration and Discourse in the Book of Genesis* (Cambridge: Cambridge University Press, 1991).
WILSON, M. K., '"As You Like It": The Idolatry of Micah and the Danites (Judges 17–18)', *Reformed Theological Review* 54 (1995), 73–85.
WINTERMUTE, O. S., 'Jubilees: A New Translation and Introduction', in *The Old Testament Pseudepigrapha II* (ed. James H. Charlesworth, Garden City: Doubleday, 1985), 35–142.
WITHERINGTON, BEN III, *Paul's Narrative Thought World: The Tapestry of Tragedy and Triumph* (Louisville: Westminster/John Knox Press, 1994).
WOLFF, HANS W., 'The Kerygma of the Yahwist', *Int* 20 (1966), 131–58.
WOLFF, HANS W., *The Anthropology of the Old Testament* (ET, M. Kohl, London: SCM Press, 1974).
WRIGHT, DAVID P., 'Unclean and Clean (OT)', *Anchor Bible Dictionary* VI, 729–41.
WRIGHT, N. T., *Jesus and the Victory of God* (London: SPCK, 1996).

YARON, REUVEN, 'On Divorce in OT Times', *RIDA* 3 (1957), 117–28.

INDEX OF REFERENCES

Judges

INDEX OF MODERN AUTHORS

INDEX OF SUBJECTS